D0222265

Chicana Without Apology
Chicana sin vergüenza

Craig Valdis

Chicana Without Apology

Chicana sin vergüenza

The New Chicana Cultural Studies

By
Edén E. Torres

ROUTLEDGE
NEW YORK AND LONDON

Published in 2003 by
Routledge
29 West 35th Street
New York, NY 10001
www.routledge-ny.com

Published in Great Britain by
Routledge
11 New Fetter Lane
London EC4P 4EE
www.routledge.co.uk

Copyright © 2003 by Routledge

Routledge is an imprint of the Taylor & Francis Group.
Printed in the United States of America on acid-free paper.

10 9 8 7 6 5 4 3 2 1

Library of Congress Cataloging-in-Publication Data
Torres, Edén E.
   Chicana without apology = Chicana sin vergüenza : the new Chicana
cultural studies / by Edén E. Torres.
      p. cm.
Includes bibliographical references and index.
   ISBN 0-415-93505-9 (alk. paper) — ISBN 0-415-93506-7 (pbk. : alk.
paper)
   1. Mexican American women—Study and teaching.   2. Mexican American
women—Social conditions.   3. Mexican American women—Ethnic identity.
4. Social action—United States.   5. Feminism—United States.   I.
Title: Chicana sin vergüenza.   II. Title.
   E184.M5T67   2003
   305.48'86872073—dc21
                                                                2003006004

Para mi mamá

Contents

Acknowledgments

I owe tremendous thanks to my research assistant Heidi Schumacher, (and all of the people she enlisted to help her). Looking up the citations for the footnotes alone was a daunting task and I am grateful for all the late nights. I want to thank the Department of Women's Studies at the University of Minnesota and Amy Katz Kaminsky for giving me the time to complete this manuscript. I am forever grateful to Dr. Nancy (Rusty) Barceló and the President's Multicultural Grant for supporting my research. Rusty, you arrived at this University just in time to push me out of my complacency and onto the faculty full time. Thank you so much for your encouragement, inspiration, and your practical help. To Elisa Facio, who spent so much time making sure this book got published, a lifetime of love and gratitude. *Muchas gracias* to professors Dionicio Nodín Valdés, Guillermo Rojas, and Jacqueline Zita who read and critiqued two of the chapters in their infancy. Your analytical comments, critical questions, and valuable insights pushed me to think in greater depth about our relationships to power in varying contexts. *A mi comadre y prima, Susana De León, te quiero mucho, mujer. Tu sabes, sin tí en mi vida, no hay corazón mexica. Muchisimas gracias por ti y tu familia–especialmente las mujeres, Patti, Idalia, Chita, Angelica, Citlali, y Tita.* Thanks to many of my students who have inspired me in ways they could not foresee. Most of all thanks to *mi papí chulo*, Michael, who started me on this educational journey and withstood its demands with more unselfishness than I had any right to ask or accept. I will always love you for this gift.

No hay tiempo ni espacio para llorar
There Is neither Time nor Space to Cry

I have spent the past fifteen years trying to negotiate the complex relationship between theory and my daily life. But I think the disjuncture between what I read and what I live began long before that. Books captured me when I was in the sixth grade. And though I loved the rhythm and flow of words, nothing I found in the many libraries I visited described my life. In junior high, I began to find African American writers, and the world suddenly opened. My wounds became visible for the first time. Many of the things I suspected about white folks, but could not voice, came off those pages and told me I was neither crazy nor alone. The civil rights movement was well under way by then. I was thrilled by the defiance and horrified by the responses of local, state, and federal police.

Though I strongly identified with black folks and their struggle, I knew the experiences of African Americans were not mine. It was just close enough to teach me a great deal about who I was in relationship to power. Some of my earliest memories have to do with white people calling me names—many I didn't understand. They were never spoken in Spanish. But I knew from the hateful tone in their voices and the meanness on their faces that they meant for me to know I was less than nothing. All of this would have been hard enough in south Texas where I would have been surrounded by my Mexican family and all the Chicanitos who made up the majority of the neighborhood and the schools. But by 1965 I was living in rural Minnesota. I made it through high school hanging on to the words of black Nationalists *por la vida*. In a few years, I would move to Minneapolis, to find not only other Mexican Americans, but also a movement of my own. Obviously, this book is an extension of that politic.

My intention has always been to broaden the scope of cultural studies discussions and practices. Some of these essays are more conventional than others. But my heart belongs to those parts of the text that are the least academic. These unexpected ways of expressing my ideas reflect both my nature (as an abstract, random thinker), and my training in several interdisciplinary programs—Chicano studies, women's studies, and American studies. But they also sometimes rise up out of this well of knowledge that was left to me by my grandmothers and great aunts. Thus, I have always tried to focus on issues of acute importance to Mexican American women. I have to confess, though, that I do sometimes stray from this center in an effort to provide general insights for all people interested in forming successful coalitions for radical political work.

Following the advice of several wise Chicana mentors, I have taken theories and concepts from a wide range of disciplines and combined them with the lessons I've learned through observation and experience. What emerges as I close my eyes to compose, listening to the voices of all the precious women in my life, is the theory and language of struggle and endurance. Though I have tried to write an academically rigorous book, there are moments when I simply must be poetic, because the emotion of those voices will not settle for simple rationality. And though I have tried to embrace the notion of multiplicity whenever I can, this is an unapologetic challenge to the traditions and systems that have tried to silence Chicanas and so many others. It makes visible to agents and targets alike the real damage to, and strength of, those who fight back.

I am old enough to have absorbed the passion and rhetorical strategies of *El Movimiento* firsthand, but young enough as a scholar to move toward wide-reaching coalition politics. I am quite sure that readers will have no trouble finding instances where I seem to contradict myself. I have made my peace with such ambiguity and hope that these contradictions will simply encourage lively discussions of the issues among readers. This is not to imply that these contradictions are frivolous. On the contrary, they symbolize ideas and questions too complex and significant to be easily decided or succinctly articulated. I would only ask that you keep in mind as you sort through these seeming contractions that both ideas might be true in a given context or in answering competing theoretical questions.

Without listing all the things that I am, I will just say here that I am a Chicana feminist. Though it has reached back to seventeenth-century Mexico for its ideological and scholarly roots, contemporary Chicana feminist writing has evolved from its early articulation within several overlapping political associations. As an intellectual, I have followed a similar but not identical path. These included the civil rights, brown power, and women's movements of the late 1960s and early 1970s, the GLBT (gay, lesbian, bisexual, and transsexual) action groups that emerged somewhat later, as well as local union struggles largely based in the Southwest. Each of these affiliations came with a set of objectives, major concerns, and rhetorical strategies—all of which have influenced Chicana feminist scholarship. I came to this specific knowledge relatively late in my life, entering the academy for the first time at the age of thirty-five. Before that, I was surviving. Working a lot of minimum wage jobs, traveling around the country for one cause or another, and becoming an unrefined Chicana feminist through experience rather than books. I miss my rough edges. But I do what I can to maintain a few, and take pleasure in knowing that some are mine for life.

Still, I owe a great deal to Chicana writers and scholars. Many of the authors who initially explored the racialization of Mexican Americans, the history of our incorporation into U.S. society, articulations of identity, and the development of a *xicana* consciousness have paved the way for my work in critical literary theory and cultural studies. This collection of essays continues the traditions of these theoretical *madres y hermanas,* and allows me to fill in some of the gaps, to answer lingering questions and explore new ideas in Chicana feminist thought. Like many of the women before me, I have consciously combined autoethnography with critical expository writing and research. Because this method has produced highly readable accounts of lived theory and practice in the past, I have used it to paint my own verbal portraits. I do not mean to imply that the life of one Chicana can speak for all others, but that it can be used as a lens through which to analyze and critique oppressive phenomena, behaviors, and symbols. In the process, the reader should see the way in which scholarly theories, artistic production, and social practices are shaped by activism and vice versa. Theory, I believe, is most useful as a framework—a means to an end, not the thing itself. To the extent that it allows us to speculate on meaning, test our ideas, *and* articulate our objectives, it may very well help us to develop various methods for actualizing our desire for change.

While the essays address a wide variety of topics from a Chicana perspective, their overriding purpose is to look closely at some of the problems involved in coalition building. There is a Mexican proverb my grandmother used to say whenever she saw something necessary that just had to get done. *No hay tiempo ni espacio para llorar.* (There is no space nor time to cry.) I think of this *dicho* when I think of social justice work, because it hints at the urgency of working toward change. In this era of intense globalization there is no time to waste in forging lasting alliances for political action. Yet the saying also implies that we might have to work through some pain in order to accomplish effective relationships. Many of us desire lasting alliances between diverse peoples in the struggle for more equitable and just societies, but personal and political differences often prevent us from maintaining coalitions. This book explores both historical and contemporary reasons why such connections remain difficult, even though we have been talking about this kind of political action for some time. I believe that once we understand the underlying causes of the ruptures that divide us we will be better equipped to either transcend or work around them.

Although this book discusses the familiar and sensitive topic of internalized oppression, it also looks at the less-studied occurrence of internalized dominance, which creates unintentional and unconscious acts of racism, classism, sexism, and homophobia (among other things). This gives us a theoretical framework for choosing how we will act or what we must do, as well as a way of distinguishing between useful and harmful approaches when working across race, class, and gender lines. In looking toward the psychological responses of individuals to both larger and personal histories, and the way in which this affects our abilities to sustain social and political affiliations, I recommend possible pathways to better deal with the anger that unjust and oppressive systems engender.

The book does not lack a critical edge, and though it is often directed at systematic and institutional oppression and its agents, at least some of it is self-reflexive. I discuss the conflict between the ideals preached in many interdisciplinary programs or cultural studies scholarship and the failures of multiculturalism and diversity. I also discuss many of the liberal constructs and scholarly trends of the past two decades, which often entertain but do not seriously interrogate imperialism nor make any commitment to activism. Like sweet-tasting desserts, such scholarship cannot nourish the needy body of a social movement—but it can add fat, which only slows us down. It seems clear that as we respond to the global economy we must produce scholarship that is useful to, and maintains our connections with, activists at every level. We must also speak many languages (English and Spanish, academic and colloquial, for instance) if we are to continue to learn as well as teach in order to create and benefit from awareness outside the academy.

While readers may find much that is recognizable here, some parts of this book are unique because I am an oddity—always somewhat peculiar in my academic institution, in my state, in my profession, and in my family. I do not say this to be boastful, nor to complain, but to imply that I have had a different experience than many scholarly writers. I tend to enter all conversations through storytelling because that is the way of knowing I learned as a child. The women in my family were and are amazing storytellers. What interests me intellectually is always something that connects to the stories I grew up with, the gossip, the tales of trouble and passion that I inherited, as well as all the crazy lives I've lived with family, lovers, and friends.

Though my socioeconomic position has changed considerably, my writing and thinking still reflects my early life in often brutal environments. It is also marked by my history within a working-class, extended family that stretched from south Texas to the Midwest, usually covering both areas simultaneously. I cannot help but think about socioeconomic structures, class assumptions, and middle-class attitudes toward the poor. Because of my continued familial and social relationships within a community and cultural milieu far removed from the genteel ambiance of the university, all of my work examines the way leftist liberal academics (including me) and other professionals benefit from capitalism.

I am a Chicana who has lived most of my life in Minnesota, which means I am not only acutely aware of identity politics, but have also had a great deal of experience with well-intentioned attempts to create political alliances between various groups of people. While my consciousness as a Chicana (as an historically situated subject or as a specific person in a particular socioeconomic location) remains solid, I try to maintain intellectual flexibility. I look for meaning in everyday occurrences in a variety of contexts. These essays reflect that process. Through this combination of personal reflection and scholarly writing I hope to help others become conscious of their own positions, just as those African American writers did for me decades ago. Together we will learn from our past, become aware of competing theories, and look for ways that we might approach our conflicts in more inventive and powerful ways.

As unique as my approach may be, however, this text joins an ongoing dialogue about the intersecting and overlapping forces of race, class, and gender as well as the futility of single-issue politics. I provide readers with examples of what goes wrong when diverse currents of thought and experience create tensions between well-intentioned people. I then analyze and interpret various responses and suggest ways in which future interactions might be made less contentious. A vital part of the progression made by ethnic studies and feminist scholars must be not only greater theoretical reflexivity, but also more effective social activism.

Like other work in cultural studies, this book treats popular culture as a text to be read and interpreted for its social meaning. Because of its attention to class dynamics, it illuminates what has often been neglected in cultural studies with the professionalization of movement politics in the academy. It pays close attention to the political economy and the people who struggle everyday with physical and psychological survival. In this way, it links Mexican Americans to other people around the globe who are being controlled and exploited as capital so easily transcends national borders. Using an analysis of popular culture in this way gives it the potential to become an articulation of the need for, and morality of, social transformation. As a politically conscious Mexican American woman, I have an interest in connecting our history of oppression to its contemporary manifestations. In the following chapter I delve into the psychological reasons why these historical circumstances make interpersonal relationships—and thus cooperative sociopolitical movements—so difficult. Many of the essays contemplate the way in which divergent theories are present in our everyday experiences. As I tell my stories and create theoretical essays I look for new ways to think about the intricacies of power and oppression. Yet, I do not hesitate to resurrect concepts that have been discarded if I find them useful. This impulse also comes from lived experience. As a child, I made far too many trips with my grandfather through junkyards and garbage dumps, ferreting out what might still be useful or transformed into a treasure. I know there is always something of value in the old stuff.

The first chapter of the book discusses the psychological and behavioral effects of historic trauma and unresolved grieving on the Chicano/a community and its relationship to contemporary experiences with racism, ethnocentrism, sexism, classism, and homophobia. It shows that the causes and symptoms of post-traumatic stress disorder can be played out in communal relationships as well as in individual lives. As women are often seen as the emotional centers of Mexican American family life, this chapter delineates some of the particular ways that dysfunction affects women. It disrupts not only the ability to function in a society by forming healthy, intimate relationships, but also the ability to become politically conscious actors in coalition with others. This chapter also shows the way in which many Chicana writers reflect both the trauma and the attempt to grieve as part of a communal healing process. My aim is not to increase the perception that the Mexican American community is somehow flawed, but to articulate how we have been hurt by—and how we have survived—a history of violent and insidious oppression. It is also an attempt to articulate how our struggle with contemporary inequality, as well as our ability to create social change, is directly related to that history.

Chapter 2 is a call to academics to maintain a strong connection between critical theory and activism, as Chicana/o studies continues to grow as a profession. In this chapter I examine an array of competing approaches to cultural studies for the ways in which professionalization within the corporate-model university may be diluting our critical edge. In examining certain attitudes and practices that may limit or enhance the possibility that cultural studies as critical theory might actually affect public policy, I ask hard questions of all liberal to radical scholars. I show how a simple desire to broaden the canon is both a tool and a barrier to any theory or method of study that begins with an acknowledged leftist agenda. This necessarily includes a critique of many institutionalized cultural studies programs, existing canons, and accepted methods of academic analysis. But, I make clear the processes by which the global economy has turned the university from a place of learning into a knowledge factory, with students as both consumers and products, as well as the effect this has had on radical scholarship.

Chapter 3 is an often poignant discussion of the power dynamics in classrooms where the majority of students are white and the professor is a woman of color. It both promotes and questions the efficacy of using a Freirean model of teaching in classrooms where U.S. students are seen by much of the rest of the world as the agents of oppression. As brilliant as they are, Freire's theories were developed in a completely different social, political, and historical context. The ideas for this style of pedagogy came to Freire through his experiences with public education and literacy programs in Brazil. He saw it as a way of bringing the oppressed to political consciousness. As such, these theories were used in a place and time where the lines between the elite, educated oppressors and the brutalized, uneducated masses were very clear.

But the social divisions in the United States are somewhat blurred by comparison to the conditions in Brazil in the 1950s and 1960s. In the United States, the teacher's authority cannot be assumed or guaranteed, especially if that teacher is female and/or a person of color. Ironically, as I and other women of color attempt to teach in a way that validates the expertise of our students and decenters our authority, we already enter classrooms as figures disempowered by the existing norms of a racist and sexist society. How then, do we translate or use Freirean notions of pedagogy when the majority of our students have unearned power and privilege in both local and global contexts? How do we teach students who already consider themselves superior to us?

While Freire speaks extensively about internalized oppression, he gives us few clues on how to deal with the internalized dominance of our students. Or, what to do when this sense of entitlement causes some mainstream students to respond with hostile and openly aggressive arrogance toward teachers who are not white, male, heterosexual, and middle to upper class. Clearly, adjustments must be made when women of color are employing Freirean models in predominantly white institutions. This chapter often asks the question "What would Freire do?" as it gives concrete examples from the classroom specifically and the university in general. It speculates on new ways to expand Freirean theory to deal with the often tense relationship between mainstream students and women of color as their teachers.

In chapters 4 and 5, I use film as a lens to explore several theories about border crossing and identity politics that have arisen in the past fifteen years. Chapter 4 looks at the way in which the border has become a grand metaphor for ambiguity and the transgression of boundaries. It also returns to Gloria Anzaldúa's notion of the border as an open wound and the borderland as a unique site for mixture. Analyzing the work of two contemporary filmmakers, John Sayles and María Novaro, I show competing images of the border from differing social locations. Their films, *Lone Star* and *El jardín del Edén* respectively, provide good examples of how the border is represented in the popular imagination as both permeable and concrete. Both directors make wonderful use of this contested site where utopian images often collide with ugly realities. In both films we see the significance of the relative sociopolitical positions of Mexicans, Chicanos, immigrants, legal or otherwise, and middle-class white folks. The often disturbing (and sometimes secret), relationships between white and brown, men and women, or some combination thereof, as well as the meaning of the U.S./Mexican border in various people's lives, provides ample material for provocative interpretation. It is clear in *Lone Star* that taboos are constructed to contain desires and create clearly demarcated lines between individuals as well as groups of people. These same human desires will often mandate the crossing of well-established boundaries. Both films, each in their own way, interrogate the diverse relationships to power that create unequal opportunities to cross or violate borders or to hide certain transgressions. *Lone Star* shows us the price disparate people must pay for those "sins." Novaro's film illustrates the effect of past transgressions on Chicana identity, as well as history's contemporary manifestations in the ineptness of well-intentioned white folks who "love" all things Mexican.

Chapter 5 is a continuation of my analysis and critique of María Novaro's *El jardín del Edén*. It is intertwined with a discussion of shifting positionality and Chicana/Latina identity, as well as the virtues of conflict within a women's studies classroom. While the Mexican women's struggle in the film is primarily economic (though this is illustrated in personal terms), the Chicana character's conflict is largely internal and reflective. She is drawn to Mexico, but both she and the Mexican women she encounters recognize that the extent of her Mexicanness is limited. The film's exploration of the Chicana's relationship to both Mexican women and her white friend was particularly relevant to the students with whom I first viewed it. Because of the intensely emotional discussions that were going on in the course, I have used the film as a way of articulating some of the issues and questions that arose. It allowed us to ask and reflect on some very difficult questions around identity, self-segregation, inclusion, and exclusion.

Since the majority of the students in the class were women of color, the film and other events prompted us to think deeply about the impulse to romanticize Mexico and its people versus being able to genuinely interact with the poor on either side of the border. We also tried to figure out ways to keep scholarly inquiry from becoming a complacent smokescreen that would prevent us from recognizing our own power and privilege and thus make us ineffective as agents of social change. I also discuss what it means to be tokenized by the well-meaning, but "matronizing" mainstream women who claim to "love" us, as well as how we might work around or solve our difficulties in an effort to forge lasting political alliances for social change.

Chapter 6 outlines the general process of political movements as marginalized groups move from consciousness to anger and protest, from complex theory to coalition politics and reform. It posits this as a cyclic process rather than a linear one, and shows the way in which a conservative backlash is always working simultaneously to maintain power and privilege for the selected elite members of the society. Though I give specific examples from Chicana/o history, I have tried to keep the model general enough so that other groups might see the way in which it is relevant to their own political struggles. As I illustrate how the prevalent modes of imperialism work to break down alliances and coalitions between groups, I try to demystify this part of the process so that we might develop more effective strategies for maintaining these relationships. And though the outcome of conservative backlash has often meant the repeal of previous reforms, I suggest that is not cause for cynicism, but a call for renewed commitments to collective action. For when the wretched at the bottom of the pyramid rise up, the few at the top must fall. And all those folks in the middle—no matter what color, gender, class, or sexual identity—they better decide to jump, or they too will tumble.

CHAPTER 1

Anguished Past, Troubled Present

The Savagery and Promise of Traumatic Memory

For most of my childhood, my father was a ghost. I loved and feared him for many reasons, and never knew when he would appear or disappear. Nor could I predict whether his brief presence would be kind or cruel. I have come to believe that he has always hated the Mexican in him. Though his parents did not speak English, he sometimes claims not to understand Spanish. Some of my siblings have also learned this self-loathing, refusing to speak to their grandparents, anglicizing their names as my father did, and reluctantly admitting only to Spanish blood. Since he and my mother were divorced, he has remarried several times, always choosing blonde women. Now in his seventies, he tells people that his first wife was also blonde. In doing so, he erases my mother from his past. I take no pleasure in revealing this. I want my father to be like Edward James Olmos in the movies. I want him to be *el hijo de mi abuelita*—the son of my Mexican Indian grandmother—but I know this will never be. He prefers to tell people the romantic story that my grandmother was the daughter of a very wealthy Spanish family in Mexico City, and that my grandfather kidnapped her. They came to the United States to escape the wrath and vengeance of her father who disapproved of their match. They chose love over wealth. Two birds, one stone. With this story, my father slips out from under the stigma of having a dark-skinned mother *and* of being poor. The impoverished Mexican has been beaten and shamed out of him. No amount of political rhetoric from me can bring it back.

Though shame-based behaviors are manifest in individual lives and ultimately the healing must be done by individuals, it is important to remember the historical source and ongoing impetus for this dysfunction. It is to be found in the practices of conquest, colonization, a concept of private ownership, and economic systems that thrive on inequality. It is also in various social processes that work in support of these hierarchical structures. These things function at all levels, dictating who is at the top and who is at the bottom of the global market, nation-state, corporation, community, worksite, and interpersonal relationships. Thus, social science studies, which focus on pathology within the subordinate community, cannot be helpful in imagining solutions to national or worldwide problems. They do not take into account the day-to-day pressures and tensions activated at the historical or macroeconomic level. Nor do these studies acknowledge the concrete damage done to the individual psyche by things wholly outside individual control.

Knowing the history of North America from the period of its indigenous civilizations through the destruction caused by conquest and colonization has helped many people to develop ethnic loyalty. Learning how this past has led to the nationalist eras of modern Mexico and the United States is an important part of understanding the cultural context that could produce both fierce pride in me and the kind of shame my father exhibits. But simply learning the dates and names or the geographical locations of that history does not enlighten us about its effect on the human soul. Our ancestors suffered the events and devastating displacements of that history, and we continue to experience its legacy, though our responses to it are much different. Through hundreds of years of upheaval, they fought—we fight—to survive. This constant state of struggle and endurance leaves little time to indulge in a ritualistic or communal grieving process for all that we have lost through imperialist processes. Our political rhetoric does not always reveal the scars we carry in our hearts heavy with this history, but our literature tells the story.

I first saw my father's pain and psychic damage replicated in the book *Hunger of Memory*. I had little patience with Richard Rodríguez's autobiographical narrative, which brought out all the anger I felt at my father for not being a proud Chicano. I hated Rodríguez for the way he spoke about his parents and their Mexicanness, but it was really my experiences with my father that inspired the passionate outrage with which I critiqued *Hunger of Memory*. Once in college and majoring in Chicano studies, I found texts that gave voice to a different kind of Chicana/o identity. Yet even in these new forms of defiant expression, the pain did not dissipate, nor did the shame entirely disappear. In analyzing this literature, I could never quite put into words what I wanted to say about this collective sense of being wounded. Each time I tried, I would be accused of "essentializing" Chicana/o experience. Yet I knew that for all the unconditional love, laughter, and joy among my friends and family, there was also profound sadness and shame.

Conventional scholarship and existing theories proved inadequate. Historical research disclosed many things about which I could express anger, but could not tell me how people responded emotionally to given events. Literary analysis has been a remarkable tool for uncovering hidden messages and discovering meaning beyond the obvious signification. Cultural studies, feminist theory, and Marxist analysis have revealed the camouflaged socioeconomic function of exclusionary practices based on race, class, gender, and sexual identity. Philosophical inquiry has yielded both simple and complex ways of conceptualizing social dynamics, intercultural relationships, and literary production.

Though I use these tools, some piece of the scar has always been missing. It seems clear, however, that much of the creative work of Chicana writers exposes the wounds, confronts those who inflict pain, and tries to exorcise the shame that some individuals feel. Thus, this work can be seen as an attempt to grieve, to express the pain, and to heal. As such, it causes discomfort in people who try to deny that the damage exists. The disproportionate hostility that has grown up around Gloria Anzaldúa's work is the response of those who cannot face the emotional wreckage of imperialism as it threatens their spiritual well-being. I have seen this resistance in my classrooms from students who cannot deal with the pain in their own lives and express quite literally their hatred toward Anzaldúa for exposing such emotions to public view. While many legitimate critiques of Anzaldúa's work may be made, the viciousness with which many attack her autobiographical narrative *Borderlands/La Frontera* is much too extreme to be simple theoretical, philosophical, or ideological differences.

Though post-traumatic stress disorder (PTSD) had been in public discourse for some time, I never really thought about its significance or meaning in a Chicana/o context until I heard Mary Clearing Sky speak at a conference in 1992. A Native American scholar and psychologist, then at Michigan State University, Clearing Sky described and outlined the basic concepts of historic trauma and applied them to Native American peoples in a way that suddenly made sense to me. When a young Chicano in my class exploded over perceived insults from another student in the class, confounding his classmates and frightening them with his intensity, I could not help but think of Clearing Sky's descriptions of possible PTSD behaviors. Normally gregarious and charming, this student almost came to physical blows with the target of his rage, who was equally explosive and dealing with his own demons. I had to step in between them on more than one occasion. The only thing these two agreed on was their loathing of Gloria Anzaldúa's work.

Through private conversations, journaling assignments, and class discussions, I learned that the young Chicano had grown up in relative poverty on San Antonio's West Side. The son of alcoholic parents, both of whom died before he graduated from high school, he was nineteen and trying to raise his younger brother and two sisters as well as attend college. He received no help from his older siblings, who seemed to be following his parents' path of self-destruction. The other student was an older man, the son of a middle-class alcoholic father who believed in using his fists on his children. While these two men should have been allies, given their sincere commitments to Chicano studies scholarship and activist politics, they could barely stand to be in the same room with each other. As we began to talk and read about historic trauma and unresolved grieving as part of the coursework and the constructive uses of anger, their demeanor in the classroom calmed. While they did not become friends, they were able to declare a truce long enough to engage in more productive discussions. This experience, and others like it, have convinced me that Clearing Sky's ideas are important to consider when thinking about ways to improve coalition politics.

Much of the language she uses comes out of psychology, both popular and professional, and literature dealing with chemical dependency issues. Though I had heard much of this discourse in regard to individual recovery programs, Mary Clearing Sky was the first person I heard speak about it in terms of a communal history. I knew immediately that this was the piece of the puzzle for which I had been searching. Hearing her speak, I recognized the shame-based behaviors I had seen for years in my family, among my friends, in the classroom, and in various political organizations to which I belonged. I also began to see the evidence and support for what she was saying, not only in Native American literature, but splashed across the pages of almost every Chicana text. Her insight made well-read narratives new to me. It added meaningful complexity to my conceptualizations of Chicana writers and of Mexican Americans in a variety of sociohistorical and economic contexts.

San Antonio poet Rosemary Catacalos addresses the communal nature of pain and the experience of being wounded in her poem "(There Has to Be) Something More than Everything." Though it deals with a personal loss, her choice of the collective pronouns "we" and "us" throughout much of the poem nevertheless gives us the feeling that this is something larger than her own discomfort. Yet at the end of the poem, she reverts to the lonely "I" as the person who runs from "mourning."[1]

Less abstract than Catacalos, Demetria Martínez, in her poem, "The Conquest," demonstrates through concrete images the connections between Mexican American history, our contemporary positions, and the personal/political dialogues in which we are involved. She identifies the three oppressive states to which we have been subject, implicating Spain, Mexico, and the United States in the process. Next she expresses her distaste toward tourists who see the Southwest only in romantic terms but fail to understand the painful histories of the old settlements or the crying of those whose stories have been silenced. Martínez also addresses a contemporary phenomenon in which Anglos express jealousy toward those of us still strongly connected to Mexican culture. Again, they ignore any pain that may be associated with that legacy. In responding, Martínez chooses signifiers (like corn and *metates* or stone bowls used for grinding vegetables), which function largely as female symbols in Mexican and Native cultures. Though the poem ends with some measure of anger and defiance, it is clear that some of this rage is repressed.[2]

Clearing Sky's emphasis on historic trauma and unresolved grieving is an approach that seeks to release that rage—to open and expose what has been hidden for too long. While I have had tremendous misgivings about some of Clearing Sky's ideas, as well as concerns that her analysis lacks any attention to gender specific experiences, I have never stopped thinking about them.[3] Once in my consciousness, they resonated with such veracity that I could not avoid them. I had actually begun writing on this topic in the early 1990s, trying to give my students in Chicano studies classes some way to think about internalized oppression and many of the problems in our communities in a historical context. Clearing Sky's ideas contributed greatly to this project, and they eventually became part of my dissertation, where I extended the analysis beyond history to show how this past trauma comingles with contemporary racism, ethnocentrism, sexism, classism, and homophobia. But I did not publicly present a paper on historic trauma and unresolved grieving until the 1994 and 1997 National Association of Chicana and Chicano Studies (NACCS) Conferences. It was not too long after 1997 when I began to find other people approaching emotional suffering from a sociohistorical perspective, showing the affect on individuals of trauma inflicted on the group (and vice versa). The number of women of color reaching for clinical information on post-traumatic stress disorder implies the existence of recognizable symptoms, a desire to diagnose the problem, and a search for ways to heal. There are many sources as well among Native American, Chicana/o, and African American authors, indicating not only an immense interest in historic trauma and unresolved grieving, but a kind of drum beat that is speaking to people of color through our mutual experiences. (See note 3.)

Renato Rosaldo reinforced my interest in the topic during an informal discussion I had with him about Clearing Sky's theories and my own thoughts on historic trauma and unresolved grieving. He suggested that we (Native American and Chicana/o scholars and writers) are simply part of a larger public discourse—though not a universal one. Everyone in Native American and Mexican American communities is in some way involved in the "same conversation," he said. "We are all trying to deal with our traumatic history."[4] While some respond by becoming hyper-Chicano or *Indio*

Supremo, others try to discard any remnants of Mexican or indigenous identity altogether.

It is important to point out some obvious cautions as I begin to describe the manifestations of trauma in our culture. Historic trauma and unresolved grieving, as well as the shame and dysfunction that accompany them, are not exclusive to Mexican Americans. Nor do they only affect one class position. I did not write about this to increase the perception that our socioeconomic and political problems are caused by pathology within the culture, nor to insinuate that Mexican American people as a group are dysfunctional. In fact, the opposite is true. However, one major source of the pain we do experience is clearly in our history and in the reality of ongoing socioeconomic and political inequality. It is not surprising that many people would be adversely affected by growing up in this sociohistorical context. Chicana feminist writer Ana Castillo says in her book *Massacre of the Dreamers*,

> The awareness that we have at times in our lives barely survived the most trying and humiliating conditions is what makes our bodies tremble, our minds flounder, and our emotional states flail in fear of the present and future. . . . we must not accept the long held premise that it is due to our inherent weaknesses and that it is our own personal failure.[5]

What is surprising is that despite catastrophic losses and continued discrimination, the vast majority of Mexican Americans have survived with our sense of Self intact and functioning quite effectively. This is a testament to the astonishing strength of our spirit. But we owe it to those who have not survived in the same manner, to those who have borne the burden of imperialism in a different way, to stop denying the effect on us as a people. We must stop seeing the consequences of imperialism as solely an individual problem with a single solution and honor the struggle of others to become fully alive in a nation that so often despises us. This is the task of a true community.

In one of the defining moments of Chicana feminist writing, Gloria Anzaldúa's characterization in *Borderlands/La Frontera* of the U.S./Mexican border as an "open wound" not only refers to its contemporary reality, but also to the historical injury done to Greater Mexico and its people. It is a place, she says, "una herida abierta where the Third World grates against the first and bleeds. And before a scab forms it hemorrhages again, the lifeblood of two worlds merging to form a third country—a border culture."[6] With similar feeling, psychiatric nurse and writer Elena Avila refers to a place where some "souls wander away due to neglect and deprivation; hide due to trauma . . . and loss."[7] This is a place haunted by both the memory and the daily reality of physical and spiritual violence.

Clinical psychologist Maria Root calls the problem "insidious trauma," because the harmful effects may begin with history, but they continue to accumulate in our collective psyche through racism, sexism, and classism, as well as other forms of oppression to which we may be subject.[8] Women and men of color suffer this to varying degrees throughout their lives. The trauma, she says, activates survival behaviors, which can be misunderstood by social scientists who cannot understand the impact of racism, hetero-sexism, classism, and so forth (unless they too are directly affected). Under these conditions, negative stereotypes in such literature may be internal-ized and have a self-fulfilling influence, which Root says is the insidious nature of stress-related disorders.[9]

Mary Clearing Sky claims that this is not just a problem for the individ-ual, but that indigenous people as a group suffer from post-traumatic stress disorder.[10] Making a link to PTSD, Elena Avila reminds us that this "dis-ease" was well known to our *antepasados* (ancestors) as "*susto pasado*," or trauma and unresolved suffering of many years duration.[11] The charac-teristics of PTSD—anxiety, personality disorder, acting out, and addictive behaviors—are clearly evident in the Mexican American community, just as they are among all Americans, even as the causes vary. While the idea of PTSD gained widespread public recognition in thinking about war veterans, few acknowledge the existence of ongoing social, political, and economic conflicts within our own borders. In her classic "Poem for the Young White Man Who Asked Me How I, an Intelligent, Well-Read Person Could Believe in the War Between the Races," Lorna Dee Cervantes makes an excellent comparison between the experience of racism and the trauma caused by daily combat. Using war-related and terroristic signifiers Cervantes shows the damage done as we experience having brown skin in white America. In these selected lines, she says,

> sharp-shooting goose-steppers round every corner,
> there are snipers in the schools . . .
> These bullets bury deeper than logic.
> Racism is not intellectual.
> I cannot reason these scars away.[12]

In choosing the signifier "goose-steppers," Cervantes ties into an exist-ing sociolect—an emotional, historical memory well known to most read-ers. But she also makes clear that the physical and psychological devastation of our historic experience is coupled with years of injustice, discrimina-tion, and exclusion. She tells us how it has harmed the community in ways that are not always visible. Cervantes alerts us to the inner fear, generated by outside hostility, that dictates how we see ourselves. Many of the charac-teristics described by Cervantes in other parts of the poem, the day-to-day fear, the remnants (or scars) of this trauma, the feeling of not belonging and of not being good enough, as well as the damage that cannot be reasoned away, mirror the symptoms listed by the American Psychiatric Association (APA) for PTSD.

Part of the reason this history has continued to take its toll on our communities (through internalized racism and self-destructive behaviors) has little to do with individual will or strength. Our people have proven over and over again that we have the desire and the tenacity to not only survive, but to become whole (or self-actualized) and to actively resist oppression. Despite our attempted annihilation, or perhaps because of it, we have continued to fight—to struggle against repression. But we cannot ignore our wounds, for they too affect the nature of our survival and the quality of our lives. While it is not an excuse for abdicating personal responsibility to family and community, historic trauma plays a role in the destructive behaviors of individuals. This has important implications for all. Part of the damage has to do with what Clearing Sky says is the inability of affected communities to grieve our losses. Hardened by the experience itself and the necessity of funneling our energy into survival, we are often unable to face the pain. For people like my father, this means displacing the source of the trauma and pain—as well as the anger they engender—onto the self or other inappropriate targets.

Much of mainstream U.S. culture has always failed to acknowledge that the actions of their ancestors have anything to do with their current privileges or the problems now present in our society. They do not want to see or be told that the oppression we experience today is part of a continuum that reaches back into that history. On the contrary, they continue to replay it from their perspective. Yet many mainstream scholars and journalists will readily note the damage in our communities even as the evidence of its source goes unnamed. Like the other implicit information we gather throughout our daily lives, the effect on our collective psyche is accumulative and has enormous consequences. Historic trauma and its relative invisibility in mainstream culture continue to sabotage some of the best efforts of our people to control their own destinies.

"In non-Western thinking," says Ana Castillo, "the body is never separate from the spirit or mind and all curative recommendations" must "consider the ailing person as a whole."[13] If we want to visualize how the Self is affected by trauma, we can imagine the four primary aspects of a person, which surround the vulnerable, as well as the secure, ego: the mental, the spiritual, the emotional, and the physical. These form a circle around the core of a person and become the first line of defense in the ego's struggle to maintain its health. In a sense, they compose the facade or face with which we operate in the world. A disturbance to, or assault on, any of the four parts of a person will push the center or the core Self off balance.

In contemporary culture we can see the pain and disturbance to these outer features reflected in the work of many women writers. Confessional narratives, like this piece written by Aletícia Tijerina, tell us about the harm that reaches in through the mind and body to ravage the core Self. It is clear Tijerina sees abuse and sexual violence, chemical dependency, and inadequate or discriminatory health care as aspects of our communal history.

> I was a junkie. Anglos have been consenting to us darkies shootin' hard drugs since the beginning of their colonization. But the white man didn't actually push the spike into my veins. I did. This act is clearly the embodiment of self-hatred. Hatred which goes back a long time. Goes back to the three-year-old girl terrorized by the knife of her father—to the white welfare woman whispering in my ears, "Your momma is a whore, you will grow up to be a no-good-whore. . . ." Individual incidents in our lives—our collective history—we North Americans—colonized and exploiter alike . . . we take from the oppressor the instruments of hatred and sharpen them on our bodies and our souls.[14]

Cognitive faculties and strong spirit are well demonstrated here, yet many authors like Tijerina confess the difficulty of maintaining mental health.[15] Poet Pat Mora, however, suggests that we can never truly know the extent of damage to the core because what we often display is the remarkable nature of our resilience. In her poem "Desert Women," Mora writes, "Our secrets/stay inside, only dried scars show/if you get close/if you dare push/against our thorns/But when we flower, we stun/Like cactuses, we've learned/to gulp and hoard."[16]

If we know ourselves well enough to read through our historical and personal memories, as well as our experiences, we may begin to understand what is being revealed and expressed. In a piece titled, "El día de la chicana," included in the Rebolledo and Rivero collection *Infinite Divisions*, Gloria Anzaldúa says that she is ready to see the core Self through the facade, through all the damage that has been done to us. "[A] seeing through the fictions of white supremacy . . . our true guises and not as the false racial personality that has been given to us and that we have given to ourselves . . . the positive and the negative seen clearly."[17]

One of the reasons Mexican Americans—Native Americans and African Americans as well—cannot be compared to other "immigrant" groups has to do with the traumatic histories to which Tijerina and Anzaldúa among others refer. We did not choose to leave our homelands as many European immigrants have, nor elect to be absorbed into the dominant culture through forced assimilation, which is a kind of brutality against the spirit. Our indigenous ancestors made no request to be incorporated into two or three national states through violence. As Mexican settlers we did not choose to lose our language and culture, to be included (yet excluded) in the original social experiment known as the United States of America. As a result of this material reality, we have been made relatively powerless over and within public and private institutions that directly affect our lives—churches, schools, governments, and the structures of commerce.[18] But the "psychological colonization" associated with that powerlessness is as devastating to the community as are the physical manifestations of systematic exclusion and discrimination.[19]

To capture the seriousness of the devastation, some people call the various events in Native American, Mexican, and Chicano history an "American Holocaust." But a double standard exists between the way the mainstream culture remembers and characterizes certain losses as opposed to others. If we think of the way the European Holocaust has been documented, or the way we have commemorated the various military losses of the U.S. armed forces personnel, and compare them to the way in which the United States remembers the history of conquest in the Americas, we can see profound differences. Chicanas/os, for instance, are unlikely to ever have a museum documenting the atrocities committed by Texas Rangers against Mexican people. We will not have a black marble wall in Washington, D.C., etched with the names of those Mexicans who died in the violent takeover of northern Mexico, or the identities of the Native women who were roped like cattle and then raped by Spanish soldiers.

In fact, the myth and the monument of places like the Alamo may testify to bravery and heroism for Anglo Americans, but to Chicanas/os such myths function as torturous reminders of what has been truly lost. These symbols serve only as white justification for the past and present dominance of brown-skinned peoples. In "Gulf Dreams," Emma Pérez writes a poignant tale of a childhood full of longing and dreams dashed. She tells of a junior high teacher delivering a lesson on the Alamo, trying to get her young Texas students to "absorb the conqueror's lies in history books." Then using her power to humiliate and intimidate the adolescent Chicana, the teacher challenges her to accept the official version of the myth and prove her fidelity to the United States. Though the young woman turns down the opportunity to collaborate with the teacher's version of the facts, Pérez writes, "In the seventh grade I wasn't prepared to argue history but I refused to renounce my mestizaje, my parents, my Mexican ancestry to comfort Anglos."[20] Pérez clearly wants to create for readers a different memory of the Alamo.

Of course, who is remembered and mourned by the nation depends on political and socioeconomic clout, as well as the way in which the victims are perceived in the mainstream imagination. The United States certainly had a history of racism and anti-Semitism firmly in place before, *during*, and after World War II. This in part may explain why it has taken almost fifty years to build the Holocaust museum in Washington, D.C., and more than a century for the Smithsonian to realize that it must return sacred objects and human remains to Native Americans.

The fact that thousands of Mexicanos and Chicanos publicly mourned singer Selena's death beyond what could reasonably be expected is evidence that we carry much grief within us. The growth of Cinco de Mayo and Dieciseis de Septiembre as important community events in the United States speaks to our longing for a way to commemorate what we have lost and how we have struggled—a public acknowledgment of our history—a reshaping of our collective memory. In addition to being celebrations of community and ethnicity, they are also part of a public discourse around victories against European oppressors—a conversation that seeks to resolve our negative feelings about being subordinate to mainstream culture. We celebrate, renew acquaintances, and take pride in our heritage. Though we do not gather on these days specifically to grieve the losses we have suffered throughout history, many Chicanas/os are now doing so around Día de los Muertos. At these gatherings we create huge public *ofrendas*, on which we place the images and names of national leaders, entertainers, beloved locals, and family members.

Cherríe Moraga pays her respects to our history of devastating losses of life, land, and culture when she connects the past to the present in a piece inspired by the 1992 rebellion in Los Angeles, which she sees as a sign of a larger upheaval that will affect the entire continent. She says, "Our rapist wears the face of death. In a suit of armor, he rides us—cross in one hand, sword in the other. And this is how they've always taken us with their gods of war and their men of god."[21] While we can read Moraga as generalizing about all oppressed peoples here, the cross and the sword imagery have specific importance to La Raza. In using rape as her metaphor, Moraga feminizes all forms of oppression and thus indicts all oppressors as patriarchs. In this way she unites the oppressed of the world under the rubric of brown women.

As many Chicana feminists have pointed out, the subjugation of the meaning and importance of the feminine principle had already begun to occur in Mexico at the time of indigenous contact with Europe. But it cannot be denied that many patriarchs in the Spanish state and the Catholic Church accelerated that process.[22] "Indian women who had once reigned as goddesses now wore the facial brands of slavery and were subjected to the imposition of a single, male, Christian god" and his only son.[23] This kind of process took many *mestizas* in New Spain beyond hope of recovery, which might have been possible in native Mexico, since they still worshiped and had faith in the feminine earth spirits.[24]

Through five centuries we have endured multiple losses: the loss of life, meaning, lands—our physical lives and a psychological sense of well-being. Pieces of our culture have also been lost, traditional and communal ways of life, family structures, spiritual customs, mythohistorical figures—especially female spirits, ancestor names, and legends. Indigenous languages and Spanish names, as well as traditional pronunciations and usage have come under attack in mainstream U.S. culture. Indian names become rare. Tómas changes to Tom, and Magdalena slips into Maggie. (My grandfather, Rafael, became Rafele on official paperwork when he crossed the border. My father, the Junior in the family, has since become Ray. Both changes represent a movement away from Mexico.) This gloss of acculturation becomes our public face. When or if it solidifies, we lose our traditional relationships with one another, to animals and their spirits (our "tonos" or representatives in the natural world), to the cosmos, and the deities. For Chicanas/os, attacks on bilingualism, English-only laws, and the elitism of European Spanish mean that our code-switching abilities are seen as colloquial and thus insignificant in public discourse, rather than as a legitimate, living language—Caló.

While some aspects of traditional practices and rituals have survived the American Holocaust, much of their original meaning has been lost or distorted through Catholic, elite interpreters and recorders. Such loss inevitably affects our sense of Self. The meaning of our indigenismo/a, of our roots in the Americas, has made us the target of ethnocentrism and racism in both countries. Mexico's ruling class has used this native past to foster nationalism but has yet to free itself of racist behaviors toward Indians and the assumption of privilege and power by those more European in appearance and lineage.[25]

The loss of both national lands and traditional spaces has neutralized the material space of communal life. Self-sustaining economies, supported by customs, rituals, and values, have given way to capitalism and subsistence jobs or migratory work. For some, the destruction of communal and self-sufficient lifestyles has robbed people of traditional parenting skills. Role models for child rearing and extended family or fictive kin for childcare disappear as social structures disintegrate and biological parents are killed, are absent for socioeconomic reasons, or suffer ill health (both mental and physical). This means that many children have lost and continue to lose the opportunity to be parented by competent individuals and nurturing community members as additional or substitute parental figures. As children grow in an atmosphere of "multiple marginality" with scarce healthy parenting, spiraling damage is done to each subsequent generation.[26] The socioeconomic changes in traditional communities and continuing poverty force people into nontraditional relationships and behaviors, increasing the chance that nurturing and coherent practices of traditional parenting will be unavailable.[27] In an autobiographical piece, Canéla Jaramillo writes of such upheaval:

> And the women—my god. We were nothing unless we could stay off drugs and alcohol or away from pregnancy. . . . Most of us didn't. All of us—men and women alike—are scarred now, our faces marred, our teeth ugly . . . and somehow paranoid. I got out early— left home at fourteen—because the violence was killing my spirit and because my mother's was already dead. A practicing alcoholic, she's been telling me since she was thirty, "My life is over." She's only forty-six. . . . But I went the wrong way . . . we didn't have the tools to make a smooth transition from the coarseness of the streets to the unblemished facade of the universities, corporate structures, whatever.[28]

Though individuals deal with and respond to trauma and massive loss in a variety of ways, as a group Chicanas/os have not been allowed to or had the time to mourn or heal. Our grief is as disenfranchised and disavowed as we have been. For many Mexican Americans, the "memory" itself has been erased in U.S. history classes. While many rally around cries to "never forget" the horrors of Nazi crimes, no mainstream angst has been noted as Chicano and indigenous histories have been rendered invisible. Thus, it is almost impossible for us to understand the link between this memory of trauma and the extent of the devastation that comes from the shaming practices to which we are currently subjected. Forced to maintain a constant position of self-defense, many of us do not fully understand that assaults on the core continue, and we are coerced into a kind of denial. This is especially true when confronted with the charge that we are displaying a "victim mentality." Such an accusation has to be one of the most brilliant rhetorical strategies in the history of argument. No one in a hierarchical culture, in a country that so prizes dominance, wants to be seen in this way.

In a competitive culture there is stigma and shame attached to losing. This is what mainstream people draw on when they say "we won, you lost, get over it." However, this is true of both Spanish and Anglo American value systems. Like many other Latinos living in the United States, we have been dominated by two European nations—by two groups of people who thought themselves our intellectual, physical, cultural, and spiritual superiors. (One of them we still carry in our blood and to various extents in our cultural practices.) Hence, we as a people have suffered what Jeanette Rodriguez describes as "layered-on oppression." For women this burden has been great, because the stigma of losing has been lain at our feet. Contemporary women still feel the impact of this violence and shame in the

form of the Malinche paradigm—a cultural model that sees women as betrayers and whores complicit in the conquest of Mexico.[29] (This is part of
the reason that Chicana authors challenge the rhetoric of nationalism, ethnic identity, or inherited collectivity—sometimes even as it is reaffirmed.)

While we have a right to embrace our status as victims, we rarely do.
Our literature is marked instead by pride in our *mestizaje*, border regions
instead of national boundaries, an emphasis on difference, ancient cultural
symbols with contemporary definitions, and experimental techniques and
styles. The two most common characteristics of Chicana subjective expression are multiplicity and contradiction. This comes from embracing an
identity and otherness we have been encouraged to despise, and working
through a maze of fragmented memories, national identities, and para-
doxical subject positions in an effort to remain connected while simultaneously dispensing with shame.[30] Rather than understanding the charge of
victim mentality as a form of victim baiting, however, we tend to become
stoic—to deny the effects of traumatic experience.

But this failure to face our pain is not just a matter of conscious repudi-
ation. Normal mourning processes have also been interrupted by the ordinary need to survive. We cannot cry out our pain if we are mustering the
strength to run from or survive violence, move our families off lost homelands, or migrate to find work. Feeding ourselves and our children on minimum (or less than minimum) wage jobs precludes the time and ability to
be self-reflective. If inadequate nutrition takes a toll on the body, it ham-
pers the mind and soul as well. Parents who try to put on a brave face for
their children when confronted with adversity disallow their own tears of
frustration and sadness. Grief held in is a wound that will not heal. Parents
who do this teach their children to stop the soul from releasing pain. Facing the humiliation of dealing with insensitive or patronizing social service
workers increases the damage to the spirit rather than allocating energy
to recuperation.[31] Working twice as hard to get an education or maintain
a decent job because we cannot be average to get ahead, struggling to preserve the vitality our families require, or fighting the stigma that comes
with assumptions and stereotypes about affirmative action policies leaves
us with little energy or enthusiasm for introspection.[32]

Occupying many social and professional locations where we seem invisible or are silenced by racism, classism, sexism, and homophobia propels
us out of mourning and into the struggle for social justice and equality. It
becomes more important for us to rebel than to focus on the well-being of
the Self. There is so much work to do. Discrimination in education, housing, employment, social services, and the criminal justice system all demand our attention. Rebuilding our communities, reclaiming traditional
communal patterns, or simply maintaining the peace in neighborhoods

torn apart by urban pressures leaves no time to grieve our multiple losses. Trying to reconstruct relationships destroyed by poverty, or to define new family models that will contribute to the health and well-being of our children *and* having to defend our right to do so, consume our creative energies. As my friend Susana De León—*danzante,* community activist, and immigration lawyer—has said when we've discussed these issues, "healing is something we must do. But as long as our children are dying, getting lost, being shot, being raped . . . I don't have time to heal, to grieve. I only have time for war. I only have time to fight."

Women forced or choosing to become decisionmakers, operating in the public sphere where we confront patriarchal structures, need to guard our sense of self and depend on our communal strength. Yet for *Lesbianas* or transgendered Mexican Americans, communalism within the larger Mexican American community can be mere illusion. For them racism and ethnocentrism are "compounded by conflicting loyalties and additional tasks in the development of [an] identity" as a woman of color and as a Lesbian, bisexual, or transgendered person. In this case, heterosexism joins racism and horizontal hostility within the community as another source of insidious trauma.[33] Chicanos who have felt emasculated by the mechanisms of conquest, colonization, continual racism, and the ensuing shame these processes entail need to reconstruct communal definitions of manhood rather than reifying European concepts of masculinity. All of us need to repair our ability to survive emotionally. But this cannot happen without facing the damage that has been done.[34]

Denial and unrealistic perceptions are well-known features of both addiction and the inability to deal with pain. For Chicanas/os denial may be self-imposed, but it can also be forced upon us from the outside by erasing our historical memory. Public schools can be sites of this kind of denial. Even when Eurocentric histories deal with marginalized communities, texts are purposefully constructed to present an "alternative" view of events and social locations on this continent. Such texts rarely interrogate systematic power. Additionally, bias is built into this additive method because it implies that some people merely have a perspective that diverges from an "objective" view of history. Another tactic is the romanticization of cultural histories outside the mainstream. This form of denial ignores the carnage that took place in the Americas, as well as the continuing pathology that exists in the dominant culture as a result of that history.[35]

In her novel set in the late 1960s, *Delia's Song,* Lucha Corpi deals with another kind of denial—the invisibility of a segment of Mexican American life. Her protagonist is faced with a college professor unaware of any life outside her own social location. The white, middle-class sociologist bemoans the war in Vietnam and the failure of the public to understand why it should not continue. Since the professor defines the public through her own experience, she says the war goes on because "we don't know what it is to have our country torn in two, to lose parents, children, brothers or sisters, our homes. To watch a mother put a rifle in her son's hands and send him to a sure death."

Corpi confronts this academic's historical amnesia and insensitivity with the thoughts and words of Delia, a young Chicana activist, who thinks not only of the history of her people, but also of her family's personal struggle in urban Los Angeles (losing one brother to drugs, one to the war in Vietnam). Delia also knows the reality of ongoing racial oppression.

> To lose brothers   Lose your children   We do know what that is   We Chicanos know what that is   Oh Mattie   We don't have to go that far [to Vietnam]   We've been at war here . . .   Maybe white people don't know what war is all about, but we Chicanos know all about it. . . .   For us the Civil War never ended. We're still fighting it.[36]

Similarly in denial of history, the Catholic Church has never fully acknowledged its affiliation with the Spanish state or the Mexican government. Though it has recently apologized to the indigenous peoples in the Americas, this might be seen as an effort to sustain its religious dominance in Latin America. If there is one thing the Church must learn, it is that one apology cannot erase prodigious amounts of pain. Priests wrote the history of the ancient American civilizations. They recorded indigenous social structures and complex spiritual practices—based on science and a cosmological view of the world—through decidedly Christian conceptualizations. This is one of the mechanisms for splitting the unified duality of Aztec deities into conflicting pairs with dominant male and subordinate female characteristics. Such denial of unity and balance closes this possible source of healing for *Mexicanas* and Chicanas. It hides potential ways of grieving for both genders. In addition to introducing concepts like sin and eternal damnation, Catholicism brought to Mexico other doctrines of denial, urging Indians to transcend the body, to see glory in suffering, to trust in God's plan that the meek would one day inherit the earth—all denying the brutality and immorality of the Spanish soldiers. Had this history been acknowledged, it may have helped the descendants of those long silenced to focus our anger in more constructive ways. It might have mitigated the shame many people felt.[37]

In order to survive with any dignity at all, many Chicanas/os have been forced into denial, have learned to look away from our devastating losses, and to repudiate the personal manifestations of communal shame. Violence—against one another and especially toward women and children—is one of the unhealthy ways that we express and inflict shame and rage, continue the trauma, and prevent grieving. Many of us learned that the world is divided into those who conquer and those who are conquered. We then become determined to take a dominant position in order to protect ourselves—even if this can only be actualized in our interpersonal relationships. This can have devastating consequences primarily for women and children. No matter how unhealthy, the family for most Mexican Americans, at whatever cost to the individual, must remain intact. Denial of the suffering we experience as a result of this impulse to protect the family is Promethean. Often our Spanish/Moorish traditions of maintaining a sense of family honor keep us silent. Religion has been used to teach women to be self-effacing, subservient, and to produce as many children as possible—all of which have served to make women subject to and dependent on men. Such doctrine denies female strength and robs women of the ability to make choices in their own best interest and in self-protection from violence.

Shame and guilt were part of the Church's arsenal of socialization techniques in teaching people what it meant for women to be sexual beings. The Church, as well as Spanish and later Anglo society, convinced men that women had to be protected from the outside or public world—that her primary concern should be the family. Priests and protestant clergy often stood by the husband and defended the marriage even as women suffered in abusive alliances.[38] The legacy of such teaching is replicated in many Mexican American families to this day.[39]

In a piece written for *Ms* magazine, Sandra Cisneros tells us that the Church's aversion to female sexuality makes womanhood a concept "full of mysteries" for those Chicanas who grow up immersed in traditional, religious culture. In describing her own body shame, Cisneros says that this combination of Catholicism and *Mexicanidad* (or what she calls a "culture of denial"), "helped to create [a] blur, a vagueness about what went on 'down there'." Thus, Cisneros says, it was not until she was an adult, able to separate in some way from Church and family, that she even realized she had a vagina. She thought her period and her urine came from the same opening.

> No wonder, then, it was too terrible to think about a doctor—a man!—looking at you down there when you could never bring yourself to look at yourself. ¡Ay, nunca! How could I acknowledge my sexuality, let alone enjoy sex, with so much guilt? In the guise of modesty my culture locked me in a double chastity belt of ignorance and vergüenza, shame. I had never seen my mother nude. I had never taken a good look at myself either. Privacy for self-exploration belonged to the wealthy. In my home a private space was practically impossible.[40]

Cisneros goes on to describe how this confluence of ignorance, shame, and the prescriptives of class have implications for women's physical health.

In Chapter 3 of *Massacre of the Dreamers*, titled "The Ancient Roots of Machismo," Ana Castillo tells us the social function of such patterns as they relate to patriarchal control. "The regulation of female fidelity from a historical economic viewpoint had more to do with man's view of woman as property and his children as heirs to his property than a transgression of morals."[41] The Church, however, acted in concert with and enforced this socioeconomic necessity through strict religious ideals. Castillo says, "the book of Genesis was and remains woman's strongest document to establish once and for all when patriarchy was installed as the modus operandi for the whole of humanity."[42]

In some cases, our denial that anything is amiss takes us into an elaborate romanticization of male/female relationships, the family or the barrio. We do not like to speak of the harm done to us by Mexicanos/Chicanos, because we know their actions are sometimes the manifestation of offended spirits, humiliation, and unresolved feelings. Aletícia Tijerina, in a coming-out piece called, "I Am the Lost Daughter of My Mama's House," poignantly shows us what it is like for a child torn out of her own culture by the effect of various kinds of oppression.

> In my memory lies the knowledge that my own father tried to kill me. He took the tool of the oppressor's hatred and used it against his family. I do not forgive him. . . . I have lost much to the oppressor. My family. My language. My culture. Still I search. Long trails of ancestral serapes flap in the winds of life carried from one generation to the next.[43]

For many of us it is also true that whatever assault we experience in our families or communities may be somehow perceived as less daunting than what we face in mainstream America. In dealing with racism or classism, family and community may be our source of strength and safety, no matter how damaged they are. That is where we feel most connected—most tied to some ancient root (as Tijerina insinuates in the previous paragraph). In terms of homophobia, however, the family can be more rejecting than the society at large. For many women, the feeling that we must choose between two spaces so unsafe leads us to a sense of hopelessness. But, Chicana writers, like Tijerina, are neither silent nor forgiving.[44]

Gloria Anzaldúa tells us in much of her work about the degree of heterosexism in Spanish/Catholic culture.[45] In Chapter 2 of *Borderlands*, she explains that a Chicana Lesbian faces all the layers of oppression, as well as censure within her own culture because she breaks not one, but "two moral prohibitions." She is sexual and she is lesbian. To come out is to risk being separated from one's home environment, to be thrown out into the Anglo world. Total rejection, however, may come only after an attempted confinement or conversion. (Though the seriousness of it might vary, few Chicanas are without a story of how at some point, her parents tried to "lock her up"—or suggested it—as a solution to what they perceived as immoral behavior.)

When I encounter these stories, I think of how overwhelmed I was in 1987 when I first read Gloria Anzaldúa's statement in *Borderlands*, "Not me sold out my people but they me."[46] It was a direct confrontation of the Malinche paradigm, but also a thought that had never occurred to me, that I could be "betrayed" because of my own culture's prejudices. Since then, in reading Chicana stories, I have found reason to recall it over and over. Anzaldúa also tells us how unsettling this realization can be. "Woman does not feel safe when her own culture, and white culture, are critical of her; when all males of all races hunt her as prey. Alienated from her mother culture, 'alien' in the dominant culture . . . her face caught between . . . the different worlds she inhabits."[47] As women of color we must face two worlds in denial: one trying to hide its history of genocide and inequality, the other trying to deny us our sexuality and equality.

It is human nature to protect the Self against such overwhelming pain. Many of us do that by becoming numb to it in one way or another. Dissociation is an act that separates us from the traumatic experience or the intense emotions associated with shame. Therapist Beverly Engel describes it as "emotional anesthesia." Similarly, addiction in any form is suppressed pain, grief unspoken, trauma unacknowledged. Sometimes this means a dependence on alcohol or other drugs. But it can also mean an addiction to work, sex, pornography, the Internet, gambling, or a variety of dangerous activities—anything that interferes with daily, *intimate* life. Working hard for many Mexican Americans means mind-numbing menial labor in order to survive. This is not an addiction in the conventional sense, but it can act as an anesthetic nevertheless—one that readily serves the needs of a free market economy.[48] As such, the pusher of this addictive substance is capitalism. When I remember or think about the people I have known working in factories or the fields, there were always those who worked harder than anyone else, went beyond what it took to survive, beyond what was expected, or even ideally desired by the bosses. They were physical and emotional zombies by the end of the day, incapable of responding to their own or anyone else's needs. Too tired to feel.

Writing of a painful life of deprivation at the margins of society, Marina Rivera, in her poem "Mestiza," shows how even the brightest of the working poor can be silenced and left numb to life's possibilities. Clearly this kind of dissociation is imposed upon us. "Even if the mind were a waterfall of life itself," she says, "they would tie you by your tongue . . . because of your poverty/you ate your dreams, learned to walk on your longings until they wore out."[49]

Other Chicanas/os—less economically precarious—get the same effect by becoming workaholics in professional or white-collar jobs, in social service agencies, and in mainstream or radical politics.[50] Both kinds of overwork can kill the spirit. But this too can be seen as an imposition. Organizations and institutions where the demand on us is great because we exist in small numbers become perfect arenas for this type of avoidance. The inability to say "no" to the ridiculously numerous requests for our time may lead to emotional burnout, physical illness, and mental exhaustion.

When we are in denial and operating in dysfunctional states, we may not teach or learn Mexican traditions or the Spanish language. Strongly political and resistant children feel and return shame when parents act out their own internalized feelings of inferiority and demand total assimilation—thinking that it will spare their children the violence of racism. Such mothers and fathers try to erase any traces of Mexican or indigenous culture from their children. Conversely, parents and grandparents who want to return to their homeland, or relatives still in Mexico, will see their acculturated offspring and call them sell-outs or *pochos*, increasing the sense of dislocation and the disfavor we already feel. Out of a desperate need to fit in with mainstream peers, some children may choose to reject their parent's ethnicity and culture, embracing U.S. mainstream culture with the full intention to discard Mexicanness. But thankfully, totally discarding or erasing our ethnicity is usually impossible. If your grandmother or your mother is Mexican, she cannot help teaching you much about being Mexican even if she does not mean to do so. This has to do with implicit cultural knowledge that is not consciously taught, or avoided, but is nevertheless learned and accumulated over a lifetime. No matter how much we disaffirm, some remnant remains.

As we continue to confront discriminatory America, layers of shame keep building across the generations, the original lacerations fester, and without mourning our losses, without tending these wounds, our bruised hearts begin to search for protection. This may mean shutting down, but it may also mean behaving inappropriately.[51] *Shame is an insidious method of social control.* It is similar to guilt and the two emotions have some parallel consequences and manifestations. (In many cases, one leads to the other.) But there is also a subtle distinction to be made.[52] People who feel guilty generally *do* things they are not supposed to do when they act out. Guilt, Vicki Underland-Rosow tells us, is associated with making a mistake. Others perceive these people as individuals whose needs and responsibilities, successes and failures, *only* reflect singular desires and actions. They do not reflect on anyone else, and it is assumed that amends can be made. For these people, there is no need to consider the larger society.[53] People who feel shame, on the other hand, generally *do not* do the things they are supposed to do. Underland-Rosow says that shame is the feeling or perception that as a person you are flawed at the core. No wrongs can be made right because the very being is wrong. "Internalized shame is experienced as a deep and abiding sense of being defective, never quite good enough as a person."[54] The Cervantes poem quoted earlier clearly illustrates this "nagging preoccupation of not being good enough."[55]

In "La Prieta," Gloria Anzaldúa speaks of being brown, queer, and poor. She illustrates the process of shaming, the way in which doing something outside the norm becomes an excuse for others to name-call. She also shows how this causes horizontal hostility among members of the same oppressed ethnic group. Following this process is an attempt at acculturation and finally an inability to act at all.

> eating at school out of sacks, hiding our "lonches" papas con chorizo behind cupped hands and bowed heads, gobbling them up before the other kids could see. Guilt lay folded in the tortilla. The Anglo kids laughing—calling us "tortilleros," the Mexican kids taking up the word and using it as a club with which to hit each other. My brothers, sister and I started bringing white bread sandwiches to school. After a while we stopped taking our lunch altogether.[56]

Carmen Morones illustrates a similar effect of inner shame in her short story, "Grace." Her protagonist is a young Chicana named Frances, who is hoping for a scholarship to UCLA. Her guidance counselor discourages her from applying, telling her that he doesn't think she can compete with other applicants. In response, she lingers in the hallway, ashamed to go back to her class. "She felt so small," Morones writes. "A nobody. A nothing. She felt angry with Mr. Lobauer for treating her like she was stupid. But more than that she was angry at herself for having let herself want something so badly that she knew deep within that she would never have."[57] In the last sentence, Morones acknowledges how shame can coexist with internalized oppression. Though Grace knows she is not stupid and is angry about being treated as such, she turns that rage inward, and instead of blaming the system, she blames herself.

Unfortunately, the United States is not the only social environment in which Chicanas/os feel flawed. As Pat Mora expresses in her poem "Legal Alien," we Chicanas/os can experience uneasiness in a Mexican context as well. Though we may have mastered smooth transitions from one to the next, we still understand that we will be perceived as "alien" in both spaces because we are, as Mora says, "American but hyphenated . . . between the fringes of both worlds." Yet, we cover our sense of dislocation "by smil-ing/by masking the discomfort/of being pre-judged/Bi-laterally."

When people who feel deep shame act out, their inability to live up to prescriptive expectations of the dominant culture is perceived as represen-tative of the entire group—as bringing dishonor to the community, ethnic group, or nation.[58] Socioeconomic status often determines who has the luxury to consider her- or himself an individual in the United States. Com-bine this understanding with thinking about who should feel guilty for the American Holocaust, as well as whom the process has shamed, and we begin to see the mainstream as a guilt culture, while Mexican Americans can be seen as a shame culture. This is one of the reasons the larger society sees a white lawyer selling cocaine as an individual, but a Mexican Ameri-can bringing marijuana across the border as symbolic of an outlaw culture, and, why we (Mexicans) automatically wince whenever people in our com-munity commit crimes that are publicly broadcast. We see it as bringing shame to La Raza, because we know that is the way it will be perceived by the larger society. We Chicanas/os are often communal actors, whose indi-vidual desire is subsumed by the needs of the whole.[59]

Thus, shame can be used to promote discriminatory actions thought to increase the public good and make criminal those behaviors that interfere with its interests. Basing his theory on the work of Michel Foucault, Thomas L. Dumm argues that the penitentiary system is constitutive of liberal democracy. That it "formed the epistemological project of liberal democracy, creating conditions of knowledge of Self and Other that were to shape the political subject required for liberal and democratic values to be realized in practice."

America—ideologically conceived as a system of "self-rule"—neverthe-less needed an institution that would encourage people to adopt its values. The threat and shame of punishment was expected to create individuals who could rule themselves. We can still see this foundational thought in public discourse around the need for longer jail sentences, more severe punishment, and the death penalty as "deterrents," though this is not borne out as a preventative in social science research.[60] Shame may work to devalue the people who do not contribute to society in the normalized way, but it does not prevent people from committing crimes. (Nor does it stop the justice system, including police forces, from criminalizing and in-carcerating either innocent people, or people of color in unfair numbers.) Shame does, however, encourage innocent people to plead guilty to crimes they have not committed.[61]

Clinical psychologist Gershen Kaufman tells us that shame is central to human life, because it has such a profound impact on all areas of the Self and thus on our interpersonal relationships. As such, it "extends well beyond our contemporary concerns with the problems of addiction and abuse, the emergent reality of dysfunctional family systems, or even the current ascendance of the recovery movement." He feels that it also plays a major role in "minority group relations, minority identity development, national identity development, and international relations."[62] To get at this idea, Kaufman draws a distinction between shame as innate affect (something all humans feel at some point), and shame that is internalized as the psyche is developing. The latter is not universal. It occurs and becomes part of the Self when an ethnic identity is in formation. This makes it an automatic or subconscious response that is constantly functioning. It does not require a specific triggering event. This means that *shame can act as a form of social control even in the absence of direct oppression.*

> It is precisely following the internalization of shame as a major source of one's identity that the self becomes able to both activate and experience shame without an inducing interpersonal event. The self is then vulnerable to shame irrespective of any external messages communicated from others. In effect, shame becomes autonomous when internalized and hence impervious to change. In the process of internalization lies the [social] significance of shame.[63]

This is why ingesting shame as a child is so significant, and why many of us seem to have a very low tolerance for any kind of slight we encounter as adults—whether it is intended or not. It is also why some of us react even in the absence of any real insult. The effects of discrimination and dominance are cumulative. And, this is internalized from the very moment we begin to recognize our difference and to see ourselves as inferior in the oppressor's eyes.

The sources of our shame are extensive. We learn it in our homes from parents like my father who has been made to feel inferior by the dominant culture. It comes to us through our social contacts, through the racism we encounter, whether it is blatant and conscious, or well intentioned, unaware, and subconscious. We learn it in schools from biased and ignorant classmates and teachers who are ethnocentric, if not directly racist, as well as from the somatic paranoids and biased individuals pervasive in the Church. They invade our homes and schools, dispensing shame along with verses from the Bible and rules from Rome. Textbooks, academic research, and statistical studies erase our histories, ignore our culture, and blame us for our overrepresentation at the bottom of the economic social structure.[64] This shame is often internalized and causes family members to debase one another in response to racism and ethnocentrism. This can happen through colorism or shade—difference, lookism, sexism, and homophobia. Children exposed to massive amounts of humiliation and contempt from every direction become ashamed of parents who seem to conform to stereotypes or display certain ethnic behaviors that have been vilified or trivialized by outsiders. People in the mainstream, and sometimes within the family or community, will stigmatize anyone exhibiting any aspect of these "negative" images.[65]

Contempt for who we are as Mexicans is perpetuated in various media representations of Hispanics or Latinos, through unrepresentative images or distorted stereotypes, and in primarily injurious portrayals unbalanced by positive ones. In our almost complete absence from film and television, except as caricatures, we get the message that we are not part of the United States (unless we are so whitewashed that we are no longer recognizable as Mexican or Chicana/o). Covert and overt messages from bosses and on job sites, at unemployment offices, welfare agencies, and anti-immigrant political speeches, or in newspaper editorials relay negative reactions to our presence and remind us of our "place" in the larger society. Through condemnation of our language usage (by both English and Spanish speakers) our very method of communication becomes a way to belittle us.[66]

This stigma is evident as friends and family members respond to prodigious humiliation with conflicting messages of hypermasculine stoicism and over-the-top emotional expressiveness. Our personal relationships suffer and become distorted in an atmosphere of unresolved grief and profound sadness, derogation, and disgrace, as well as anxiety about our social location and safety. When we are not clinging to one another in our mutual fear and frustration, we distrust those most like us. Anzaldúa says, "Chicana feminists often skirt around each other with suspicion and hesitation. For the longest time I couldn't figure it out. Then it dawned on me. To be close to another Chicana is like looking into the mirror. We are afraid of what we'll see there. Pena. Shame. Low estimation of self."[67]

This internalized shame leads to conflicts within the Mexican American and larger Latino communities. Hostility between those who want to assimilate or embrace mainstream culture and those who disparage it, for instance, is really a contrast between two responses to racism and shaming. One is defiant of the master; the other acquiescent or complicit. (Neither is to blame.) In some cases, the one who wishes to join the mainstream will not accept it, or does not perceive it, as a dominant force. For others, joining to whatever degree it is possible is a way of appropriating some of the power and privilege we recognize.

Whatever its source or manifestation, elitism has a deleterious effect on the psyche in terms of social relationships. Trouble often erupts between Chicanas/os and Latin Americans who have grown up as part of the elite or mainstream in their own countries. This happens because these Latinas/os do not understand how shame—as the legacy of conquest and colonization and as an ongoing process—has affected working-class Mexican American people. Nor do such elites know what it means to internalize shame at an early age. "Many Latin American countries do not have a middle class as we know it in the United States. Thus, elitist attitudes, based on dichotomous social class divisions, are transplanted to the United States" by upper-class Latinos.[68] They sometimes fail to perceive the depth of injustice and social inequality in this country or to understand our need to respond with intense anger. Even if they encounter racism or ethnocentrism in the United States, they do so as adults. Their psyche or sense of Self did not develop in a climate of hatred, as it has for Chicanas/os. Hard feelings will develop if these Latinos are recruited—or decide on their own—to take advantage of affirmative action programs even if they come from wealthy families and have not lived a lifetime of disadvantage.[69]

Though this conflict grows out of European, hierarchical structure, racism, and culpability, it does not lessen the sad fact that assimilated Mexicans and elite Hispanics can reinforce feelings of shame in those that cannot or will not assimilate. Such people may join the mainstream in its demand that we forget about the past, which is a denial of history's connection to continuing discrimination. Since it tends to place blame for the failure to rise on the individual, it is also a disheartening example of victim blaming.

When we do not mourn what we have lost, or deal with the shame, when we deny our emotions, avoid any thought of the events in our lives or memories of our past that cause us pain, we only increase or prolong the symptoms of PTSD. If we avoid grieving, which necessarily includes thinking about the trauma, then we never face the injured Self. Failure to do so can result in inappropriate emotional responses to stimuli in our everyday lives. We may feel overwhelmed by little things that go wrong, yet unaffected by a major crisis. We can be filled with enormous grief over insignificant events like the loss of a soccer game, but express or experience little emotion when someone close to us disappears from our life. Rage may be directed at a child who spills milk, while we exhibit numb indifference in response to spousal violation.[70]

Such dysfunction plays out in our families, where only the needs of the people most severely afflicted by stress disorders get met. This can result in the abuse, neglect, and abandonment of children. Without healthy parental skills or role models, there is no one to foster, maintain, or repair our self-esteem. The lack of extended families due to migration can mean there is no one to teach us our personal and collective history from a Mexican perspective, no one to combat the shaming processes nor empathize with our pain. When we do not see our inherent and individual value reflected in the eyes of our parents, it is very difficult to learn to protect ourselves. In dysfunctional households we only learn to internalize more shame. There is no example of dealing with trauma or doing grief work for us to follow, no one to talk with about our unresolved feelings. In fact, when the need to express or explore our emotions is constantly stifled, we learn not to speak— cutting off a potential path to regaining our balance. Feeling and subjective need become taboo. No emotional life is possible in an atmosphere where intensity is either forbidden or misdirected.[71]

The whole Self, capable of so much more, is denied, lost, or forbidden. *"Sin alma no puedes animarte pa' nada."*[72] In this state, personal needs or desires become unnecessary. Lacking an entire range of emotions, we have no reason to set or learn boundaries or limits. If we do not learn how to defend ourselves or see the need to do so, we may give others access to us in unhealthy ways—simultaneously closing down our vulnerability to genuine, human connection. At the same time we may trespass on the rights and safety of others or take advantage of their weaknesses and insecurities.[73] For some this leads to promiscuity, a way of experiencing intensity without having to feel it. Canéla Jaramillo writes:

> I used my body against the way my mother used hers: fucking but never cooking, cleaning or loving. Until I realized it was the same kind of poison . . . I fell in love with a woman—first in a long string of "broken children" I began to collect, trying to nurse my own pain, to rock it to sleep . . . we unleashed a lot of fury and terror on each other, just trying to be vulnerable enough to love.[74]

Professional scholars may become stuck in thought and analysis. Practicing a kind of intellectual promiscuity they separate themselves from old community ties and responsibilities in the process. This may not appear on the surface as dysfunction, but it can be a way to avoid intimacy. If we wish to push down the emotional residue of oppressive or painful experience, we may avoid talking to people with whom we grew up or deny our working-class roots except as it is politically expedient to remember them. It can also mean sharing the bulk of our lives with people with whom we are in no danger of forming truly intimate relationships. For Mexican American women who respond in this fashion, *Chicanisma* is no longer a piece of the soul, but merely a rhetorical tool.

Internalized shame "forms the foundation around which other feelings about the Self will be experienced . . . until finally the Self is engulfed. In this way shame becomes paralyzing." While we may avoid some pain in the short term by shutting down, no positive emotions can be experienced either.[75] Emotions—good or bad—are an essential part of a life fully lived.

Without them we cannot move or grow. We can exist, but it is not the abundant life to which we are entitled. Elena Avila tells us that "Without soul, we feel empty . . . and homeless. We look into space and long for 'something' that will give us that childlike innocence, joy, and creativity. Some of us become cynical, withdrawing and isolating ourselves from each other. Or we [find a way] to escape."[76] Finding alternative "fuels" that can substitute for life energy—anything to which we may become addicted—further assails the Self. When the feelings get erased you cannot experience attachment.[77]

Unfortunately, this way of dealing with anguish does not stop with any individual. We pass it all on to the next generation, the effect of the original trauma, the unresolved grief, the shame, the dysfunction, and the addictive behaviors. You do not have to be actively engaged in the addiction to pass on the spiritually crippling turmoil. "Dry drunks" can transmit dysfunction through emotionally debilitating behaviors that show up in the next generations as physical or sexual abuse. Such things add to the original wound even if we have no conscious connection to the memory, because they continue (or begin for our children) the assault on our bodies, minds, spirits, and emotions. The inability to experience intimacy, to feel or give love unconditionally can spread across the community as it is expressed in violence toward others—(re)creating trauma for all those involved. In this way children in families who have managed to become relatively healthy, can reinherit dysfunction through public behaviors and social contacts. Members of the family still vulnerable to stress can then fall back into familiar dysfunctional patterns. If the problem is in the community it can be passed on.[78]

Like African American and Asian women, Chicana authors have been assailed for revealing the pain and inequality that exists in our lives. As men, Chicanos may feel personally blamed by revelations of abusive relationships, chauvinistic paternal figures in the community or tyrannical fathers, preferential treatment of our brothers, and other manifestations of cultural sexism. This perception (not the criticism itself) only adds to their own guilt and shame, as well as reinforces the notion of women as traitors—in this case, the betrayers of "family" secrets.[79] But the major problem with stories that reveal the suffering of Chicanas is that some readers tend to fixate on it, not understanding or looking for the origins of this heartache in anything but individual choice, response, and conduct. Other readers who are themselves "victims of catastrophic events" or dysfunctional behaviors "may suffer from sudden flashbacks that disrupt their lives and catapult them back to the abusive situation. Remembering as they do, having their lives disrupted so, they feel isolated and different. . . . They may also despair that there is no hope, that there is nowhere to turn."[80]

Such people do not want our vulnerability and shame exposed because it is too painful to confront. Neither do they want to be judged by outsiders because of it.

Despite the dangers involved, Chicanas cannot and will not abandon this work. Rarely do they leave readers without hope—even as they express their own pain. Over and over in Chicana narratives we see the memories, the personal and communal effects of our historic wounding, unresolved emotions, and daily struggles.[81] We see characters, which resemble the people in our communities, suffering what we do, acting out of internalized shame and displaying incongruous behaviors. But we also see personal journeys through the pain—women confronting the "shadow beast" of a painful past.[82] Chicana writers seem to know that pain, anger, and fear—as well as their corollary inappropriate reactions—will not dissipate without exposure. It will only grow more intense and explosive as contemporary stresses exacerbate the problems that began with social and political injustice.

In the United States, the social unrest that explodes out of our pain quickly becomes a battle between mismatched opponents. The government has the most effective weapons of annihilation and control. People responding to an oppressive regime rarely have more than our bodies. Thus, psychological distress will never sustain an effective, ideological revolution. Unfortunately, rage and grief are more likely to implode rather than explode. In the land of the free, radical action is easily contained. Chicana writers are more apt to commit to a war of words, to cross figurative lines in the sand, to deliberately engage in arenas where change is slow, but physical death or incarceration is unlikely. As agents in a discursive struggle, Chicana writers must reveal how we are affected by inequality wherever it exists, despite objections and trivialization by male (or male-identified) critics. While intrafamilial tensions as subject matter can be universal themes, we must make them ethnically, nationally, culturally, and historically specific. *The connection between historical memory, dysfunctional behaviors, and oppression must be clear.*

Elena Avila says that the place of our healing is embedded in our cultural heritage.

> We are not strangers to trauma, oppression, and loss. We . . . have had to fight long and hard to preserve our culture. I thank our ancestors for knowing that we are more than a body . . . we are also a soul. Our soul is our unique essence, our life force . . . when our soul is present, we accept dualized and fragmented parts of us as a paradox . . . we understand the paradox. We are a proud, Chicano people who no longer tolerate the injustice and oppression of a

society that does not recognize the earth wisdom of her indigenous people.[83]

It is this aspect of the literature—this resilient *indigenisma*—that is most often missed by mainstream audiences and cultural critics seduced by the promise (and sometimes economic rewards) of multiculturalism and diversity. But Avila goes on to point out that identifying with this *indigenisma* has a communal function beyond a romantic longing for post-modern complexity.

> our culture is rich with healing and our words can become Yerba Buena words when we tap into the old wisdom of our antepasados. Our souls are deeply embedded into that simple earthy knowledge, and we can find ourselves "back home" when we open up to all that we are.[84]

History and tradition are part of our present *and* our future. Neither problems nor solutions solely originate with the individual. In order to be effective in public life, however, we must be healthy enough to think critically about our past and to form sound alliances with other people. Genuine social change depends on both. Masculine movement politics, focused solely on economic inequality, do not encourage us to reveal our human needs, our psychological distress, or emotional pain. Our own defensiveness sometimes inhibits our ability to create connections with others. It teaches us to hide our vulnerability and causes us to distrust. (Of course, this may be a learned survival strategy.) But Chicana authors seem to understand that acknowledging the loss, the disgrace, and the pain in our lives—and learning to trust—is a major step toward eradicating the kind of vulnerability that grows out of dysfunction. In "Corazón de una anciana," Edna Escamill writes of her need to deal with the psyche, not just ideological struggle.

> ¡LA RAZA! Sometimes all it means to me is suffering. Tragedy. Poverty. Las caras de los tortured santos y las mujeres en luto, toda la vida en luto. La miseria is not anything I want to remember and everything I cannot forget. Sometimes the bravery in facing and struggling in such life is too little. The courage with which a people siguen luchando against prejudice and injustice is not glory enough. I am not content with that picture—I am only crazy.[85]

In order for us to be able to help succeeding generations make healthy connections to our spiritual mothers and blended cultural traditions (Indian, Spanish, Mestizo, and the United States), we have to deal with our own wounds. As Gloria Anzaldúa begins to move toward the new mestiza consciousness in *Borderlands*, she says:

> I acknowledge that the self and the race have been wounded. . . . On that day I gather the splintered and disowned parts of la gente mexicana and hold them in my arms. Todas las partes de nosotros valen . . . I will not be shamed again / Nor will I shame myself. I am possessed by a vision: that we Chicanas and Chicanos have taken back or uncovered our true faces.[86]

If we understand that oppression is not simply about political or institutional discrimination, but that it is also a form of mental, physical, spiritual, and emotional abuse, we can cleanse ourselves and stop internalizing the hatred and humiliation we experience. We can celebrate, without apology or qualification, the strength it has taken to survive this history. Realizing that we have this power makes obvious our duty to feel and express our rage over what we have lost. To explode rather than implode.

Mexican Americans who learn the "truth" of our history must either deny it or face the intense anger it engenders. This is not easy for damaged people who have learned to suppress feelings. But, we must do so in ways that do not add to our adversity and pain, but will renew us.[87] Avoidance mechanisms drain us. The effort it takes to keep our feelings down saps our strength. "Anger," Beverly Engel maintains:

> [I]s energy, a motivating force than can empower those who feel helpless. Anger is your way out. By releasing anger in a constructive way, you will increase your ability to truthfully communicate what you feel. Speaking . . . will prevent the build-up of tension [that has exhausted your supply of energy]—energy that could otherwise be used to feel and express love and compassion.[88]

Our displaced spirit "is so resilient and forgiving. It will come back to us when we take the time and courage to look for it. It will come back when we commit to care for it and allow it expression."[89]

Perhaps the first step is to realize that this anger is justified. As Chicanas, we have every right to be angry with our oppressors, to feel rage at family members or friends who act in similar ways or in collusion with those who dominate us, to be repulsed by anyone who excuses or protects the institutional and personal tyrants in our lives. We are right to resent those who express sympathy with our plight but refuse to act concretely when they have the power to do so. It is legitimate to feel hostile toward anyone who does not believe that we have suffered or who trivializes our experience. Irritation is the only sane response to someone who tells us to transcend our pain or forget it. People who blame us for our own oppression deserve our exasperation and wrath when they fail to acknowledge or see the extent to which we have been damaged—or conversely, they expect us to constantly act out of that damage, ignoring our strength and ability to self-direct our lives. We have the right to be angry no matter how long ago the original trauma occurred or how different things were then, no matter how much progress has taken place, no matter how ignorant or well-intentioned our oppressors have been, no matter what change is promised in the future. Our fury is justified anytime we are ignored, silenced, negatively stereotyped, incorrectly labeled, or otherwise not respected. Any occasion in which our history is omitted or lied about deserves our indignant dismissal.[90] Until equality and justice become reality, we have a right to be angry.

But, in order to respond in healthy ways, we must learn to understand anger as separate from other emotions and to recognize with whom or with what we are angry. This is not always easy because the shame and anger often get mixed up. Or the anger over the traumatic events in our personal lives often becomes intertwined with political outrage. People who have suffered trauma in their interpersonal relationships may misdirect their rage over social injustice onto family members. Or, people angry with intimates who have hurt them may project their rage onto potential allies in a political struggle. Sometimes the level of paranoia and distrust among activists is stunning.

In some cases, shame can take the place of anger in our understanding of what we feel. This is especially true for women, who, are told as children and as adults that we are not really angry, that what we think is anger is really fear, jealousy, or insecurity. Thus, we learn to replace our anger with other emotions thought more suitable to proper female behavior. As adults our anger is trivialized as PMS or vilified as bitchiness. For women of color this bind may be reinforced by messages about appropriate or safe behavior based on race and ethnicity.[91] (Because those with whom we get angry could be dangerous to us.) Chicanas also face the dilemma that when we get angry, mainstream people often do not hear what we are saying because they are listening to us through stereotypes that paint us as hot-blooded and explosive, or we are equally dismissed—as loud, animated, intense, and easily agitated.

Destructive releases of anger help no one and may hurt us, or people close to us, especially if it is displaced and we strike out at someone who has not harmed us or is not the cause of our anger. Furtive or covert retaliation falls into this category, as do vengeance and manipulation. Any indirect method fails to truly express justified anger. Directing anger inward by suppressing it or trying to ignore the feeling is equally counterproductive.[92]

Expressing anger takes courage. We have to overcome the fear of rejection (in a society that does not value constructive disagreement) and fear of retaliation (in a nation that is hostile and violent). Nevertheless, we must try to do so, because the release of anger has many benefits. It can alleviate much of the shame and self-hatred we have accumulated because the more we stand up and face the source of our anger the more likely we are to stop blaming ourselves. The resulting improvement in the way we see ourselves lifts our hopes and allows us to dream. It also releases the energy we spend suppressing anger to be spent on more productively resistant activities. Once this physical tension eases, our bodies may be less prone to the corporeal manifestations of stress. When we discharge anger and shame it frees us to recognize and express other, more positive and pleasurable emotions. Each time we express anger constructively, our inner resolve strengthens and we get better at clarifying our positions, directly expressing our needs and making our boundaries clear. We can move from casualty to survivor, from someone controlled by the trauma and unresolved feelings to someone self-directed and able to work effectively for reform in genuine alliance with others.[93]

Constructive release of anger requires understanding that anger is a normal human response—that it is part of the affective system with which we are born. It is neither good nor bad. This does not mean we blame others for what we feel, though their actions may have triggered the response. But simply blaming (rather than identifying and expressing our feeling) fuels the anger, turns it inward, and keeps it from dissipating. If we hold people and institutions accountable for their actions, rather than simply blaming, we are opening the door to possibilities, to negotiation and problem solving.[94]

While the history of trauma and survival (that necessarily displaces normal grieving) is something most Mexican Americans share, responses to such stimuli vary. That is the reason some people seem unscathed and continue to function without apparent difficulty, able to sail smoothly the ups and downs of everyday life. Others respond moderately, neither fully functional nor dysfunctional, but somewhere in between, depending on the circumstances, hitting rough water with some failures, but surviving relatively well overall. Still others seem to bear the full brunt of the traumatic experience, those of us whose whole lives seem dark and destructive, damaged people who capsize even in calm seas.[95] While the offspring will similarly respond individually to their own experiences with traumatic events or the legacy of dysfunction in family and community, some will have a better chance at survival than others. But a chance is not a guarantee. Thus, the children of emotionally healthy parents may still end up in gangs, just as some children in dysfunctional families succeed at building their own seaworthy ships and sail out of the destruction.

As I said elsewhere, if the problem is in our community it can be passed on. But so can the ability to heal the Self. For Chicana authors that pattern is provided through the strong sense of self present in autobiographical prose, or it is passed on from the (literal or figurative) grandmother to a feisty protagonist. We can see, both in literature and in our lives, models for defying authority and subverting the dysfunction of the parents. Chicana writers are taking major steps toward recovering the lost self, or as Anzaldúa and Castillo have both suggested, healing the split. Though few of us will grieve or seek healing in as poetic or ritualistic a way as the writers, we must acknowledge the links between our collective and personal pain. We can only do this by studying history to discover the true nature of the American Holocaust. This may include exploring similar histories and the common elements of oppression among other peoples.[96] In doing so, we begin to see patterns shared by possible allies. We also need to learn about the socioeconomic and political devices of oppression and the way that problems in our communities are exploited or used as justification for continued neglect. As historian James Diego Vigil writes, "Making people feel inferior because of how they look, speak, and/or act is clearly a mechanism to keep them socially immobile."

As many women of color have pointed out in texts on the value of testifying, our stories of abuse and addiction should be told outloud, because both individual and community histories can provide us with survival strategies. Though often in textual form, this information does not have to lose its collective meaning, because it can always be returned to oral forms. This kind of witnessing or testifying has always been part of the healing process—and it is crucial for marginal communities and previously silenced voices. When we speak, we explode our sense of isolation and create new patterns of behavior for our children. We take the first steps toward healing because we let the pain escape. We are not numbing it or pushing it down. Eventually we will allow ourselves and others to remember and (re)experience the pain, to grieve the losses, and to know that we can survive traumatic events with a full range of emotions.

"When we experience grief, the grief is palpable, the sounds of the grieving are not blocked and the individual sobs and cries with every cell of the body."[97] Such a cry can be cleansing, provide release, and help heal the hurt. It helps the soul know what to do with so much pain. An old Mexican saying warns us to "Cry, child, for those without tears have a grief which never ends."[98] Like babies, if we cry hard and long, we sweat. We no longer hold our grief in conscious thought—blocked in our heads. The pain is released through the tear ducts and our pores.[99] Sometimes the release comes the other way around. Sweat and ceremony lead to tears. Anita Valerio describes this process that occurred for her when she was sixteen, attending her first Indian sweat.[100]

I cried inside that sweat, it seemed as though I could never stop crying as though my heart was being tugged at and finally torn loose

inside my chest. Other people cried too. So much emotion is expressed in the sweat and in the medicine lodge. And the weird thing
about it is—you don't really know what it is you're crying about. The
emotions seem to come out of some primeval cavity—some lone-
some half-remembered place. It seems when I cried it was more than
an individual pain. The weeping was all of our pain—a collective
wound—it is larger than each individual. In the sweat it seems as
though we all remember a past—a collective presence—our past as a
Native people before being colonized and culturally liquidated.[101]

When we learn and share our documented and oral history, we can release our anger and tears with confidence—with the support of our ancestors, with the knowledge that we are neither crazy nor alone, not stupid or
out of control. Insidious forms of oppression have brought us to this place
and continue to exist, and we have a right to be furious about that. With
these feelings no longer forbidden, we become eligible for true joy. This
leads to more appropriate emotional responses to the events of day-to-day
life, and lessens the desire to numb ourselves with various addictions.[102]

Beyond what we do as individuals, says Juan Garcia-Castañón, "other
interventions need to be made in both social, political, as well as psychological arenas."[103] Lobbying for continued and improved mental health fa-
cilities and services, fighting the cuts in entitlement programs, offering
greater services for PTSD and other stress disorders through community
organizations are some things that can be done. Latino organizations and
sympathetic foundations must recognize the need for the community to
heal itself and to develop ongoing programs and necessary resources to deal
with existing problems as well as preventing the spread of dysfunction
from one generation to the next. One approach, Garcia-Castañón suggests,
is through the school systems. Those can be used as a site for diagnosis and
treatment as well as a channel for public funding. Such monies may already be funneled into these locations as drug and alcohol prevention subsidies or funds for the deterrence of gang-related activities. Both of these
problems may be connected to PTSD and other forms of stress and dysfunction in the lives of the children. Thus, it makes sense to use this money
for treatment and prevention programs.[104]

A business or corporate approach to education, however, will never recognize the need to reduce the sources of insidious trauma in the lives of
children. Consequently, organized political opposition and continuing
public discourse against such management approaches are absolutely necessary. And this is our dilemma. Sustaining this kind of work is difficult for
the healthiest of people. For those of us who are fragile and stressed to the
limits by the demands and disparagement we face every day, taking on

such a task is both irrational *and* compulsory. (Is it any wonder we some-times feel *loco*?) Yet this is our burden, and perhaps our gift—to be able to confront outrageous and damaging public issues as well as the savage muti-lation within us at the same time.[105]

Regaining the ability to create and maintain closeness and attachment, it is very likely that we will lessen the amount of dysfunction we pass on to our children and be in a better position to help them in their journeys through insensitive public institutions. If we improve our capacity for compassion, we can also help other people. Compassion makes it possible to forgive—to understand that we are all acting in the world with the tools and the strength we have available. Part of the healing process involves forgiving ourselves and those around us for all of the problems and unhealthy behav-iors of which we have been a part. When we see dysfunctional behavior in action we must listen and respond through our knowledge of trauma and shame. And though we must set limits and protective barriers, we can per-form in ways that do not increase the shame and guilt of others who are simply acting out of their own pain. We must know that some of the people who have hurt us are behaving defensively or coldly because they do not know how to behave otherwise. All of this is essential to being able to inter-act with sometimes difficult people in social and political organizations.

But forgiveness is not necessarily a simple action and must happen for the right reasons, as part of a recovery and/or healing process and a commitment to action. It cannot be done because we feel guilty, think it's the moral thing to do, simply to smooth surface relationships, or out of self-sacrifice. When the abusive behavior responsible for part of our "insidious trauma" (racism and sexism), is still occurring, we cannot be expected to forgive those who continue to harm us. This is one of the reasons that any kind of "therapy" we receive or engage in must be experientially and culturally embedded.[106]

Sometimes our parents and guardians have had pain and experience in damaged families that have made it impossible for them to parent in healthy ways. We do not necessarily have to let them continue to bruise us, but it is in our best interest to forgive and feel compassion for them as human beings. Anzaldúa says, "We . . . can no longer let defenses and fences sprout around us. We can no longer withdraw. To rage and look upon you with contempt is to rage and be contemptuous of ourselves. We can no longer blame you."[107] But it should always be clear that this forgiveness does not mean they can go on hurting us. Part of healing includes being able to set boundaries for our own protection. What it does mean is a movement away from holding so tightly to pain that we cannot release it.

In her piece "Notes on Oppression and Violence," Aletícia Tijerina makes this choice to move from pain yet toward love. She talks about the way in which hatred and fear make us weak and leave us empty and alone, whereas love makes us "alive with feelings." It is a place in which we connect to others to "perform human acts," building more love in the process. She closes the piece with the political implications of such a life choice, "Each moment we recall the vision of love *we commit an act of resistance against the oppressor*." [emphasis in original] [108]

Making this choice may require that we become our own protectors, nurturers, and givers of unconditional love if we find ourselves surrounded by those who cannot act responsibly. Networking with other healing or healthy people may be a part of the process. Seeking community support and alternative families is another strategy. Surrounding those who are not yet on the path, rather than excluding them, is always preferable, as long as we are not putting ourselves in harm's way by doing so. When we define ourselves, we must remember that they are part of who we are. Though my father's shame is not mine, it does play a role in how I respond to certain people. We cannot separate such people from our identities. Setting boundaries and protecting ourselves need not preclude intimacy, empathy, or compassion. We must learn to live knowing the battle will never be completely over, knowing that no human being is pain-free, but confident that we will not only survive historical and insidious traumas, but thrive as individuals and as a community. [109]

Chéla Sandoval, a cultural critic interested in the formation of an oppositional consciousness, in response to social hierarchy, has said that women of color share an understanding of how power works. This understanding allows us to identify experiential peers and potential political allies. [110] What we know of power makes manifest our ability to empathize with the sorrows of others dominated by it. We recognize historical mutilation in one another. This means that if we can learn to heal—to make good use of our pain, memory, and rage—the potential for strong and lasting alliances in various political struggles may well become a reality.

CHAPTER 2

Rich in Culture, Low on Capital
Cultural Studies and the Global Economy

Fifteen years ago, when I first read Lorna Dee Cervantes's poem "For the Young White Man Who Asked How I, an Intelligent, Well-Read Person Could Believe in the War Between the Races," I felt as if I could have written it. I was thrilled to see that someone had finally given voice to my feelings of being at heart a poet—and a lover of good literature—who was forced by the circumstances of my birth to become, and remain, politically conscious. In her poem, Cervantes says that she would rather not have to think about racism, instead she would love to be able to spend all of her time studying esoteric subjects and contemplating the beauty in the world's classics, but because she and her children are daily victimized by racist people and institutions, such a delicate and cerebral life is not possible. Thus, while the young white man can ignore racism as a problem (because he is not the one being victimized) she is forced to be aware at every moment that "there is a war going on."[1]

Like Cervantes, I would love to be the kind of cultural studies scholar who spends her time analyzing literature or films on their aesthetic merits, or searching for meaning in the classics. But because I am a Chicana, I have no choice but to constantly monitor my surroundings for ethnic, racial, class, and gender biases. And because I grew up noting the differences in the daily lives of people close to me, I have no choice but to study the impact of the economy on people in various social locations, from the precarious positions of agricultural workers to those earning a living off the books in the informal economy, from the relatively stable financial situation of those in civil service to the unionized, working-class members of my family. While I do not claim to be an expert on the topic of global-ization—I confess most of what's written about it puts me to sleep—I feel obligated to speak out. Once I knew something about the historical develop-ment and context of capitalism, as well as the mechanisms that are supposed to police abuses within the system, it was much easier for me to critique those cultural elements that either support or symbolize the rise of transna-tionalism and the imperialist impulse.

As Masao Miyoshi has said, the world's political economy is a factor in all of our lives now.[2] While it profoundly affects millions of people on a daily basis, those of us in the First World either have the luxury to ignore it most of the time, or to be entertained by a thousand diversions designed to keep us from caring (or knowing) what is transpiring. This is as true today as it was prior to September 11, 2001. Perhaps the only difference is that when I began this book the economy was booming and now it appears to be on a downslide. Having lived long enough to experience several bull and bear markets, I know that individual lives can indeed be profoundly affected by these fluctuations. I also know that as classes, the rich have continued to rise and the poor have continued to slide further behind throughout these ups and downs in the economy. I further know that a downturn in the economy has historically coincided with a rise in nation-alism, allowing leaders to take us into war as a cure for their shrinking investment portfolios.

One of the reasons I believe those of us in the humanities must become amateur economists is to pay attention to the implications of the widening gap between the rich and the poor, the threat of war, and the disappearance of civil liberties due to the rise in nationalism, because the traditional num-ber crunchers will not. Traditionally, economics as a field has not been the science of economies, but the science of capitalism.[3] While economics is valuable and necessary as information, most people in the United States have neither the attention span nor the education to care about statistics or to un-derstand the jargon of conventional economists. That is one of the reasons that interdisciplinarity is so important. We should welcome the shift in sta-tistic-laden fields where some scholars are beginning to understand the im-portance of maintaining a public voice, which can be understood outside one's field if we truly believe in social change. We need to be accessible in order to dissuade the general public from swallowing without question the valium-like messages about the nature of contemporary capitalism.

Many geographers, political economists, cultural studies scholars, and political activists seriously interested in forming lasting alliances between various social groups crave unifying visions like those that existed during the civil rights era or the antiwar movements of the late 1960s and early

1970s. In terms of my own scholarship, I believe an important and radical political vision once existed in the newly created Chicano studies and women's studies departments. I also believe this vision has grown cloudy and diffuse, not just because our thinking has become more complex, nor because of the necessary critiques of masculinist nationalism and mainstream, liberal feminism, but because the unifying themes have been continuously attacked and trivialized in some very insidious ways. Whereas critiques have helped us grow, the assaults have often served to divide us. One consequence of these attacks has been a rush toward professionalism and the simultaneous dismissal of those who dare to do work that profoundly differs from what the academy accepts as legitimate.

The lure of high theory and scholarly validation through traditional channels can make it easy to develop languages and ideas undecipherable outside the academy. Staying within these boundaries can lead us to produce scholarship, which may be grounded in philosophical traditions or previous theoretical constructions but not the material reality of the global economy. And as I have already alluded, it is often easier for poets and humanities professors—sometimes one in the same—to read, interpret, and analyze texts than it is to engage students in a discussion about the economy. Yet, I have found no matter what I am teaching, that is exactly where the discussion eventually leads. Though students rarely go there willingly, it is built into my courses from the beginning.

In teaching a course titled "Women and Work," I focused on the political and cultural implications of the female workforce in the *maquiladoras* along the U.S./Mexican border. In contextualizing these women's lives for the students, it was imperative that I know something about the historical development of the global economy. Beyond this particular class, it became abundantly clear early in my career, that the way I wanted to teach—as well as the way I wanted to critique literature, film, and popular culture—meant needing to understand the mythology around capitalism in the late twentieth century. This has become ever more important as we have moved into the twenty-first century. Though one could write many books on this topic, I am devoting only one chapter to it here. I want to at least outline the things that have become important for me to know as a feminist cultural studies scholar and teacher.

Nasrin Jewell, an economics professor at Macalester College, helped me to identify and articulate some of the common myths about the global economy held to be true by the majority of people in the United States. I hear my students repeating these myths all the time. Thus, it is useful to deconstruct some of these notions and provide a clearer vision on how we got to this point in our economic history.

The first of these myths is that the global economy is a natural phenomenon—the result of basic human impulses as well as the supply and demand principles of free enterprise. Part of this myth includes a peculiar kind of cynicism and acquiescence. If it is natural, then there is no use trying to change it. But, the current state of the global economy is not the naturally occurring result of free enterprise. While it is true that some form of capitalism has existed in most societies from our earliest recorded history, what we experience today, like all social, economic, and political systems, is constructed. There is nothing "free" about it. It is manipulated, planned, and supported by both business interests and governments. Whereas government was once envisioned as a mechanism for making sure that powerful men, organizations, and companies did not accumulate too much centralized control, it has now become the means by which corporations ensure their right to more than their fair share of resources and wealth.

While it is not impossible to control the effects of giant corporations, it has become increasingly difficult for nations and communities to mediate them. Control over such operations diminishes daily as wealth and power transcend the boundaries of any specific nation. Corporations themselves thus have no loyalty to any one community nor its collective values and greater good. Never in our history has it been more important to elect representatives who care more about working people and the environment than they do about corporate wealth. The only entity large enough to reign in runaway greed and exploitation is a strong government. But if people are to make a difference in the way their governments operate, they must be educated and involved. This does not necessarily mean being a part of the mainstream political parties as they currently exist, but it does mean active organizing.

The second myth I encounter in discussions about the global economy is that we are all affected by it in the same way, that because it is global, no group is better or worse off than another. (In many ways this is related to the U.S. mainstream myth of equal opportunity and the false notion that hard work automatically equals adequate monetary reward.) Many of the past decade's phenomena contradict this myth—the growing poverty and chaos in the world, the increased transnational migrations, the continued underemployment of many U.S. workers, the feminization of poverty, growing unrest in the Third World, and the continually increasing gap between the rich and the poor. Clearly race, nationality, class, and gender make a difference in how various peoples experience the political economy.

Because transnational corporations (TNCs) have the power to make or break whole countries, or to profoundly affect the daily lives of entire regions, hatred naturally grows toward nations that have the most power to either support or to reign in the corporate operations but fail to do so. The largest global enterprises have operating budgets many times greater than some countries. It is widely perceived that these huge corporations are responsible for the misery engendered by unequal participation in the system. Because they have no national allegiance and only view governments as allies or enemies, TNCs are free to take the wealth anywhere they want, no matter where the natural resources or labor forces exist. In an effort to attract that wealth in terms of taxation as well as consumerism, governments become tools for achieving and maintaining corporate-friendly rules and regulations. Yet this quest is fool's gold because corporations, and the individuals who profit most from them, are quite capable of avoiding taxes. This can undermine the social welfare systems and infrastructures of whole nations.[4] We are not affected equally, but differently along national, ethnic, class, racial, and gender lines (among other social and political categories).

Related to the previous myths is the idea that the global economy is gender and race neutral. To some extent the falsity of this assertion has been answered in the previous paragraph, but race and gender differences are evidenced in definitions of what constitutes "work" and what is valued as "productive labor." The things that women traditionally and necessarily do around the globe will never be valued by a consumer culture or corporate economy. Everything from cultural expectations for who fulfills certain roles in the new economy to how pay scales are determined in Third World countries by TNCs is gender based. The growing development of prostitution as a service industry for tourists (as well as the increase in mail order brides from poor nations to men in the industrialized West), is testament to the fact that the global economy is not gender or racially neutral. That the workers who are forced to migrate from their homes in order to earn even low wages are overwhelmingly nonwhite means that no claim of racial neutrality can be supported.

In this country, nationalistic pride is founded on the belief that we live in the greatest democracy in the world. This is related to the next myth about the global economy, that no acceptable alternatives to the current forms of U.S. democracy and capitalism exist. There are scores of people who understand the falsehood of this core value. Few people who have been victimized by racial-profiling and a decidedly unequal justice system believe we live in a free society. No one who has aspired to national political office believes this is a great democracy. They know it is a republic, and that one can be elected without the popular support. No serious political activist, or member of a sovereign nation within U.S. borders, nor anyone else who has either studied or lived in a more communally based or mutually shared culture believes that no alternatives to this form of government or economic system can be found or constructed. But for many mainstream people the fairness and greatness of this system cannot be argued.

Their faith in it is unshakeable and it is a deeply emotional issue. When politicians want to shape government in a way that increases profits for corporations and investors, all they have to do is outline the virtues of democracy and unquestioned loyalty. As a signifier in the U.S. sociolect, democracy already encompasses free enterprise, which many people equate with capitalism. But it is the rhetoric around "democracy" that brings tears to their eyes and elicits feelings of pride. Precisely because it is so linked to this affective response, it is almost impossible to get people to listen to rational alternatives, or even care about how the economy really works.

Nor can such loyalists imagine that democracy might be totally superfluous or unnecessary to the current transnational corporations. The truth is that no particular form of government—even U.S. republicanism—is needed for capitalism to continue to operate in much the same way as it does now. Today's global commerce and industry not only operate well within, but also are adequately compatible with, Scandinavian democratic socialism, Japanese consensus politics, South Korean or South American military dictatorships, as well as the communism of China. As long as it has the support of the people in power globally, the system by which the people are governed locally matters little. Yet many citizens remain addicted to the notion that democracy and capitalism are inseparable. Like those addicted to other feel-good substances, they remain in denial of the evidence to the contrary.

The next myth involves an incomplete or faulty sense of history. People assume that the current global economy is the same economic system that made the United States such a powerful nation in the first place. While the roots of today's capitalism can be found in the feudalism of Europe—and has been a part of U.S. history almost from its inception, the current situation has a relatively contemporary beginning. Capitalism is based on the principle that the means of production should be privately held and that personal wealth can be acquired through investments and the exploitation of labor. It has never assumed that monetary success and the accumulation of the greatest wealth comes from hard work. It comes from owning factories, buying and selling stocks, and holding down the wages of those doing the work. In the early nineteenth and twentieth centuries this thinking began a general reorganization of work, family, and community around the needs of the manufacturers.[5] This also meant a shift in consumer patterns, and the effects are still in evidence today. What has changed, and generally peaked in the past fifteen or twenty years, is that these early industrial revolutions were generally contained within defined regions, nations, or states and that is no longer true. Whereas all aspects of a particular industry once remained in a certain area, they now exist across regional and national boundaries.

As the Industrial Revolution (which began in the eighteenth century) progressed, landowners lost their socioeconomic and political power to bankers, investors, and industrialists. Companies began to merge and these larger entities began to displace small merchants. Yet, neither production nor technology proliferated on a global scale for many decades. Though colonialism as a mechanism for obtaining raw materials and opening new markets seemed to touch every imaginable location, there were in fact vast regions of the world that remained relatively untouched by the reach of capital and its concomitant, Western culture.

However, in those colonized areas most affected, the uneven distribution of technology and industry set up patterns of exploitation that continue to this day.[6] The so-called Third World is the legacy of this economic and cultural imperialism. But even in the West, people who were female, brown, poor, and/or uneducated were similarly ripe as victims of this exploitive system. To these basic patterns the new system has added additional hierarchies within these larger groups based on nationality, regional location, sexual orientation, physical abilities, and so forth. Our understanding of oppression has become more complex as a result. But the ideological diffusion of potentially important alliances—as increasingly diverse groups are forced to compete over scarce resources—has often meant the disintegration of effectively resistant coalitions.

At the same time that poor and oppressed people around the globe are kept and encouraged to remain relatively separate from one another, the technological revolution since World War II has meant instantaneous communication between the elite. Combined with the spread of Western culture, this means that wealthy and powerful people from differing nations have more in common with one another than they do with the working classes within their own countries, racial, or ethnic groups. Thus the marriage of the Mexican daughter of the head of PEMEX Oil to the son of George Bush, Sr., can create an easy alliance between two elite oil-producing families despite their obvious racial and ethnic differences. In terms of cultural and class differences, it would have been *more* difficult for Jeb Bush to marry a working-class Tejana—born and raised in his own state—than it was for him to marry a privileged woman from Mexico.

Instantaneous communication and the technological revolution have also meant that labor need not be done in a centralized location. The old Ford plant idea, where all necessary materials and parts are brought into a central location and many workers in an assembly line turn out a final product has exploded—its various pieces now located around the world. The "spatial and temporal compression" provided by technology engenders an international, elite culture organized around the accumulation of wealth.[7] The formation of transnational organizations has been necessary in order to avoid the "tyranny of structurelessness," and from wreaking havoc among the elite.[8] Under the guise of political, military, or trade alliances, these organizations also cleared the way for corporations to do business across international boundaries.

But in the past two decades, such border crossing has become more than merely transgressing national boundaries; it has obliterated local laws and undermined the very meaning of national borders. The General Agreement on Tariffs and Trade (GATT), which eventually became the World Trade Organization (WTO) because business leaders thought GATT lacked sufficient power, and the North American Free Trade Agreement (NAFTA) made a mockery of the whole concept of national sovereignty. Members of the WTO do not represent the national interests of any one country. These global decision makers were and are all former CEOs of large corporations. Their primary interest is not how well our nation fares or building a just society, but in smoothing the road for high volume corporate traffic.[9]

I admit I see the world through a complex array of philosophical and ideological filters—Chicana feminism, union activism, working-class intellectualism, historical materialism, socialist feminism, and institutional scholarship—none of which have included formal studies of economic systems. I am a Chicana from a working-class family in the humanities by talent, temperament, and choice. My knowledge of economic imperialism has an experiential base. Though this experience is largely tangential now, I still witness the effects of the global economy on a daily basis through my family, friends, and acquaintances who are here without papers because they could not survive in any other way. It is clear to me that WTO members cannot possibly care about the way current economic forces betray the social reforms of the 1960s and 1970s—especially those designed to create opportunities for disenfranchised populations. Nor are they concerned with the sheer numbers of people who must leave their homes and travel great geographic and emotional distances to work. I cannot imagine that these corporate representatives think at all about the people who contributed their labor to the previous eras of full-steam growth in manufacturing—people whose children and grandchildren cannot now earn a living wage because such jobs no longer exist. I feel sure they do not consider the workers who have been forced to make so many concessions—in effect paying for CEO bonuses. Nor do I think they care about frightening workers into accepting lower wages by threatening to shut down plants as the voracious economic machine demonstrates that cheaper labor exists elsewhere. I do wonder how they live with themselves knowing that these moves toward ever more desperate and exploitable workers have not been done to save companies from extinction, but to earn ever higher profits for stockholders.

Under capitalism the goal is never sustainability, but acquisition of wealth. Any publicly held company that only continues to earn its shareholders a steady income over the years is considered a failure. In order to be considered successful, the company's stock must generate higher and higher rates of return. Greed is far more often the motivation to move operations to a new location. Unlike the capitalist ideals of the past that fiercely advocated a laissez-faire approach, today's business leaders not only demand government intervention, but expect it. Now "hands-off" refers only to any official questioning, judicial action, or legislation that might curb profits. Yet corporations have their hands firmly extended for government bailouts and favors in the forms of tax subsidies, credits, and incentives as well as any other type of financial support that might be available.

But why is any of this economic history and development significant to interdisciplinary scholars like myself whose primary personal interest is in cultural production? Why, like Cervantes, can't I just immerse myself in the aesthetics of literature and film? From the beginning I have interpreted and analyzed texts through the eyes of the Other—someone outside mainstream culture, someone who grew up on the margins of many overlapping social locations. The more educated I have become, the more impossible it is for me to view any of the differences with which I am marked—race, ethnicity, or gender—separate from how these categories function in a class-based society.

Somehow, I have known from a very early age that the hierarchies I encountered on the playground or in the classroom were not based only on skin color or gender or ethnicity. Even as children, I knew we were also being judged and either granted or denied certain kinds of power on the basis of our class positions. I learned that the shifting nature of these categories depended on context, and that although having a family with money might mitigate the meaning of being brown for some Mexican Americans, it could not do so in all situations. In grade school, I had regular screaming matches and fistfights with Diane Chávez—who always had lunch money and shoes without scuff marks or holes in the bottom. The white teachers seemed to love her thick shiny hair—always expertly cut and well-combed. They touched her, unafraid of getting lice. My girls and I made fun of her for her perfect pleated skirts, white blouses, and unmarked saddle shoes. Yet I did not hesitate to fight for her against the white boys who called her a "dirty Mexican," and kicked at her from their bicycles as we walked home from school.

Similarly, whereas my being light-skinned might have bought some privileges in a certain space or time, it could not always make up for deficiencies in socioeconomic class. Though I could not articulate any of this as a child, I understood it. I felt it in the form of shame and humiliation as I learned my place in the world and figured out where I was welcome and acknowledged, and where I was ignored, hated, or invisible. I had early experiences that cannot be forgotten, like being the only Latina asked to a slumber party and being amazed to learn that a child my age could have her own room. Though I am ashamed to admit it now, I felt proud to be with those blonde, blue-eyed girls. Then I realized that I was the only one asked to bring her own sheets. I was mortified, but still I went for the sheets. There were no extras in my house. Such memories have given me a lifelong concern for the cultural aspects of class as it overlaps with race or ethnicity. They were the source of my thinking about our varying relationships to privilege. As I studied the history of Chicanas/os and the processes of conquest, colonization, and neocolonialism, I came to understand the importance of capital and its relationship to various forms of government.

Past leaders with grand visions of building the United States into a globally dominant empire could never have succeeded because ultimately they were confined to national territories. Those leaders wanted dominance in order to accumulate wealth and power, but their desires were hindered by land spaces and economic systems independently governed. This new form of capitalism, however, makes that Western dominance a reality without having to legally colonize other nations and with a minimum of military intervention. (I say minimum not to diminish the importance of U.S. military actions around the globe, but to include the mere threat of military action as a significant instrument of control. It is also "minimum" because economic dominance does not require fully annexing other nations through military means.) While this brand of Western economic and cultural imperialism may be invisible to mainstream U.S. citizens, it is a familiar pattern to people of the Third World. It is an ideological and threat-based form of colonization most subalterns easily recognize. The cultural implications of such dominance are legion.

This kind of economic domination sells, maintains, and insidiously promotes Western culture worldwide. It pushes "a dominant set of cultural practices and values, one vision of how life is to be lived at the expense of all others. And it has serious practical consequences," for traditional and regional practices. Even in relatively developed nations, "it often kills local film and television industries which are so vital" to maintaining a nation's sense of itself.[10] Luckily, this is not an entirely successful enterprise. Despite capital's considerable cultural imperatives and its often-seductive power over non-Western populations, the dominant society also changes as it comes into contact with new labor forces and markets. Much has been written about this hybridizing process[11] and its role in cultural resistance, identity formation or expression, and social agency. Unfortunately, the most visible and exciting aspects of cultural production will be commodified if at all possible. All things Latino, for instance, become a desired ideal only as it can be marketed and used to sell everything from music to clothing. (This exists simultaneously with some of the most intense anti-immigrant social hostility and law enforcement in our history.)

However, some people do struggle against this commercialization of culture. When we look at politically charged, underground artistic production here, or the popular culture in other nations, as well as intellectual production in the Third World, it is easy to see that many people are resisting global imperialism both at the grassroots and theoretical levels. In some cases, resistance is neither politically organized nor the result of critical theory. It is lived culture. Despite the silliness of such things as "Latino Chic" or the 1990s being declared the "decade of the Latino" in various national media outlets, the prevalence of large Mexican and other Latino populations is changing or hybridizing local Western cultures. José Antonio Burciaga, in his book *Drink Cultura,* tells us that he found a prediction that this would happen carved on a Mayan stone in Mexico. He translates the inscription as "They conquered us, but our culture conquered them."[12] In addition to the force of singular groups, there is a merging of African American and Latino, Native American and Mexican, Asian American and Latino cultures going on that escapes most mainstream attention. At least four things facilitate this recognition and sharing of similarities between these groups' social rituals: (1) intermarriage; (2) living together in low income housing; (3) appreciation of and the fusion of each other's music; and (4) the commonalities of oppression each group experiences.

This cultural *mestizaje* or mixture could eventually go beyond simply changing and influencing Western or mainstream U.S. culture to displacing it from its current powerful position.[13] But, if this coincides with learning capitalist culture then some mechanism for maintaining the value of traditional communal styles must be in place. Part of the problem with the necessary and useful critique of nationalism is that it cannot conceive of a group loyalty position that is not masculinist, patriarchal, capitalist, supremacist, xenophobic, and homophobic among other things. But many Chicana writers, from Gloria Anzaldúa to Michele Serros, are trying to create such a space,[14] where you can express a kind of cultural nationalism and still make room for the mixing of cultures. This is very much in the Mexican Indian tradition of receiving the values and beliefs of the people you encounter, making an effort to understand them, and figuring out how their rituals or beliefs might be incorporated in, or work with, your own cultural values. It is not about appropriation and imperialism because the shift is neither forced upon, nor stolen from, an inferior Other—it is an exchange between equals.

In terms of scholarly resistance, Asian intellectuals among others have contributed greatly to understanding what this new form of colonization—the global economy—means to people. Through these critiques of the West, many mainstream U.S. theorists have come to realize that the liberal humanist notion of human rights as an ideological struggle is not parallel to a discourse of survival. It often seems counterproductive to be talking about the way in which we all at some point, or in some context, inhabit either oppressed or oppressor positions, when there are people without the simplest of human dignities like "food, housing, and basic sanitation" as well as the right to preserve "one's own identity and culture."[15] Yet this is something many U.S. scholars of color and/or feminists have known for some time. Many women of color, born in the United States, have been writing from a subaltern or postcolonial position for the past several decades, though under other terms.

We must continue to use these critical tools if we are to imagine more amicable societies with diverse people living together in a mutually beneficial world. But outside cultural resistance and critical theory—in strictly economic terms—globalization does not take note of either hybridizing processes or social agency. Foucault's theories about the bottom-up flow of power aside, economic globalization only works one way. This is an especially poignant fact for Mexican migrants who cross the border in search of employment. Whereas giant corporations have free access to any land space in the world, the poor are expected to respect national boundaries. Indeed, laborers can only be exploited to the extent that their movement is restricted and controlled. If Third World workers, for instance, could cross all national borders freely to find better paying jobs, who would be left in those countries to exploit? Whereas corporate spatial relocation and growth is limited only by the profit motive, that same consideration for free access and unfettered movement expels and constrains the majority of humanity. NAFTA was sold to the public with a rhetorical appeal to openness and greater opportunity for all. It was touted as a way to bring poor countries into the global market place. But, as Masao Miyoshi has said, "The 'global' economy is in fact nothing but a strategy of maximum exclusion."[16]

So how is it that the majority of citizens in the developed world have failed to be alarmed by this exclusionary project? What opiates within U.S. culture keep people so pacified that they are stunned to learn that people in other parts of the world hate the United States? If the critical theories that so permeate cultural, ethnic, and feminist studies are based on Marxism, then shouldn't scholars in these fields be supremely interested in how the machine sells itself? Shouldn't we be focused on the mechanisms by which elite politicians, academics, administrators, conservative think tanks, right-wing organizations, fundamentalists, entertainment executives, and others who most benefit from unrestricted economic growth operate in this world? This would seem the ideal project around which to create alliances between scholars and activists—to describe in simple and somewhat entertaining terms how this global economy seduced us, made us dependent on it, and continues to hold us captive by successfully drawing our attention away from even the most scandalous behaviors and repercussions.

Whatever we write or teach, analyze or interpret, class and the political economy should be a subtext. Ziauddin Sardar has identified three significant tidal waves that brought us the current economy and are of interest to cultural studies theorists. First was the unearned, but nevertheless zealous, pride in being "American" that accompanied the economic liberalization of the Reagan-Bush years, which saw not only the crumbling of the USSR but also the rise of NAFTA. As markets became free of legal constraints and employers began to move out of the United States in search of cheap labor "Americans" were focused on moral and family issues.[17] Similarly, September 11 gave the new Bush administration the perfect excuse for pulling our attention away from the economy. He had only to revive the strategy of promoting nationalist hysteria—and punishing or vilifying anyone who did not go along—to win the Republicans control of the Senate in the elections of 2002. The sons had clearly learned from the grand patriarchs the value of flag-waving and calling into question your opponent's national loyalty or morality.

In the 1980s, as multinational corporations were being handed huge tax exemptions, voters supported candidates who ironically talked of getting big government out of our lives. Indeed, poor people being abandoned by the government in favor of multinational welfare came to be seen as a good thing by mainstream Americans. As U.S. consumerism replaced production as the chief economic activity of the country, no one seemed to question the notion that we could spend our way out of any economic crisis. The cult of individualism preached at all levels of U.S. culture—from government to the entertainment industry—left many people waiting in vain for some economic good fortune to trickle down. But the only thing that fell from the top was their real wages. No one in this era of "feel good" politics seemed to notice or care that as privatization, disguised as democracy, was becoming the norm in developing nations, poverty and starvation increased at alarming rates worldwide.[18]

The second broad trend pushing globalization forward was the worldwide exportation of U.S. middle- to upper-class values and ideals.[19] This brand of liberal democracy and sophisticated metropolitanism as portrayed in U.S. films and television programs became the new norm for cultures around the world. Satellite technology has made Western culture instantly universal. Pop music and fashion trends can be beamed out in seconds to tell consumers everywhere what they should want, what they need beyond the necessities, and how they should look.[20] Since what we consume is often predicated on what we desire and fear, rather than on what we need, capitalism means the introduction of new ways of thinking about one's self in relationship to others.

While it is true that certain films and advertisements exported from the United States have paid some attention to human rights issues or environmental causes, they have done so as a means to an end. They are often simply plot vehicles for telling familiar tales of the lone hero against the evil empire, not serious critiques of U.S. foreign policy or corporate exploitation of the world's resources and its labor force. Most films, after all, depend on corporate money to be made at all. This does not mean a complete dearth of critical art, however. Some filmmakers, even as they ultimately reify Western supremacist, capitalist, patriarchal culture do manage to raise interesting questions and significantly challenge colonial impulses and motives. Still it is far more common to find that United States productions demonize radical political movements and trivialize the experience of being victimized by racial, gender, class, or homophobic biases—making fun of even the most benign efforts to organize around social justice or environmental issues. At the same time, the people's power—as well as the government's power—to raise questions around these issues has withered in the face of global capital.[21]

You needn't look much beyond two facts to understand why the culture industry would create these messages against those critical of the system and the norms that exist. Most of the movies and television programs successfully exported overseas are products of heavily invested individuals and corporations—many of whom directly benefit from the transnationalization process. This is connected to the third factor in understanding how this new form of capitalism has expanded so rapidly. In addition to Hollywood, pop music, and other consumer products, Sardar tell us, global news networks "like CNN, News International, and the BBC World Service have hastened this universalization of Western culture."[22]

Big stars from Latin America are encouraged by recording executives and seduced by the promise of greater stardom into "crossing-over" and recording in English. Never mind that the most commonly spoken language in the Western Hemisphere is Spanish. In order to be considered a legitimate star in this totalizing culture, people like Enrique Iglesias and Shakira must sing in English, even though neither is originally from the United States. Though the accompanying music videos are essentially artistic advertisements for the CDs, they, like the larger film industry, help to promote a U.S. worldview. Any resistant musical message from Latin

America or Marxist Spain will be long gone by the time it airs. As sociologist and cultural critic Ben Agger says, this is a moneymaking enterprise that "exists in large measure to represent capitalism as a rational social order."[23]

Previously, the idea of a national culture was manufactured by the middle to upper classes in the West as a way of ordering various nations hierarchically. If you could label, know, or define another's culture, you had the means to dominate or control that nation. Myoshi says that "a culture was selected, edited, and privileged to represent each nation around the end of the 18th century and throughout the 19th century."[24] Like Myoshi, many scholars have described the effects of orientalism, the white man's view of the Indian, Western portraits of Africa as the Dark Continent, and similar constructions. Now, even these shallow or artificial "cultures" are increasingly irrelevant as identifiers. The global market means an international bazaar to which all elites have access.[25] The white suburban U.S. mom can have a dream catcher hanging in her mini-van, learn to salsa from an exercise tape, and wear a tee shirt embroidered with the Chinese symbol for happiness. And, she can do all these things without ever having to learn anything about the people or cultures from which these artifacts or expressions emanate. This kind of insatiable appetite for the exotic is less about hybridizing or changing mainstream culture than it is about the prerogatives and frivolity of the dominant class.

In some ways, the disappearance of these "traditional" cultures—officially sanctioned and defined by the West—may be a good thing. But the theft of a people's unique rituals or creativity as well as the destruction of their way of life is altogether different. How can we expect such people to trust in political coalitions with U.S. mainstream participants? Unfortunately, the current socioeconomic steamroller is far more abhorrent than the older forms of cultural imperialism (the Western anthropological constructions of the Other), have been. It makes the relatively more recent manifestations of multiculturalism (with whiteness or U.S. middle-class values still at the center), look revolutionary. Yet I think both the impulse and source of various kinds of imperialism are always the same—a belief in one's superiority, a sense of entitlement, an inability to fully understand the worldview of the oppressed, and a desire to dominate. While the constructions of the colonial powers obscured and lied about peoples outside the West (as well as those marginalized within it), such stereotypes only slightly directed the shifts in the cultures themselves. But the new economy signifies the "triumph of consumerism over local life," a shift in the meaning of geographical differences and the devaluation of *indigenismo*.[26]

Few things could be more dramatic than the cultural upheaval that has resulted from globalization. Altered gender and interpersonal relationships, different methods of child rearing, and shifting identities, as well as ethnic loyalties, have occurred rapidly wherever transnational corporations have set up shop. One has only to look at the U.S./Mexican border to see glaring examples of this shift. But those nations and people excluded from the machine because they have been deemed unprofitable (and are thus forsaken by industrialized elites), do not escape the nightmare of globalization. These areas do not enjoy the police forces and other governmental structuring devices necessary to keep order so that capital can continue to operate efficiently. Such countries—many of them in Africa, Asia, and Latin America—are left vulnerable to the many forms of social violence and all of the ills that crushing poverty can engender as the most aggressive forces within them rise to power.[27] Because nations like the United States that might step in to keep innocent people from being slaughtered have become a world police force in service to transnational corporations, no actions will be taken unless peace in the region is necessary to capital interests.

Director John Sayles in his film, *Men with Guns,* shows us how local life is disrupted and forever changed by this feature of globalization, as well as how little it is understood by any country's elite. He also makes clear that the middle to upper classes cannot entirely escape the violent effects of this change, which to some extent they have either set, or helped to set, in motion even if only through their complacency or apathy. Sayles also tells us through his narrative that even when the rare elite member of mainstream culture becomes politically conscious, s/he will likely look for the source of social upheaval in the wrong place and aim their good intentions in the wrong direction. They cannot succeed in changing the lives of the poor by leaving their golden cities for the nearest ghetto or the rainforests of the Third World. They would do better to alleviate chaos in other societies if they fought their own governments, which have become mechanisms of corporate greed. A research trip to Central America or Chiapas may actually make it easier for the oppression to continue because it does not serve to change any of the larger reasons for the conflict.

Yet this traveling outside their own social locations is exactly what many cultural studies scholars have done. Like the doctor in Sayles's film, they have become so fascinated by *indigenismo,* the promise of a life different than one's own, as well as the mysticism of the Other, that they have lost sight of imperialism. If it is true that people in cultural studies are "committed to a *moral* evaluation of modern society and to a *radical line* of political action,"[28] then surely these recondite—yet profound—effects on local cultures should garner scholarly attention beyond observation and ethnography, or even simply reporting on the terrible conditions.

Traditionally, cultural studies has never pretended to be objective, nor metaphorically soulless. We have an agenda, a perspective, and to some degree an ideology. Most of us are impervious to the criticism that real scholarship must be value-free. We know it never has been. Our predecessors have not been just coincidentally some of the most influential thinkers over the past few centuries in economics, philosophy, human and natural sciences, linguistic theory, and literary criticism as well as feminism and critical race theory.[29] Each was committed to social change through theory, to deconstruction and reconstruction of social orders, to understanding and destroying the mechanisms of dominance. Whether this was done with a primary focus on race, gender, class, or some other category, the purpose for many of them was to critically expose how industrialist capitalist societies create, reproduce, and maintain unequal access to power and social locations.[30]

Such theorists have been at the forefront of many resistance cycles (which I describe more fully in chapter 6). In brief, these cycles include: achieving consciousness, developing a critique, active resistance, coalition building, empowerment, and eventual reformation. Yet with each round of successful paradigm shifting a philosophical, rhetorical, ideological, and material backlash develops among elites and their supporters. (This too is more fully articulated later in the book.) In a brilliant strategical accusation from the right, aimed at trivializing the experience of being oppressed, conservatives accuse radical scholars and activists of having a victim mentality. This has forced many cultural studies scholars to shift their focus from critique to justifying the kinds of theory we produce, especially when it does not always resemble the traditional or canonical work of past scholars. Responding to charges of perpetual or even professional victimhood, as well as their own weariness of continually feeling victimized, some cultural theorists have given themselves over to the notion that "theory is power."[31] But the emphasis in this kind of self-reflexive, free-floating world (where all experience is relative and we are all fragmented and decentered) is seldom on the critical part of what once was "critical theory." The emphasis has shifted to the legitimization of cultural studies as a worthy, scholarly enterprise through the creation of complex theories, which in the end have no real connection to those who must struggle for mere survival under global capitalism. This kind of purely intellectual culture studies, Ben Agger tells us, has become impotent scholarship—a regressive movement that "defeats its political purposes."[32]

In her article "Response: Cutting/Edge," Debra Castillo discusses this difficult and pragmatic contradiction, where critical theory and radical language become prized and privileged by the academy because they demand that we think more complexly, yet they substitute for oppositional action even as they allow us to cling to the binary thinking of Eurocentrism.[33] A Disney-does-diversity approach that analyzes the company's movies for children in terms of race and/or gender, or looks at the cultural influence of its theme parks outside the United States but never criticizes the corporation's business practices will not do. To fail to illuminate the company's insidious hold on a major portion of the media and its dominance on prime time television—especially news production—is an example of how some theorists can use the right language without making any commitment to radical action.[34]

While I believe the theory we produce can provide a structural framework of ideas that might be useful to activists, it must be more than an exercise in complexity—it must speak to the specific concerns of oppressed groups. In fact, the proliferation of postmodernism often comes with the avoidance of words like "opposition" and "resistance" or even "oppression." The whole notion of a dominant/subordinate binary is dropped from the theoretical vocabulary, blurring insider/outsider distinction and obliterating the solidity of Otherness. As I have written elsewhere, this can no longer be considered critical language because if everyone is oppressed then no one is, if everyone has power then no one does.[35] This is easy to believe in the new global economy because there are so many victims and no one is totally outside its reaches.[36] But this is no more than a linguistic wet dream. The fact that the vast majority of the world's population is excluded from globalization's ability to create great wealth and power, as well as the reality that it is forced upon populations with no desire for it, means that oppressors and oppressed still exist in binary relationships.

While theorists struggle to analyze everything through a postmodern lens and carry on great debates as they self-referentially police one another to make sure to enforce the disallowable binary, they actually contribute to its continued existence in several ways. First, they spend much more time and energy criticizing each other, as well as potential allies, than they do denouncing the system itself. Second, when they do critique globalization processes, they do so in language that only intellectuals understand or care about. Despite voracious denials to the contrary—and the positions of thinkers from Wittgenstein to Foucault—the inaccessibility of such ideas will always create outsiders.[37]

While cultural studies and critical theory have been one of the few success stories of interdisciplinary inquiry throughout the humanities, we cannot ignore the fact that there is little interest in "literary and theoretical discourse" outside its own participants.[38] In part, this is a consequence of the shift from the university as a site for research and teaching, to the university as corporation.[39] Students are no longer expected to be inquisitive learners, rather they are forced to become efficient consumers of education. They are constrained to wanting a degree, not a learning experience. Administrators can only diversify the faculty to the extent that tight budgets will allow, despite what might be best for educational purposes. Whether or not this is intentional or a subconscious choosing of what is most comfortable or the result of fiscal imperatives, traditional Eurocentrism continues to be "inextricably built into the very structure" of a "basic" education as well as what is accepted as rigorous research.[40] Even in feminist studies, scholars seem to want it both ways—to keep their original status as resistant outsiders but to be seen as legitimate scholars. They deny a Eurocentric canon and teach students to critique such a centering device. Yet there is a strong feeling among some faculty members that there are basic, or classic, women's studies texts and theoretical constructions—or a history of Western feminism—that every major should know. In subtle and overt ways, it becomes clear that U.S. and French feminist theorists have more cache than do Native American, Latina, or African American thinkers.

In addition to the obvious racism involved here, French feminist approaches, postmodernism, deconstruction, poststructuralism, postcolonialism, cultural materialism, and a variety of permutations and hybrids of these theories are attractive to scholars precisely because they are so lofty. They are prized because their complexity is intellectually exciting, their difficulty produces exclusivity, and mastery of the language creates the illusion of genius.[41] In my own experience it is also more often successful in generating research dollars and scholarly sabbaticals, even though grant applications generally request the limited use of jargon. Because this conformity to, or, practicing of, elitism "represents an abandonment of and indifference to people outside the academy, especially the poor and the uneducated," Masao Miyoshi claims, it is "simply not credible as resistance." In fact, it "furthers the exclusive enterprise and supports the profiteering of TNC's, thus it fits very well in the new corporate environment of the University."[42]

I want to make clear that I do not wish to write an "anti-theory" essay. Theory itself is not the problem, and in fact serves many activist purposes—especially if authors are brave enough in this era of blurriness and fragmentation to name the oppressors and the oppressed. As a graduate student pointed out in a seminar discussion on this topic, we should not be mad at theories themselves but at an educational system that does not make it possible for everyone to understand and use critical theories and academic terms.[43] (Of course even this represents a Eurocentric bias as it presumes everyone should or would want to understand the world through these particular lenses.) But I often think we cultural theorists resemble ostriches with our heads in the sands of inaccessible ideas and languages. Somehow we've come to think this will protect us from extinction as the humanities become less and less revered in this new corporate culture. We simply don't seem to recognize the immediacy of the ideological shifts in this nation's sense of itself and what it means to be educated. A consumerist student body facing the realities of becoming white-collar proletariats in this economy cannot afford to desire a "traditional liberal arts education in general, and literary studies in particular."[44] Grappling with cultural issues can seem profoundly irrelevant in a business/consumer model of education. Yet it is easy to see who benefits from the undervaluing of cultural studies, as well as its increasing professionalization as it seeks legitimacy within the corporate model.

Postmodernism, for instance, feeds right into the corporate university's desire to cast all conflicts, criticism, and disagreements between all manner of ideological adversaries as differences of opinion. Relativism—where there is no right or wrong, weak or strong, dominant or subordinate—can make great use of postmodern theory. Diversity can be celebrated without really looking at power differentials and the unavoidable difficulties of true inclusion and coalition when inequality continues to exist. When the university engages in what Barthes called "neither-norism," it appeals to academic excellence by claiming to value diversity, but hastening to add that it wants neither white nor people of color on the faculty, but simply the best. Thus, they are not choosing between conflicting social locations, but only choosing excellence. This means they do not have to address the fact that historically excellent candidates have been routinely rejected in favor of the mainstream applicant, and that unless forced to break their established patterns, most institutions will maintain the status quo. Thus the "neither-nor" statement simply endorses the system as it currently exists.[45] It does not criticize or try to change what is in practice unfair and discriminatory. Those who use neither/nor statements can "appear to take a 'higher' moral ground and make no commitment to move in any alternative direction. This seeming neutrality encourages" complacency and supports inflexible practices.[46] Thus it satisfies the corporate desire to maintain a relatively homogenous campus climate. This illusion of multiculturalism allows the institution to preserve its authority through systematic hierarchy, producing acquiescence in conservatives and liberals alike. By using "academic excellence" as its slogan it can simultaneously appease the advocates of the status quo, maintain stifling hierarchies, and silence its opponents.[47]

As long as the most critical, revolutionary, and activist work can be kept in small, and consistently under financed departments and labeled as diversity, such theory will produce little anxiety for administrators. If numbers of majors are the bottom line, then even these departments can be threatened with, or subject to, extinction in the name of economic efficiency. Further, if this work must be stated in undecipherable language in order to be considered legitimate scholarship, then the university has no cause for alarm about what radical notions faculty and students might have, because their ideas can never be taken up at the grassroots level.[48]

Recently in a course on identity development, we had been defining "Chicano" not just in terms of race and ethnicity, but also as a signifier for a radical politic. A student asked, "after all we've learned about our history and our contemporary situation, is it possible for me to live as a Chicano in a capitalist country?" Another student answered, "No. I don't think it is. Our very identities are always under attack." They understood that in a postmodern corporate system, a subversive identity is a difficult thing to maintain—especially for those on the edge. Since the Reagan-Bush years we have known that every business—even the university—is prepared and able to downsize at its convenience. Cost and efficiency can be accepted reasons to expel, deport, ostracize, exile, or replace "whomever it finds undesirable," unproductive, or simply irrelevant in today's economy.[49] Any scholar understands that the numbers game has replaced critical thinking skills as our institutional priority.

This has led us to become what Ben Agger has called excellent bureaucrats instead of revolutionaries.[50] Indeed, Masao Miyoshi claims that corporations pay little attention to what remains of radical or subversive speech heard on college campuses today. Making celebrities of successful subversives and rewarding them appropriately tends to dull the revolutionary "content of their character." The comforts and privileges afforded by the corporate "star" system turn even the most vocal critics of the system into hot commodities. Miyoshi says it is this circumstance that makes CEOs sleep easy. While right-wing columnists and think-tank essayists may rant about the liberal nature of most faculty members, "the university may in fact be among the most conservative institutions, with TNC interests firmly entrenched and protected."[51] Even for those who do not become stars, staying alive as ethnic, feminist, and cultural studies scholars within higher education "obligates [us] to develop a protocol of technical procedures that are fetishized for their own sake."[52] For those of us who are largely treated by colleagues and administrators as token hires, this can buy us some measure of legitimacy as acceptable scholars in a way that radical resistance and subversive activism never will. While acknowledging that self-professionalization may be necessary in a hostile intellectual world, critical theorist Ben Agger insists that it keeps us from "solving real empirical and political problems."[53] Yet to ignore the needs or demands of the institution for "academic excellence" can mean remaining at the bottom of the pay scale, neither time nor money for research, and in many cases not getting either tenure or promotions.

Writing of any kind has been described as a lonely process, yet, the university-employed scholar's need to publish is legendary. This duality does not make a life outside the institution easy—particularly for those of us with large families, who come from cultures in which social interaction is as necessary as food. While it has always been essential to produce scholarship—especially in large research universities—the current emphasis on publishing a book in order to get tenured or promoted eclipses any concern for teaching or public service. The corporate university has discovered that donors are almost as impressed by academic all-stars as they are by winning quarterbacks. That means that the more books a faculty produces, the better—even if they are unreadable outside an academic audience. Yet, because the demands on our time have increased due to reduced staff and increased student to faculty ratios, scholarly writing can be a particularly isolating endeavor. It is much more difficult to find colleagues willing and able to workshop articles or critique various drafts along the way. Like other kinds of professionalization, writing for publication demands a price. Ironically, for even the most sincere critic of the political economy and earnest cultural studies scholar, it often means separation from the very communities where the most compelling and politically relevant work is being done. We find ourselves with little time to participate in, or even keep up with, resistant popular or underground culture that is in a constant state of creation and renewal.[54] Thus, what we write may be irrelevant by the time it is published.

As a Chicana, I struggle to satisfy many needs—to jump through the institution's hoops for legitimacy and to stay connected to the many social locations outside the academy to which I have access by virtue of my friends and family. The fact that I am educated is part of my privilege and power. Yet, I see this as continuing an intellectual tradition that began in the indigenous Americas long before European arrival, rather than as use of the "master's tools." Combined with my ethnicity, racial mixture, shifting class positions, and gender, being educated puts me in this liminal space where I am simultaneously insider and outsider. Yet my conscious political loyalty to a working-class, Chicana identity never wanes. (And yes, I am also a feminist, postmodern postcolonial decolonial subaltern subjective voice—though this is not the sort of thing I can declare over Christmas dinner. I can, however, say with ease, *"porque soy Chicana."*)

While my personal/group history and experience, as well as the many social locations I inhabit, can be combined with education to give my voice as a Chicana a unique brand of social agency, it does not give me equal power in the corporate academy. Language and deed continue to marginalize Chicana/o and feminist scholars (through tokenism, isolation, Eurocentric and patriarchal criteria, minimization of our work, suppressing organized resistance, misunderstanding the interdisciplinary enterprise, trivialization of activism, ignoring critical challenges to the system, invalidating our credentials, and a host of other subordinating mechanisms).[55] We are reminded on a daily basis that we lack foundational membership—that we are merely visitors in someone else's house—that the common national identity so insisted upon by U.S. capitalists does not include us except through violence and seduction.[56] It uses the justice system in the first instance, the market and the media in the second.

Though a multiplicity of social locations may be valuable in theorizing difference, and certainly necessary to understand how power works, we must face the dilemma that no radical politics can be built upon such shifting sand. We've had almost two decades for this kind of postmodernism to reshape the academy and the reality is that alternative ways of knowing, work from non-Western sociolects, and Third World feminist texts have never succeeded in displacing the false universal culture that permeates the U.S. university.[57] As a Chicana feminist I may provoke some guilt, shame, and defensiveness as I denounce a shared or common culture. I may come to symbolize an ethnicity, gender, sexual orientation, regional or national space even as I refuse, *and* strategically use, such essentialism. I am constantly sublimating the lack of *cultura pura* and fighting off the violence of cultural confrontation with the mainstream. Both processes wound me deeply. These wounds, which will not heal, characterize an intellectual space that serves the needs of the university as a corporation but leaves oppositional scholars to bleed. Especially wounded will be those of us upon whose bodies capitalism—as it was with earlier forms of colonization—is played out. These cuts dig deep into political minds and resistant spirits and create festering sores on those with any kind of political consciousness or Other identity.

Were we to truly become visible beyond the rhetoric of diversity and multiculturalism, we would make obvious the insidious methods by which Western culture reproduces itself and the damage it does to people in the process. This is not a new idea, but something subordinated voices have always tried to posit. From our often token positions we and our work continue to define the cutting edge of oppositional scholarship until our theories are consumed, digested, and returned in some benign form by the mainstream writer, well-known expert, or a scholar with "proper" credentials.

As a Chicana, I cannot afford the luxury of what Ben Agger has called a *New York Times* postmodernist approach to cultural studies.[58] Nor can I join many feminists in their rush to postcolonial studies. Though many postmodernists insist on being considered both insiders and outsiders because they see themselves as being on the cutting edge of theory (and thus anticanonical), they may fail to recognize the limitations of their cerebral projects. Miyoshi[59] calls them "TNC intellectuals," because they are primarily focused on each other's work rather than on the material conditions of the world outside the university. Such scholars spend much of their creative energy on catching the next new theory, the latest vocabulary, and anything else that will make them sound innovative as they present papers at professional conferences or publish in journals no one outside the academy reads. They obsessively engage in tedious arguments over ambivalent statements or contradictory concepts—evasive language and blurring points of departure—while "passionate concern with the forgotten and underrepresented" is abandoned."[60]

I find it disconcerting to have to speak in opposition not only to TNC-thinking administrators and legislators—as well as those who either willingly or unwittingly support them—but also against people who would probably claim to be my allies. But we cannot work in coalitions unless we are willing to dust off the language and concepts that once so clearly identified oppressors and the oppressed. Of course I know that is problematic—isn't everything? How is it that scholars would allow themselves to be so distracted by blurring lines, fragmentation, intersectionality, multiple agency, hybridity, and a host of other *pedos puros* that they can no longer recognize victims and victimizers? Good thing the Mothers of the Plaza del Mayo were not postmodernists. Lucky that Malcolm X didn't speak the language of poststructuralists. Miracle that Rosa Parks didn't understand that the bus driver was oppressed too or she might not have insisted on keeping her seat.

While technology makes it possible for theories, new ideas, and critiques to circulate around the world with great speed, we do not have to be riveted to an intellectual style that erodes our connections to the very people we know are most oppressed, underrepresented, and silenced. And even the most philosophical mind must admit that in the transnational market, identifiable hierarchies exist. Perhaps we should stop training graduate students in the fine art of critiquing scholars who essentially agree with one another but have different ways of reaching the same conclusions, and teach them instead that even in postmodernist, postcolonial, postfeminist discussions, our major purpose ought to be questioning and challenging and disrupting unmediated elitism, exclusion, and most important, unregulated enterprise.[61]

Cultural studies should be used to analyze what we see and experience in everyday life. Film, literature, television, advertisements, news programs, and music videos among other "texts" should be read for the way in which they both reflect and construct the dominant ideal. But we also need to be vigilant about the way they distract us from world events and international politics, as well as the global economy and its consequences. We need to be writing about the way in which these artistic and informative productions serve as the rhetorical devices of capitalism. It is important to interpret and expose the messages they convey, and the manner in which they urge us to conform, adapt, acquiesce, and accommodate the needs of the global economy. U.S. mainstream popular culture "should be exposed for what it is—an ambassador of modern day imperialism."[62]

In one sense, the corporate culture of the university has arrived just in time to revive the passions of the once radical activism and scholarship that gave rise to ethnic studies and women's studies departments. Chéla Sandoval calls the tendency to create theoretical domains that keep knowledge within the academy a kind of apartheid, within which scholars busy themselves developing new terminologies. Or, white middle-class liberal academics go about reinventing what she calls "the methodology of the oppressed," by reworking theories already posited by activists and scholars of color. All of us are hoping for some kind of interdisciplinarity that works.[63] At some point it should become obvious to us that one reason why writing in plain language would be preferable, and perhaps why it is eschewed by the academy, is because it would make coalition among like minds easier. The establishment of theoretical domains and reinventing ideas take time and energy that could be focused on making revolution. While we can critique certain concepts, or point out the limitations of various claims, our enemy is not "essentialism" or "cultural nationalism" or "identity politics." It is not even second-wave feminism. Our enemy is the global expansion of capitalism and consumer culture. And for scholars, the evidence is all right here in our river city—the academy.

CHAPTER 3

Wisdom and Weakness
Freire and Education

Farms are everywhere in Minnesota and its neighboring states. In twenty minutes you can drive from the central core of the largest metropolitan areas and encounter vast fields of soybeans, corn, sugar beets, and other vegetable crops. Each requires manual labor to plant, tend, and harvest. Most farmland in Minnesota and Wisconsin (stolen in various ways from indigenous peoples), used to be owned and worked by small families—some still are. Since the Reagan-Bush years, these farms, most less than five hundred acres, have increasingly given way to agribusiness. These larger operations now number acreages in the thousands. Mainstream people from the Minneapolis/St. Paul area drive by these fields on their way to vacation homes on the shores of the many lakes with which the glaciers have blessed the landscape. They travel to cabins and campgrounds squatting in the pine forests and visit fancy lodges on the shores of Lake Superior. Breezing past vast fields that once were prairie land on their way west, they pass the valley of the Jolly Green Giant. All vacationers hold their noses as they drive through the ammonia-laden stench of hog farms in the southern half of the state and into Iowa.

Few of these travelers think about the growing food or notice who bends over or squats between the verdant rows—hoeing, weeding, or picking—tolerating extreme temperatures and biting flies or giant mosquitoes for very little pay. Mainstream folks give little attention to who butchers and packs the pigs and turkeys, or what it might be like to slop around in blood for very low wages at meat processing plants in places with peaceful-sounding Indian names like Owatonna.

But I cannot help but think of farmworkers and meatpackers. Childhood summers with hay seeds stuck to my sweating, burnished brow, strawberry-stained fingers, and ears numbed by the sound of tractors, balers, and combines keep them near to my heart. Many memories have lingered: slimy and steaming pig innards that spilled out onto the ground after their bellies had been slit open; chickens running on nerves, around and around the yard once their heads had been cut off; tugging at the blood-stained white feathers after the birds had settled into death. These memories are not as horrifying as they might sound. I grew up with the slaughter of animals for food, though we often could not afford to buy the prime cuts of that meat. We had instead the sweet smell of *barbacoa*—the head of a cow set onto coals in an earthen pit. Even as I walk the polished halls and well-tended lawns of my university, it is the men and women mowing the lawns and trimming the shrubs who catch my eye. When they are planting, the smell of freshly-turned soil and manure are familiar as I pass. Rural fields, and the people who work them, will always be part of me.

A short, round-bellied man with muscled arms stands behind a wheelbarrow. He looks like my grandfather. I want to talk to him. As I pass, I smile. He looks down and away. I know that to speak to him would only make us both uncomfortable. "Buenas tardes," I say anyway, unable to resist. He looks surprised and confused, but repeats the greeting back to me.

Some might think that by getting college degrees and an academic job I have achieved some measure of success. But what have I gained if I cannot talk to the person I once was? What have I earned if people like my grandfather automatically show me deference—when at the same time some students will disrespect me at every opportunity because I am a Chicana? I know that the word "oppression" has fallen out of fashion, and that many scholars will cease to listen as soon as they hear it. Nearly everyone (including me) has embraced the idea of complex and multiple positions from which we all negotiate our oppressor/oppressed identities. But almost every day I witness or experience the starkness and clarity with which I can still draw a line between oppressor and oppressed.

I am on my way to give a paper at the University of Wisconsin in Madison. I love the drive from Minneapolis because it takes me past some beautiful landscapes. For the first time—though I have made the drive on too many occasions to count—I pass a large field where more than a hundred workers are bent over the crops. I am thrilled to see so many Mexicanos to whom I immediately feel related. But the reality and contradiction of what we are both doing slams into my heart, and I begin to cry. I want to talk to them. But I know that I cannot. I know I am no longer a person who goes into the fields, no longer a cousin they just haven't met. I am a professor. And, that is not the person I would want them to talk to. I ache for this lost connection.

Will the line between oppressor and oppressed that I recognize so easily hold under scholarly scrutiny? Certainly not, I can theoretically erase it as quickly as I draw it. Yet, theory cannot take away the pain of what I understand to be true. Theory cannot make my conversation with Mexican workers easier. Neither can it mitigate the hostility with which I am sometimes treated by mainstream students who see themselves as my superior, who see me as one in the same with those workers, even when we know how far apart we have become. I cannot abandon the word "oppression," cannot let go of its still cruel meaning in my life.

Reading Paulo Freire's *Pedagogy of the Oppressed* some two decades after it was first published had so profound an effect on me in the mid-1980s that it still guides me in the new century as I try to deal with these issues. As a working-class child coming to Chicana consciousness in the politically charged 1960s, I closely identified with the oppressed masses Freire sought to liberate. I began to see the possibility of education in a less cynical way. I learned it did not have to be just a tool for socializing citizens of the state. Public education could be a process of critical thinking that had the potential to create rebels. I hoped it could empower people unwilling to accept the socioeconomic and political positions into which they had been born. Neither would they tolerate the hierarchical systems that maintained these social locations.

Rereading the book in the mid-1990s, I began to realize that I was an expert on my experience in the world. In keeping with what bell hooks has called "theorizing through autobiography,"[1] Freire's work has continually made me consider the irony of being a Chicana from a working-class background *and* a teacher in a major research university. What does it mean to be a woman of color committed to Freirean and feminist pedagogy in an institution where the majority of students and faculty come from relatively privileged social locations? How do I think about my authority in the classroom in one moment—only to be caught without it in another?

I am on my way up to the Campus Club to treat my friend Lupe to lunch. A well-dressed white woman enters the elevator and smiles. She seems amused that we are speaking a mixture of English and Spanish and keeps looking at us as if she is included in the conversation. Lupe asks what floor we are going to. "Mierda," I say as I realize I have forgotten to push the button. Too busy catching up on the latest chisme. The woman who stands between us and the control panel pushes the wrong button. "Oh no," I say to her, "we want the fourth floor." "No you don't," she corrects me, "this one opens the door to the kitchen." Lupe and I look at each other and laugh, rage and sad amusement bubbling up in us like lava. I do not tell the woman that I am a professor at this University. I just reach around her and push the right button. She seems embarrassed as it becomes obvious to her that we are going to same place she is. As we sit down, she is still staring at us. Still trying to figure out why we are there amidst the white linen tablecloths and banks of windows overlooking the campus—especially as she watches Lupe casually flirt with the Mexican bus- boy who cleans the tables. This woman's mistaken assumption that we must be going to the kitchen becomes one more tale I will tell about what it feels like to be a Chicana professor at a major research university.

Tom Heany, writing in an online article titled "Issues in Freirean Peda- gogy," concludes that the great thinker's methods have little potential outside the chaotic revolutionary circumstances under which they were developed. Only as nations undergo tremendous upheaval or periods of great change, Heany charges, can Freire's ideas come to fruition.[2] Yet as a Chicana student, I flourished in courses with teachers who had been influenced by his theories and methods, whereas I had always struggled in traditional classrooms. (While I could do the work and get good grades, they stifled my critical thinking.) Once I had read Freire's work for myself, I was convinced that I could teach in no other way. Though he was clearly using Marxian language and a materialist approach, Freire knew that oppression was about more than the effects of capitalism.

As both a product, and a proponent, of Freire's work, I have used his methods in both formal and informal settings. While they work wonderfully for many students—especially those who identify with oppressed groups— they are not as successful with those who either consciously or uncon- sciously identify with the oppressor. While it is true that most people in the United States—due to their power and privilege on a global scale based on nationality—are constantly negotiating shifting positionalities, I think it is still valuable to think of "the oppressed" as a category for strategic reasons. If I might be granted this moment of reductionism, there is a difference be- tween those students who enter the classroom already engaged on a daily basis in an active struggle against overlapping forms of oppression and those who see themselves more closely aligned with mainstream society. The first group is much more likely to see Freire's ideas as a continuation of their daily sociopolitical struggles and developing consciousness. They will accept what he is saying and incorporate his ideas into an ongoing process that precedes and extends beyond any one classroom experience. Those who do not iden- tify with the oppressed—even as they may be experiencing it—will be reluc- tant to see the usefulness of his work or the value in "questioning the structure of society for one semester."[3]

Numerous and intense conversations with colleagues who have shared similar experiences and concerns about teaching mainstream students inspired this essay. Among this group were four Chicanas, three African American women, one Puerta Riqueña, two Native American women, three Asian women, and a woman of mixed Chicana and Filipina heritage.

Most are working-class and some are lesbian. I have also discussed this topic with several men of color teaching at the university level. While most of us love teaching, have received good to excellent evaluations, and maintain wonderful relationships with many devoted students, we all have encountered difficulties with arrogant and often openly hostile mainstream students. While all teachers may deal with such hostility, we have all agreed that this goes beyond the occasional misanthrope. We know that racism, sexism, classism, and homophobia reflect, create, and maintain a particular kind of hostility that is not in evidence when the instuctor is white, straight, male, middle class, or some combination thereof. With a sense of entitlement that comes from deeply internalized dominance, such students eagerly display their assumed superiority, social authority, and their belief that they can afford to dismiss us.

The son of a nationally known public figure comes up to shake my hand the first day of class. This young white man asks where I am from as he does not assume I am a native Minnesotan. I tell him I have lived in South Minneapolis most of my life. "But, where are you from?" *he asks again. Knowing what he wants to hear, I say, "my grandparents were from Mexico, but live in South Texas. My parents were born in this country." I turn to talk to a Chicano who has been in my classes before. The young white man interrupts the Chicano as he begins to tell me what he's done over the summer. "Hey," says the white student, "do you know Henry Cisneros? I met him once during a campaign trip with my father." I laugh and look at the Chicano when I say, "no, Henry and I don't travel in the same social circles." The Chicano laughs with me and says in Spanish, "yeah, I went to Henry's house all the time when he was mayor of San Anto. I went with my dad to cut the lawn." The young white man looks confused. "You know, not every Mexican American from Texas personally knows Henry Cisneros," I say, "especially poor people." The young man pulls back. He understands now who I am. He makes some remark about affirmative action making it harder to tell the difference between the rich and the poor. For the rest of the semester he ignores me. On those few occasions when he bothers to show up for class he does a remarkably good job at reciting liberal democratic rhetoric. But he turns in a one-page final paper, hastily scribbled during the last class. I give him a failing grade for the course. The following year, he is admitted to law school.*

None of the curriculum adjustments and shifts in teaching styles that have taken place on campuses in the past two decades due to the dissemination of Freirean ideas had prepared me for this. As brilliant as they are, Freire's theories were developed in a completely different social, political, and historical context. One in which the lines between the elite, educated oppressors and the brutalized, uneducated masses were very clear. They did not necessarily consider how the process would work once the oppressed became the teachers, the subjects became the authors of their own experiences, and the privileged became the students of the historical Other. The Freirean method calls for teaching in a way that validates the knowledge of our students and simultaneously decenters us as the only authority in the room. But as women of color, we enter the classroom already disempowered by existing gender and racial relationships, which may or may not be accompanied by class differences.

How do we translate or use Freirean pedagogy in any U.S. classroom where the majority of students have unearned power and privilege in both a local and global context? While Freire speaks extensively on the problems associated with internalized oppression, he only gives us vague clues on how to deal with internalized dominance—that peculiar intellectual infection that tells students that only college professors who are male, white, heterosexual, and U.S. born deserve to be taken seriously. Can we take the instruction of a man whose experience-based theories were formed out of a concern for the poor in Brazil and use them with students who often cannot even imagine what it means to be poor in their own cities let alone in Latin America?

At the very heart of his methods, Freire counsels us that an effective teacher must give up authority in the classroom and must create a setting in which the students will take responsibility for their own education and become authorities on their own experiences. Much of the literature on feminist pedagogy similarly problematizes the power differential between teachers and students. But both theories assume that all teachers automatically have authority conferred upon them by all participants in the educational system. While this is true in the formal sense—in that we will ultimately assign grades at the end of the semester—informally, I often enter the classroom to discover students who are neither willing to grant me such automatic power, nor even show me common courtesy in some cases. Such students will stubbornly resist participating in the process or look for ways to sabotage it.

I've seen little if any research done on power differentials within classrooms where certain students may in practice be more politically and socially powerful than their teachers. I've read no studies of students who possess not only the tools, but also the brashness, that comes with the ability to access power at levels generally closed to marginalized students.

I am teaching a class called "La Chicana." Because I want the Chicanas in the class to feel that their experiences are central to our theorizing, I set up a "fishbowl" discussion. I ask the self-identified Chicanas and Latinas to place their desks in a central circle to talk about Gloria Anzaldúa's work. The white students make it clear that they do not like having to listen to these women, without comment, through half the class. When they do speak, they are angry. They do not talk about Anzaldúa, but about how unfair it has been to "privi-

lege" Chicana and Latina opinions. The Chicanos and other students of color in the class do not object, and are surprised by the responses of the white students. Arguments break out as the white students try to redirect the discussion to their experiences with "reverse racism." I explain again one of the purposes of the course—to put Chicana experience at the center in order to better understand their social locations and worldviews. The white students complain that I am oppressing them. The next day I am informed that the Dean's office wants to discuss a disturbing phone call from a parent about my "discriminatory" and "inflammatory" teaching methods.

What would Freire have done with a student who could easily bypass a department chair and any number of other steps on his or her way straight to the dean's office to complain about a teacher's methods? How would he have handled power dynamics within the classroom between students from historically disenfranchised populations and those determined to maintain existing forms of inequality?[4] Did Freire ever think about the ways in which the authority of the teacher and her intellectual ability could and would be challenged with such hostility by students with unofficial power greater than her authority as the professor?[5]

Symbolic of our lack of authority is the students' ease with calling us by our first names. On the personal level and because I am trying to create a learning community, I ask and encourage my students to do so. But many do it long before I state this preference. And, I cannot help noticing that students of color, especially students from Mexico, Southeast Asia, and Somalia, will continue to call me Dr. Torres or Professor Torres, while white students seem to have no problem adapting to the informality of my first name. Even as we interact outside the classroom in friendly social settings, or in those cases where the relationships have changed to more familial or intimate ones, students of color will continue to defer to my authority. Whereas white students will easily drop any hint of deference outside the classroom. Some of this is cultural difference, with U.S. students generally socialized to have less respect for their teachers than do students in other national or cultural groups. This informality could even be a good thing if it were indeed a sign of creating an equal learning partnership between us. But it is less indicative of successful decentering than it is an outgrowth of their belief that I am not equal to a "real" professor and thus not worthy of either false or genuine respect.

Mainstream students rarely question my factual knowledge base, but will freely attack the content or the entire premise of the course, even though they signed up for it, knowing full well from catalog descriptions what the course would entail. This tells me that they have had a negative reaction to seeing me and hearing me lecture—that I am not the person from whom they expect to learn. Indeed, until the very recent past, University of Minnesota college students would never have had the opportunity to see someone like me as the expert or authority in the classroom.[6] For many of our students, who come from rural communities outside the Twin Cities metropolitan area, I am the first Chicana with whom they have had contact. (Unless they have lived on or near farms that have hired migrant workers. Though this too has changed for some small town kids in the past decade, as many more Mexicans and Mexican Americans have moved to certain areas of the state.) But in many cases, I am the first person of color to whom some students have spoken. Like their suburban counterparts, they come to the central city with a host of stereotypes, incorrect assumptions, and misinformation. Not all of them exhibit the disrespect I have described. In fact, many of them are eager to transcend their ignorance and open their minds to the reality of a diverse world. They are the ones who are willing to be embarrassed by what they do not know in order to sort through difficult concepts. They are the students who struggle through their personalized white guilt to political consciousness and activism. Indeed, I have seen remarkable transitions from identifying with the dominant culture (even without realizing it) to taking on an antiracist, antisexist, antihomophobic, anticapitalist identity.

But, I have also seen my share of students who will not budge from their precollege ideas about race, gender, sexual orientation, and class or economic systems. I do not expect all students to see the world from my perspective, nor do I desire conformity. While I certainly hope there will be opinions, ideas, and theories that differ from my own—precisely because this kind of dialogue creates a better learning environment—I do not expect to be treated with either contempt or condescension. I require active participation in the process and a demonstration of critical thinking skills. If they are going to critique the course and its content, the texts, and my skills as an instructor I do not want them to do so passive-aggressively by pouting or refusing to engage in learning activities. Nor do I want to be subjected to an attack on my personal appearance, the tone of my voice, my speaking style, or the fact that I occasionally respond emotionally with a word, phrase, or sentence in Spanish. Nor do I want to be charged with straying too far off the topic when using teaching techniques they do not recognize from their years in banking style institutions. And contrary to a few students' beliefs, I am neither "too feminist" nor "too sensitive" to racism. Nor do I hate white people. I am, however, guilty of the charges that I am bitter, angry, and the ever-charming "bitchy" when it comes to thinking about, and experiencing, the historical and contemporary systems of oppression. I will not apologize for passionate responses to racism, sexism, classism, or homophobia.

I have found the experience of teaching in the university to be a prolonged psychoanalytic project—though I have no training in the field of psychoanalysis. But continuing to grow as an educator and a political activist has meant trying to figure out what the barriers to consciousness are. What mechanism exists in the minds of my students that makes them so sensitive to their personal pain and sense of alienation in the postmodern world, yet unsympathetic to the exploitation of others? What takes control of their minds and emotions to make it impossible for them to see through any other lens than that of the dominant position, while I and other people in historically oppressed groups have had to, for our own survival, learn to look through a variety of lenses and filters, including the dominant one?

If it is true that we inhabit many different subject positions, and that identities and roles are constructed and can therefore be deconstructed, then why is it so difficult for these students to step out of an identification with the dominant elite? Why is it so difficult for them to accept or assume that a woman of color as a professor is analogous in terms of a knowledge base and expertise to that of a white male professor? Is it impossible for me to get reluctant students to engage in the process without reintroducing Tayloristic principles of management or reinstituting a strict code of control that demands respect for authority, memorization, and repetition rather than critical thinking?

To do this would be antithetical to the Freirean philosophy. He was engaged in a process of teaching that produced not only useful, routine knowledge, but also critical wisdom and consciously political citizens.[7] While I believe that this method allows the oppressed to grow in a way that makes them envision and demand more for themselves and to resist the social locations imposed upon them, I am not sure how his method works on those already in or identifying with a dominant position. Certainly the process must be altered in some way because experience has taught me that at the same time students in oppressed groups are finding their voices and becoming increasingly politically conscious, the mainstream students feel threatened and attacked. When they are no longer the center of discussion, concern, or study they feel completely off balance. They feel wrongly accused. And because no person in this society is without some guilt in having made racist, sexist, homophobic, or classist remarks at some point, or having such thoughts on occasion, they feel exposed. So frightening is this for some students, they cannot react in any other way except with defensiveness, aggression, or self-protective withdrawal. This response at best does not allow for growth, and at worst causes them to become even more entrenched in a very narrow, but powerful worldview.

Because these students do not identify with the oppressed masses Freire sought to empower, but instead identify with the oppressors, they may not recognize their position as a political one. Every critical remark I make from or about a subordinate location is viewed as an attack on them personally, as well as an attack on their assumed objectivity and neutrality. I become political but they are not. Whatever I say from this position threatens their personal comfort, their endowment of privilege and power, and their commitment to the ideology of whiteness.

Such students come into class with not only opinions but also desires that conflict with my own. They want a passing grade with as little psychological discomfort as possible, and I want them to learn in a way that will resonate for years to come. When students cling to their power and privilege, it is difficult to resolve the tension between their desires and my goals. Like any teacher, I bring a specific subject position into the classroom (albeit a shifting and fluid one in many ways). This means I can teach certain topics with more than words, texts, or carefully memorized facts. When I speak about oppression, I teach with emotion, personal stories, body language, and fluctuating tones of voice that indicate some visceral response on my part. All of this grows out of my history (both personal and communal), as well as my day-to-day experiences in the contemporary world. I do not hide behind false objectivity because I want my students to understand the toll of racism, classism, sexism, and compulsory heterosexuality on real people. I want them to see the way in which intertwining, overlapping, intersecting, or simultaneously occurring forms of prejudice, and exploitation actually wound people. I want to show them my scars, to disrupt the socialization processes that have made it so easy for them to disconnect from the ways people are harmed by various oppressive systems. I want them to understand the difference between and the sameness of the physical devastation and the psychological damage caused by the increasing disparity between the wealthy and the poor.

I also teach from this experiential base because as Native Canadian educator Rick Hesch points out, Freirean "pedagogues assume that knowledge is constructed by individuals in a social context. That is, knowledge does not (solely) exist in books. . . . Rather, we each interpret words differently, based largely on the nature of our previous experiences in life."[8] But this style often conflicts with the mainstream students' desires to see only themselves and their experiences reflected. They want flawless bodies at the head of the classroom, or at least ones they recognize. Scars and wounds do not make sense in a society they've been led to believe offers equal opportunity to all. To believe otherwise leaves them little choice between admitting that this unequal system functions in their best interest or becoming politically active. Thus, their having the temerity to disparage me is not personal. It is a defense mechanism that allows them to remain in their comfortable rut and continually validates their dominance. If they can dismiss me, they can dismiss my concerns.

Classroom dynamics often become skewed by unequal relationships to power. Though I am supposed to be the authority, I often share with the few students of color in the room a feeling of isolation. As often happens in predominantly white settings, which feel oppressive even when no overt acts are taking place, we brown folks are just happy to see each other. We have in common a sense of alienation when we hear our lives and our experiential knowledge being trivialized, ignored, or disputed. I do identify with disenfranchised students when false universals are employed. I automatically resist such normalizing mechanisms. I am linked to the students of color by our presence at the margins of society, by stereotypes that limit us, and by our experiences with unaware, unintentional racism among other things. We bond immediately when it is clear that we simultaneously recognize the expression of power differentials and oppressive tactics. Consequently, the mainstream students sometimes notice this affinity and assume that I am "playing favorites." They are not entirely wrong about that. I often see friends, family members, or myself in the marginalized students and my instinct is to protect them, fight on their side of an argument, and form alliances with them. Yet I know this will never be manifested in assigning either unfair or unearned grades, and that my responsibility as a teacher is to all the students in the room. I also know that alliances built solely on skin color, class, gender, ethnicity, sexual identity, nationality, religion, or any other single characteristic are often folly and usually dangerous.

This does not mean that I have to pretend to be objective. Being mainstream and expressing the norms of the dominant society is not being objective either. One of my favorite fortune cookie messages—one of very few I have saved—says, "Do not practice moderation to excess." Part of what makes me an effective teacher is that I am open about my passions and politics. My agenda is not hidden. I own it. While I believe in much of what postmodern theory has to offer, I could never transmit the relativist assumptions that often come with it. Like most Freirean practitioners, I see teaching as a political act. Anyone who pretends otherwise is lying. Again, this does not mean I expect to convert all students to my way of thinking. My only objective is to teach them to be politically conscious, critical thinkers. If this means that conservative, mainstream students become acutely aware of power differentials and the meaning of their own social locations, and then decide to own that space and take responsibility for working diligently to maintain their power and privilege—then I'll be sad. But at least I'll know that they are doing so consciously. Such an enemy is much easier to fight than the apathetic, well-intentioned, but still supremacist student who claims to see (or do) no evil. What I do expect is to be able to enter into discussions with them in which we will all test our assumptions and ideas. To talk in an atmosphere of experimentation, and

mutual trust that our major goal is learning. But this task is especially difficult with students who have internalized dominance to the point where
they cannot recognize the existence of systematic hierarchical arrangements based on arbitrary physical and circumstantial characteristics or
cultural beliefs and practices.

One of the biggest barriers I face with these students is what Bannerji
and Ng have called "commonsense isms." Understanding this concept gets
us "away from the notion that sexism and racism are merely products of
individuals' attitudes." Though the authors acknowledge that "isms" can
never be completely separated from people's attitudes and individual behaviors, they emphasize "that racism and sexism are systems of oppression
which give rise to structural inequality over time." This is not something
that people who have internalized dominance easily hear or understand. So
much of the oppression we experience has been normalized, has become
entrenched in the culture as a way of being and acting in the world, that it
is taken for granted as the right way to act. The sexism or racism or classism inherent in such behaviors has been successfully disguised because
they have continued to be practiced for decades (even centuries) without
serious consequences or negative social sanctions.[9]

It took two years of women's studies and ethnic studies classes before
one of my white students finally understood that dressing up like an Indian
princess for Halloween was not the same thing as donning a ballerina cos-
tume. She was under the same spell as the University of Minnesota fra-
ternity students who advertised a "South of the Border" party and asked
guests to show up dressed "like Mexicans." The common sense of internalized dominance told them that this was analogous to having a toga party.
In both cases, the idea of pretending to be something or someone you are
not for Halloween or a party seemed to them to be what the holiday was all
about. It made sense to them. The notion that such images might be hurt-
ful to a large group of people did not occur to them. They did not think
about the way in which such costumes might be trivializing whole cultures
or perpetuating myths about the groups. Nor did they consider that such
stereotypes were part of a long history of oppression and therefore of great
insult. Despite years of education by people of color since the civil rights
movement, the dehumanizing effects of such playful imitation had totally
disappeared from their consciousness.

Once challenged, this commonsense or normalized way of seeing,
thinking, and acting in the world as an oppressor, is often defended and
disguised as a "right to one's personal opinion."[10] This is especially true if
you can find one or two others at a minimum, if not the majority of other
discussants, to agree that you have a right to think that it is ok to dress up
as Aunt Jemima on Halloween and that equal weight will be given to the

opinion of anyone who thinks this is racist. Similarly, anyone with an interest to do so could easily find supporters for the idea that those who want Indian nicknames for their sports teams simply disagree with those who claim the practice is disrespectful to Native Americans and racist. Thus the oppressive act itself has no harmful ramifications for the practitioner, because even the people who might abhor the practice are silenced by this seemingly common sense approach, this doctrine of differing opinions. Without negative sanctions the behaviors become routinely indulged, are seen as either traditions or historical, and any criticism can be dismissed as political correctness run amok. (You can see this in arguments over the flying of Confederate flags on government buildings.) But, this is not just a matter of equally weighted opinions, because the historical and contemporary victims of oppression are in a better position to determine what hurts or demeans them or their cultures. Of course, it does not seem harmful to either the oppressor or anyone who has internalized dominance. They are not the ones being hurt.

As many scholars including Freire, Susanne Pharr, and Roxanne Ng have pointed out, once these subtle, everyday acts of oppression become normalized they become the standards for objectivity. In this loaded atmosphere, to see a difference of opinion—rather than a racist, sexist, classist, or homophobic act—is to be considered objective. This sets teachers like me, striving to make clear and understood a complex Chicana (Marxist, feminist, anti-homophobic) perspective, the purveyor of "biased knowledge."[11] The oppressive "isms" remain normal and I become suspect—someone not to be trusted or believed because I have an agenda. Thus when I try to point out these taken-for-granted or commonsense "isms" I am seen as having subjective knowledge shaped by my biased opinions. Mainstream biases simply disappear in this process.

To acknowledge that normalized activities are as oppressive or more oppressive than overt acts of domination is to ask students with internalized dominance to admit that something is terribly wrong with the very social structure that affords them privilege and power. Such an admission threatens them to the core. To know that something is wrong and to choose to remain politically idle turns their apathy into an unjust action by default. It makes them culpable, not just as inheritors of an unequal system, but as active participants in maintaining that inequality.

My teaching style, which revolves around discussion and tries to honor each student's learning style, motivations, and level of consciousness, includes a variety of in-class activities designed to encourage participation. Because it is also spontaneously student-directed in many ways, it is sometimes perceived as being unorganized. Students uncomfortable with self-direction, active participation, and dialogue will critique these methods as if they are rooted in my individual personality rather than in feminist or Freirean pedagogy. Though I hand out an extensive syllabus, which explains and outlines not only the objectives of the particular course, but also the purpose of such teaching methods, a detailed schedule, and rules for effective discussions, some will still be plagued by a feeling that I am disorganized. While I explain that we will remain flexible and I encourage creative approaches to learning, I also try to make it clear that an organizational framework exists for those who need more structure.

Resistance from students desiring the traditional banking style of education—put information in, get information out—is not always a symptom of internalized dominance. Some students simply do not like change. For others, such freedom can be extremely anxiety producing. Certain grade-dependent, concrete sequential thinkers need clearly defined rules, succinctly written expectations, and criteria for performance evaluation, as well as concrete assignments. Resistance can run the gamut from pouting to assertive critiques and questioning, which can be helpful rather than simply disruptive if the students really want to sort through possible answers. Admittedly my teaching style works better for abstract random thinkers who more easily make spontaneous leaps and thrive on creative approaches to critical thinking and theory making. But I always try to accommodate the needs of students who think more sequentially. Still, there are always those students who reject these methods, not because of their innate learning styles, but because the activities are being offered by a Chicana. The resistance level of students who want to maintain the status quo goes up as the teaching methods seem to have a profound impact on classmates no longer willing to accept things as they are. Rejection and apathy often become something more than mere anxiety. While they may be careful about what they say, with often overt hostility such students will find a way to let me know that they not only reject my perspective, but that they feel superior to me in every way.

I have been teaching a course in the American Studies Department called "Creative Americans and Their World," for six weeks. The course is designed to focus on artistic production within an historical and cultural context. The course content changes with each instructor and reflects their expertise. I have built my course around Chicana/o art and literature. A group of five white men, who always sit together, talk to each other constantly through short lectures, films, or group presentations at every class, but do not actively participate in discussions. When they have become too disruptive, I call on one of them by name. He is so disengaged that he does not hear me ask him a question. I say his name again. "Yes, darling," he responds and the others laugh. I ask the question. "I don't know, sweetie, why don't you tell me," he says, putting his hands behind his head. He stretches his legs out in front of him and strikes a relaxed pose. The others laugh. "I haven't been able to tell what the fuck you think I need to learn from you," he mutters to his buddies as I turn my attention to someone volunteering an answer. As the students leave at the end of class, I hold the young man back and set up an appointment for him to come to my office. His tone is condescending and overly polite. He leaves and joins his buddies outside the building. His hand raises in a one finger salute toward the classroom as they walk off.

This posturing does not frighten me personally, and on a good day I understand how completely these young men have been indoctrinated. How frightening it must be for them to have to face—for even a few hours a week for a small portion of this one year—a strong, socially conscious Chicana constantly challenging their unearned power and privilege. But politically, it chills me to the bone. I know there is a whole system outside my classroom that values them and the way they think. Generally, I expect, and am thus prepared to deal with, this treatment from conservative mainstream students, but they are not the only practitioners of internalized dominance.

Because we all grow up learning hierarchical structure and the behaviors of commonsense oppressions that function in complex ways, elitists of all genders and sexual orientations, as well as select men of various colors, ethnicities, and classes can exhibit hostility toward women of color as professors. While few white feminist studies students will question my credentials or abilities on the basis of gender, they can be every bit as condescending as the most rigid white male student in the classroom. Because they have studied race as a category of oppression, women's studies students sometimes self-righteously see themselves as experts on the subject—if not experientially then surely theoretically. Yet they often harbor suspicions that faculty of color don't really have the theoretical chops that some of their white professors or they themselves have.

This exhibits itself in the classroom as annoyed impatience with conversations around racialized experience and emotional expressions of the pain and anger felt by students of color. It takes the form of trivializing these testimonials by calling them anecdotal and insisting on a return to data or theory. This may work for them in other classrooms. Yet, I know that this appeal to theory is not a call for the expertise and writing of scholars of color, it is a desire to return to their comfort zone or the centrality of European and Euro-American theorists. While I do not hesitate to use white theorists wherever I find them useful, I refuse to let this kind of scholarship be the only authority in my classroom. Nor do I want it to dictate how we will read various texts or interpret knowledge. Like Freire, I want students to read and to think about what is being said through the lens of their own social location, to ingest, reflect, and develop critiques relevant to their lives, but not to the exclusion of all other perspectives.

If marginalized students happen to cross the same path in their thought processes as did Foucault, Derrida, Mohanty, or Butler, I will point out to the class that they have done so. But I prefer to let students find their own path through the process rather than being led by a well-quoted theorist of a quite different social location and experience. While other theorists and I may help them organize what they have thought, written, and spoken, or push them to ask ever-deeper questions, we will do them no favors by simply letting them follow an already worn path. To impose theory and method upon them is to destroy their incentive to discover and create theory of their own, as well as the joy of finding theories that validate their ideas. It may also cause them to skip many vital steps. Psychologically they benefit more from making it through a thought process to formulate or discover a theory than they do from having that theory handed to them.

But woe be unto any instructor with students in a single classroom at vastly different stages of learning high theory. Nowhere is this conflict more evident than in the women's studies classroom. Any hostility caused by internalized dominance toward a professor will be magnified in this situation. Almost all of the colleagues with whom I have spoken about this have told their own stories of women's studies students who have acted out in class and disrespectfully questioned the teacher's competence. Dr. Gwendolyn Pough, an African American colleague in my department, shares with me the experience of having our graduate students patronizingly offer to show us how to teach generally, and how to teach certain theorists specifically. This kind of behavior leads me to some major contradictions. First: feminist studies students are often the brightest, most assertive, and hard-working students in the classroom. They usually are great critical thinkers. This makes them wonderful participants in discussions and reading their essays can be a joy. But they can also be the most elitist, insolent, and self-righteous of students. Their dismissals of women of color can be vicious and are often based on erroneous assumptions about our knowledge and the extent to which we understand high theory. To criticize it is to be thought incapable of using it.

The second contradiction is at the heart of this essay on women of color using Freirean teaching methods. At the same time that we are trying to implement critical teaching and humanize the classroom by decentering ourselves as authorities, we may be forced to assert that authority in order to keep our personal and human dignity in the face of the constant recreation of white, patriarchal, homophobic, capitalist superiority.[12] Daily we must cross that minefield of demanding respect and earning it, yet trying to make our authority as insignificant as possible in the classroom. We must constantly search for ways to help students who are intellectually opposed to various forms of oppression, yet still practice entrenched models of discrimination and exhibit internalized dominance. This often means looking for ways to overcome their defense mechanisms while trying to quiet our own. I am not interested in teaching white women how to improve their individual lives if this means simply working within the existing system.

One of my goals is to help these students discover how they have been manipulated through popular culture, the media, and others in their own social locations to accept commonsense forms of oppression and to internalize dominant behaviors and beliefs. I want them to understand that words like "freedom" and "individuality" are largely rhetorical devices disguising the many ways we have been shaped by culture to see and think of others and ourselves. This keeps us from recognizing that the occupation of certain social positions, and our varying relationships to power, are wholly constructed not just in overt ways but also in very subtle and often invisible ways. This leads to unrecognized, but highly functioning internalized oppression *and* internalized dominance. It is crucial that mainstream students come to understand it is neither the accusation (nor the proof) of racism, sexism, classism, or homophobia that creates guilt, shame, anxiousness, or defensiveness within them. Rather, it is living the lifelong fiction of superiority and unearned privilege that causes discomfort.[13] It is also important for them to know that although they can never change their experiential reality within their own social locations, they can change their unexamined identification with the dominant culture.

Cultural theorist George Lipsitz might call this adopting or developing an antiracist identity as opposed to a mainstream one. But this is not necessarily a position one comes to through objective reasoning alone. It requires what Freire, and subsequently Ana Castillo and others, have called *conscientizaciøn.* This is a consciousness of their own political positions in the world and what that means in terms of finding ways to create change. As many writers and scholars have suggested, a critical look at one's own suffering and the ability to feel empathy may be required for making this transition from one identity to another. If you cannot face your own pain, James Baldwin has said, "you can never really grow up—because there's no real change you go through."[14] Hostility can be a symptom of staying within this figurative childhood of internalized dominance, of not growing beyond one's guilt or developing the ability to see someone else's pain.

bell hooks says that she is always looking for "the confessional moment," a flash of vulnerability or tenderness, an easing of hostility and defensiveness, which she says can be used "as a transformative moment."[15] Being able to feel and confront your own suffering makes it possible for you to identify with the oppressed and empathize with the position of the Other. This helps you to understand their political struggle, though not their experience, as your own. From this level of consciousness, students can choose to reject the rewards of an unequal social system and identify instead with antiracist, antisexist, antiheterosexist, and anticapitalist goals. Though this means abandoning the considerable socioeconomic bounty that often comes with mainstream privilege, they may be able to live a more spiritually gratifying life that has its own exquisite gifts. As a teacher I must remember that going through this transformation is often painful for students. They lose the person they have been and thought themselves to be for so many years. They must redefine almost all of their relationships with family and friends. As the transformation continues and sociopolitical consciousness increases, lifelong companions may no longer be part of their lives. Such losses must be grieved, and such consequences of change can be saturated with insecurity, sorrow, and wounded feelings.

Even short-lived moments of consciousness can be painful. When a mirror is held up and you see with clarity your life of privilege and power reflected in the words and experiences of an oppressed Other, the ugly image can be extremely difficult to look at. If these students do not have the will and desire to bear that pain and to face the ugliness, they will attempt anything to avoid it.[16] Hostility, abusive language, and disrespectful behaviors function as avoidance mechanisms. If denial continues and mainstream students refuse to participate in the process, they will remain children of privilege playing powerful games with very real social consequences. Should they choose to live fully within mainstream culture, no one will ever hold them responsible for their role in perpetuating an unequal, oppressive system.

Like bell hooks, I am constantly looking for that human moment when transformation becomes possible. An instant of consciousness when avoidance subsides and they might be persuaded to look away from their investments in privilege and join in the process of creating a world that does not yet exist.[17] When the moment presents itself, I must push beyond what already exists in many feminist, cultural studies, and humanist classrooms across the country—beyond postmodernism and relativism—to personally connect across our socially constructed differences. I must find ways to validate, but not romanticize, what they already know and think on the basis of their experiences and perspectives while not alienating the oppressed and the already politically conscious students in the room. In those moments when their defensiveness is replaced by curiosity about the meaning of their lives and a desire to rid themselves of internalized dominance I must find ways to help them recognize and challenge commonsense "isms." This can lead them to questioning their own motives and behaviors, and to read even the most familiar texts with a more critical eye.[18]

Though I have adopted, experimented with, and developed varying methods for creating learning communities in which learning/teaching partnerships can arise, I often resent the necessity of constantly having to ask myself, "what would Freire do" during difficult conflicts with resistant students. The task would be much easier if my colleagues were not often purveyors of the same internalized dominance from which the students suffer. Trying to practice Freirean pedagogy is an exercise in futility if I must spend all of my time trying to deal with the disrespectful behaviors of unaware, unintentional oppressors, while at the same time my mainstream colleagues are free to practice the very same commonsense "isms" as they focus on their areas of concentration and create exclusive canons in women's studies. Dealing with the sensitivities, hostility, and defensiveness of privileged students cannot be my full time concern. It robs marginalized and oppressed students of my attention and takes valuable time away from their engagement in the learning process. While many of the mainstream students are new to the process, politically conscious students of color grow petulant and impatient as they are forced to listen to and participate in the same discussions over and over. For them, such discourse becomes merely an exercise in oppression and a restatement of the existing hierarchical relationships as white experience always demands center stage.

When the greatest of my energies must be spent dealing with the anger and pain mainstream students are feeling (and the behaviors that engenders), the lives of the oppressed continue to remain invisible. Their major function becomes serving as a brick wall against which the internalized dominance of the mainstream students continually bumps its ugly head.[19] As a Freirean pedagogue, my first loyalty must be to the oppressed students, though I cannot totally abandon any student. As a facilitator of the dialogue I have to show respect for all students. But I cannot let those who have internalized dominance mistake that respect for weakness. To do so is to invite them to take advantage of their opportunity to be heard, which often results in their attempting to control the conversation. This "neutralizes the critical nature of the dialogue."[20] I do not want the role of facilitator to be reduced to referee. My primary focus must be attacking the social and political conditions that create and maintain various oppressions and helping all students to understand what different "isms" have in common so that they might come to view one another not as members of static groups but as human beings capable of enacting change through broad-based coalitions.[21]

Leslie G. Roman in her article, "White Is a Color!" claimed in a quickly familiarized quote that the final question was not "can the subaltern speak," but "are the privileged willing to listen to what we say?"[22] Freire maintains that oppressed peoples suffer from a condition that he called *cultura de silencio,* or culture of silence. Many U.S. educators, since the addition of ethnic and women's studies departments, have focused on the way in which this silencing mechanism has caused oppressed peoples to internalize negative stereotypes of themselves. So much so that when the alienated person finally speaks, their comments often seem bereft of critical attributes. But I would argue that at least some of this apparent absence of critical thought is a communication problem—a failure on the part of mainstream participants in the dialogue to correctly interpret what the subaltern is saying.

I have been asked to respond to a paper given by a Chicana graduate student as part of a public forum at the Humphrey Institute. The other papers being presented represent the latest trends in theoretical language and concepts. It is clear the students have worked hard to impress this largely academic audience. The Chicana's paper is autobiographical. It traces her amazing history as one of only three female workers in a steel plant in Gary, Indiana, in the early 1970s. The audience members seem less than impressed by this presentation. They exchange glances across the circle, and a few raise their eyebrows as she becomes the authentic voice of experience—a factory worker rather than a graduate student doing research. It is clear from the questions people ask that their interest is voyeuristic at best. They want more details about the woman's life and no one asks her to critically interpret the meaning of her experience or tries to see what she is saying as theory. I respond to the paper, contextualizing her experience within the history and failures of Lyndon Johnson's "Great Society," affirmative action initiatives, and the subsequent shifts in the global economy that led to her unemployment. The audience questions grow more scholarly and the comments more sophisticated. The Chicana's animation and excitement subside and she becomes silent. I see the waves of anger coming from her body like heat off a tar road in the sun. As we leave the room, one of the participants comes up and thanks me for an interesting presentation. "I hadn't realized," she says, "until I heard you speak that her paper was about so many things. Could I have a copy of your comments?" The student, who had linked arms with me—in that conspiratorial comadre way we Mexican women have—lets go of my arm. When we get outside, we yell and scream out of frustration. "That," she says, "is what happens when the subject becomes the author." We cross the Mississippi, our hands flying as we speak, still raging at the whole pinche *process.*

Internalized dominance does not allow mainstream students to hear the substance of what is spoken by the subordinate members of the society. Since they belong to the class, gender, race, or sexual identity group that creates, determines, and imposes its own language, ideology, and value system on others, they only hear in that language. They cannot be still, listen, think, or reflect in the Other's language in order to become at once less and more self-reflexive. Nor will they understand the theoretical complexity of what seems to them merely anecdotal testimony or storytelling. My friend is right. This *is* what happens when the subaltern speaks.

In course after course it becomes my job to cross the border that dominant culture students have constructed between us (because they see me and the students of color as inferior) and act as a translator. Contrary to the dialogical method Freire advocated in which all participants are simultaneously teachers and learners in a cooperative process, this can cast me as the "expert" on all of society's Others. It is a role I deeply resent and am unqualified to fulfill. The time and patience it takes to translate to a mainstream audience what is obvious to marginalized students often causes those oppressed students to see me as a *malinchista*—a traitor. Unfortunately, that is often exactly what I see in the mirror, because it is how I would feel in their place. But because I am committed to the humanization of the entire class, rather than replicating the authority and hierarchy of the existing system, I have to approach each student at their level of consciousness, not where I want them to be.

As I rage against oppression in many forms, I sometimes lose faith. I wonder if a Freirean pedagogical method can help mainstream students to see personal experiences (others' as well as their own) in a historical context? Can it awaken in them, as Freire hoped it would for the oppressed, "an expectation of change," engendering in them the collective power necessary to transform an unequal social system?[23]

Ironically, it is often in the most reluctant of bright students that I see some of the greatest potential for critical consciousness. They have tools that could develop into the skills and competencies necessary for dismantling hierarchical social models, challenging authoritarianism, and struggling collectively to transform the social order. But their internalized dominance traps them in "bootstrap" mythology and visions of individual empowerment, rather than believing in the power of collective action.

According to Freirean theory, there are several stages of achieving critical consciousness. The preconscious condition is linked to biological necessity. He felt that the perception of an individual whose primary interests necessitate a focus on basic survival is bound to be limited. But in the case of many of my students, their perception is limited by never having had to think of physical survival at all. The extent to which they are willing to experience a loss of privileges (even when they agree in principle with liberal democratic values), also limits their capacity for achieving consciousness. Freire posited the idea that such people react only to isolated events, to specific and immediate circumstances, from a provincial perspective. Hostile students clinging to their power and privilege can be just as rigid and provincial. Unlike Freire's oppressed masses, however, the social locations of these students do not require them to focus outside their local cultures. It is very difficult for them to progress to the point where they gain the capacity to question their own lives, to hear a critique of their power and privilege as something other than a personal attack on them as individuals, and to respond to the larger scope of any problem rather than to the specifics of it.[24]

Even when there is progression toward critical consciousness it is very difficult in a U.S. context to link this awakened political sensitivity to collective action. Freire's theories developed in a specific geographical space and historical time period. Revolutionary organizations and liberation groups existed to provide structure for the collective actions of critically conscious minds. Physical action could easily be linked to liberating ideas. While the university makes an effort to provide students with service learning opportunities and supports some vaguely political student organizations, neither it nor the U.S. national political scene offers much opportunity for the collective action newly conscious students crave. While some students of color, women, and/or GLBT students may find active political groups focused on some sort of social reform, there are seldom organizations directly involved in transformative political action where mainstream students can direct their political energies. This is compounded by the institution's continued rhetorical reliance on individual empowerment.[25]

Unlike many marginalized people who have been trained by their parents or have discovered on their own the futility of seeking validation from mainstream sources, white middle-class students have to work much harder to develop an antioppressive identity that necessarily requires a sense of alienation. While there is much in contemporary, capitalist U.S. culture from which to feel alienated, students with internalized dominance still crave validation from their peers and the institution in the form of good grades. Unlike many people of color, they lack the capacity to endure mainstream society's rejection and seemingly endless social problems. A consumer culture of instant gratification cannot teach them to wait for long-term solutions nor small changes that may take generations to implement. Nor does it teach them to think beyond individual action and change. They have no gift for tolerating the ambiguity and sense of constantly being outside the center that Gloria Anzaldúa describes so brilliantly in *Borderlands/La Frontera*. Thus it is more difficult for mainstream students to consciously seek out an alienating activity and to create dissonance in their own lives than it is for a student who has grown up as an outsider to do so.

Embedded in Freirean theory is the notion that social activism is a natural consequence of critical consciousness. Yet I often see that while some students seem to achieve such awareness in the classroom, their internalized dominance reappears in full force once they leave the protection of the university for field work, actual demonstrations, political organizing, or internships. All of the codes with which they have grown up overwhelm their newly acquired critical thinking skills as they seek familiarity, comfort, and validation in an unfamiliar environment. They miss their opportunity to enter into the history of social justice, civil rights, and feminist organizing through transformative behaviors, relying instead on their unearned privilege and power. This is often a crucial moment for students. Hopefully, the skills they've achieved in the classroom will help them to reflect on these experiences self-critically, will help them recommit to change rather than give up on it.

At all points of the process, and with every encounter, I am forced to bargain with students afflicted by internalized dominance. With each outrageous moment of commonsense racism, classism, sexism, or homophobia, I must ask myself not "What would Jesus do?" but "What would Freire do?" If he could remain hopeful and optimistic despite being surrounded by and subject to poverty, repression, and political exile, then surely I owe it to my students and myself to continue to try. I must remain committed to helping not only the powerless, but also the privileged, to understand their relationships to power.

Some might still question whether or not Freire's methods can or should be used at all in a country that holds so much power over the rest of the world. But in addition to his own experiences in Brazil and Chile, Freire was profoundly influenced by his tenure as a visiting professor in the United States during the politically charged 1960s. The violent conflicts between activists and emissaries of the state during the civil rights and antiwar movements convinced him to expand his definition of the Third World from a geographically specific reference to an ideological one. It was during this time, as he witnessed this struggle for socioeconomic and political equality, that he penned his most influential book, *Pedagogy of the Oppressed.* Clearly, nothing about those middle-class students protesting the war and demanding civil rights gave him reason to despair. On the contrary, it seems to have inspired him. Of course, a more cynical person might say that his tenure as a visiting professor in the United States simply gave him the time to write down his thoughts on the way in which a new kind of teaching could play a role in revolution. I prefer to think he saw in those students the hope that even the children of privilege could attain critical consciousness given the right conditions.

I have finished teaching the Introduction to Women's Studies. My evaluations have come back and I open them with some dread. It is a class with more than one hundred students. This has made the use of Freirean methods almost impossible. As I look at them, I notice what has been consistently true over the years—the numbers are lower than I get in my smaller classes. Still, 49 percent of the students think I am an exceptional teacher. Another 39 percent rate me as satisfactory or slightly above. That leaves 12 percent below. One student says I am a very poor teacher. The numbers improve as they rate my overall knowledge of the subject matter, respect and concern for students, respect for diversity, and success in getting them to think. Almost 80 percent give me an excellent rating for encouraging students to express their views. As I read their written comments I try to focus on those that are positive and those that offer constructive criticism. While these far outnumber the negative comments, it is the bad ones that rivet my attention.

"This is the worst class ever. I don't feel I learned anything except how to complain and to feel guilty about being upper-class, white, and American."

"We didn't learn anything about the history of women's rights (except in a few lectures). We only listened to you whine about women of color."

"I got sick of hearing about how shitty the lives of colored people are without any substantial evidence. The U is an institution that values scientific fact. You made statements in lectures without citing credible sources. And when you did, the studies were from places that can't be trusted."

"We talked too much about race and homosexuality or sexual orientation. I didn't feel included in those discussions. I was expecting to learn about women."

"Please focus on women, with race, class, and gender as a complement— not the whole course. Too much race. I would have liked to feel comfortable focusing solely on gender issues and not feel obligated to always think about the race or class of a woman."

"I wanted to focus on women rather than societal problems as a whole."

My own idealism in the face of such comments often embarrasses me, and cynicism sometimes feels more comfortable. How could they go through the whole course and not understand that all women in this society are raced, classed, and gendered? That all of us have a sexual orientation? But I cannot afford discouragement. I will go on employing Freirean methods because I believe they empower students of color. And not incidentally, because of the few mainstream students who come through my classrooms and end up making life-altering decisions about the way they want to live and what they want to work toward.

"I loved this course. It really opened my eyes to so many things! New things and other social issues that I hadn't really thought were important. Now I know how they affect real people. For the first time, I think I'm beginning to know what 'critical thinking' means."

"I learned a lot and definitely look differently at things. Now, I feel connected to everyone. Anyone who wants a better society should take this class."

"This course made me reflect on everything in ways I never have before. It opens so many new doors even as it closes some old ones. Not once did you tell a student their opinion was wrong. You let us speak out and I learned so much

from listening to what everyone had to say. Thank you for affecting the way I see myself as a woman among so many women."

"The friends I made in the class were great. We're going to keep meeting together and are joining some student groups fighting for social justice. I can't wait to go to Washington for the antiwar rally! Thanks for making me THINK."

!Viva la conscientizacion!

CHAPTER 4

Desire on the Line

Sexual Transgression and the Border as Grand Metaphors

When I think of the U.S./Mexican border region, my head fills with multi-dimensional and overlapping illusions. Primarily memories of south Texas, these disconnected images shuffle and swing through the years. Like the pieces in a kaleidoscope dream, they fall into patterns, which although ever changing retain some measure of predictability. The strongest of these impressions have been with me since childhood. The tiny house where my grandparents lived in Mercedes, where they raised fourteen children of their own and looked after several grandchildren as well. The sweet taste of fresh-picked oranges that my grandfather cut and used to pacify us. The glistening sweat on brown, smiling faces in the front yard as my father and his brothers played baseball like a religion.

I remember digging through the crushed seashells that would go into the bottom of the septic tank, and *mi tía* Rosa finding the prize—an unbroken scallop shell. Though she was my aunt, she was my age and my best friend in the whole valley. But the pinkish shell was not treasure enough to soothe the welts my grandfather raised on her thin legs with a rope when he found out that she had been playing near the men who were drilling the new well. Tyrant that he was, my grandfather always induced either screams or silence—nothing in between. But amid the tears, I also remember *mi tío* Hector, who turned us all into laughing hyenas with his impressions of *Cantínflas*.

When we least expected it, he would come riding out of the corral on a little brown burro that bucked and kicked to get that *menso* off its back. Texas dirt swirled in the sunlight as Hector tumbled to the ground, his dark skin lightened by dust. *El burro* gave a disgruntled look over his shoulder as he trotted away. Similarly, the ever present and comforting smells of corn tortillas and churros from '*uelita's* kitchen still linger in my waking dreams and make me smile. And perhaps most vividly, I am haunted by the recurring image of the Ku Klux Klan waiting with lighted torches as we returned on Sunday nights from visiting family across the river.

I had not seen this mixture of ordinary life on the border—in all its beauty and horror, gentleness and brutality, simplicity and confusion—represented in mainstream culture until I saw the film *Lone Star,* by writer/producer/director John Sayles. This extraordinary movie has generated many critical essays, and much of what I have to say may not be new. But the passion of my memories for the landscape Sayles describes forces me to speak. Perhaps because the territory is so familiar and the subject matter so personal, I will succeed in adding something to this body of criticism. Overall, my impression of the film falls somewhere in the middle of a dialogue—somewhere between cultural theorist José Limón's optimistic view and feminist film studies scholar Rosa Linda Fregoso's more cynical perspective.

While *Lone Star* can easily be discussed on its own, I want to explore its themes in comparison with the Mexican film, *El jardín del Edén*, by María Novaro. Both films deal with the conflicting desires and perspectives of people from various social locations along the border. They also illuminate the contradiction between the daily pleasures and the frightening realities of life on the line.

In both films, viewers see the power, as well as the limitations, of desire to change the antagonisms between Anglos and Mexicans in the borderlands. Exploring the themes of sexual transgression and the borderland as a multicultural space, Sayles and Novaro offer them up as grand metaphors for interracial, intercultural, and international relationships. I am not using the word transgression here as many cultural studies theorists have used it to only mean a kind of resistance to hegemonic impulses. I am also using two related definitions of the word transgression: first, to pass over or go beyond a boundary; and second, to violate, infringe, interfere, or disturb. While I feel certain that Sayles did intend his film to be a challenge to long-held notions about borders, I think that Novaro's perspective is more related to transgression as an aggressive act by the powerful against the oppressed.

While much of the past decade has been littered with references to crossing borders, especially in academic scholarship, many of us in Chicana feminist studies have been horrified to see Gloria Anzaldúa's elegantly defined notion of ambiguous, complex, mestiza space sacrificed on the altar of postmodernism. Whereas "borderlands" once described both a physical space and a bicultural experience unique to Mexican Americans, it has grown into a convenient concept describing all manner of fragmentation and breaking the rules. Stripped of its origins in Mexican Indian thought, the concept of a borderland space, as opposed to a borderline, now occupies much of our popular culture. In thinking about the films in which this grand metaphor appears, I am reminded of what East Los Angeles poet Olga García Echeverría has said about such images from the perspective of someone who lives in this space. On the CD, *Raza Spoken Here*, she traces the brutal history of Mexicans and Chicanos and dismissively sites many of the euphemistic metaphors that describe the border. "Forget them," she says, and focus instead on the colonial history. Look at the contemporary discrimination against, and exploitation of, immigrants and citizens of Mexican descent. Their "*sangre* ain't salsa, and the border ain't no metaphor," is Echeverría's call to focus on the material reality of the border for Mexicans and Chicanos.[1]

The political boundary that exists between the United States and Mexico constitutes a central symbol in both Novaro's *El jardín del Edén,* and Sayles's *Lone Star.* Both filmmakers seem to understand that this space is simultaneously permeable and concrete. Each shows us a geographical location with its own community and culture. In *Lone Star,* Sayles emphasizes the importance of geographical location by letting us get a good look at the land before he ever shows us any faces. Novaro's artistic eye strategically stops the camera on specific features of the environment, or pans across the landscape in a way that adds nothing to the plot of her film. Yet she uses the physical presence and atmosphere of Tijuana and the rural desert on both sides of the border to give us a sense of the solid earth, and a feeling of the immediacy in a place where, as Anzaldúa says, the Third World rubs up against the First.[2] Sayles and Novaro represent their spaces from different world perspectives and social positions. Novaro is Mexican and female, Sayles is U.S. American, male, and white. This makes both the similarities and differences in the two films interesting.

Like Novaro, Sayles deals with the conflict between immigrants and law enforcement. Each filmmaker looks into the political and economic realities that motivate people in this borderland space and impel them to cross legal or ideological boundaries. But they also pay attention to the crossing of social boundaries. Thus, each focuses on both physical and psychological movement.

In this country, we are encouraged to think of immigration as something that an alien "Other" does, and that this act is outside of us—its only effect might be a negative economic impact on the social system. But in Mexico, as well as in Novaro's film, immigration is seen as something that affects everyone—individual, family, community, state, and nation. Focusing on the present, Novaro takes the history of immigration from south to north for granted. She assumes her Mexican audience knows and understands this context. While Sayles seems to understand that the movement of people from one location to another has a ripple effect for generations, he cannot take for granted that most people know this history with any complexity. He must unravel history as well as a personal mystery and its ramifications for his audience.

Lone Star

Sayles leads viewers to understand the profound impact of immigration on everyone's life, even if many of his characters remain unaware of it or try to keep its effects a secret. Like Novaro, John Sayles seems to understand that as immigrants move the whole landscape and everyone in it shifts in some way. But because he knows that mainstream America has little knowledge of the Mexican diaspora and Anglo colonization processes in the Southwest, he must find a way to show viewers the relationship between the past and the present. He does this through the visualized memories of his characters. In an unusual narrative structure, multiple voices tell us the history of the region. Using flashbacks that glide from present to past and back again with no fade-out or interruption of the narrative, Sayles makes us aware of the intimacy between historical moments. Though his flashbacks confuse viewers in the beginning, this structure perfectly manages our response as a particularly cryptic truth is slowly revealed. As the action travels back and forth between time periods, between the United States and Mexico, and between fathers and sons or mothers and daughters, we learn the depth to which the act of crossing the border infiltrates everyone's life if not their consciousness.

Like the ubiquitous John Ford of an earlier era, Sayles is a white man used to confronting the mythology of the dominant culture. In *Lone Star*, as he has in other films, Sayles uses mood and mystery to manipulate how we will see certain aspects of that culture.[3] Sayles filmed *Lone Star*'s exterior scenes in Eagle Pass, Texas, but does not give his fictional land space this name. Instead he calls it "Frontera," signaling his focus on the borderlands as a particular geographical and cultural place. His flashbacks intersperse seamlessly with the present as Sayles exposes the historical distortion and the immoral ground upon which white supremacy has been built generally and in this geographical location specifically. In doing so, he attempts to portray the descendancy of the white patriarchal order in south Texas, where people of Mexican descent are the majority population.

Because this is generally the case along the border, it has been easy for politically charged Mexican Americans throughout the country to see this space as a kind of cultural homeland for *Chicanismo*, or the material site on which an imaginary nationalism might be based. It has been political/cultural nationalism without an existing or historical "nation" in the Western sense of that word—neither Mexico nor the United States, but a third space, home to a culture that is more than the sum of its parts. Some people have implied that Chicanas/os have falsified, embellished, or exaggerated their link to this borderland space and culture through references to Aztlán as well as our imagined relationship to the experience of crossing over. We have been accused of illicitly yearning for, and naively creating, an identity that is indigenous to the Southwest but has no real ties to existing tribal groups or recognized indigenous nations. We have been charged with the cultural misdemeanor of looking to a Mexico that no longer exists, of not understanding what it really means to be Indio or mestizo in modern Mexico. But for many Chicana/o activists, identifying as indigenous to this land space is absolutely necessary to our political perspective. To be grounded in this space shapes our view of neocolonialism.

It is difficult to know where Sayles stands on this issue. But rather than a Chicano cultural dreamer, Sayles provides us with the militant reporter, Danny, whose nationalism is firmly rooted in Texas rather than Mexico. His outrage and concerned knowledge of the area's history come not from the perspective of an immigrant, but that of an original inhabitant, someone whose land, resources, and traditional life have been stolen. He understands that this process—begun in the past and continued in the present—hurts the people he sees as his "nation," even as it does not directly affect him personally. Like many mainstream media portraits of radical activists, this character's behavior seems strident and stubborn. He won't give up, hounding the town's leaders as he refuses to let them forget about the Perdido land development.

Sayles chooses the signifier "Perdido" or "lost" to describe the project that destroyed a Mexican settlement in the creation of Lake Pescadero. This name comes from the Spanish verb *pescar*, which has two meanings, both relevant to the story. The first means "to fish," which seems fitting for the name of a lake largely created for the benefit and enjoyment of the town's elite, who ended up with lakeshore property after the dam was constructed. But the second meaning, to catch unaware, is far more significant to the Mexican residents who lost their homes and community. One might conclude from this choice of signifiers that Sayles sympathizes with Danny's rage and his attempt to correct the mythology created by the town's leaders around the project. They had justified the project by denigrating the displaced residents and downplaying the negative aspects of the development. Danny wants to replace this skewed view of history by restoring their subjectivity and testifying to whom they were as human beings, deserving dignity. But interestingly, Sayles shows the reporter's behavior as confrontational. For the mainstream audience this may close more minds than it opens since internalized dominance would make them identify with the town leaders who are the targets of Danny's accusations. Yet Sayles balances this rather stereotypical character with historical information that supports the Chicano's political message even as he asks us to disapprove of his "in-your-face" demeanor. Is this ambivalence on Sayles's part? Or is it just an attempt to accurately portray the complexity of the region?

While his part in the movie is minor, Danny reinforces one of the movie's major themes—that those with the most power have the greatest investment in remembering history in a certain way. Sayles goes to great lengths to show us what some folks "will do, say, manufacture, and fantasize to suppress that knowledge and keep history moving," to their advantage.[4] Full of self-righteous bravado, this Chicano functions not only as counter to false histories, but also as a specific type. He represents a political position and a voice well known in Texas, rather than a fully developed character. Fortunately, *Lone Star* is filled with a broad range of Mexican American types responding to the environment with differing levels of consciousness and a variety of sociopolitical desires. This is part of the movie's attraction for Chicana/o viewers. Rarely have I seen a movie that so captures the socioeconomic and political diversity of Mexican American life in south Texas. Historian Vicki Ruíz agrees. Responding to a question about the film following a public lecture on an unrelated topic, she said that it is particularly this aspect of the film that Sayles "got right."

Yet, while they are sometimes portrayed as annoying or obsequious, no Mexican or Chicano ever becomes the bad guy. The villain comes in the form of an old Anglo sheriff who has been murdered. Sayles lowers his camera to shoot Kris Kristoferson as Sheriff Charlie Wade, making us feel short by comparison to this overpowering figure. He also backlights him with dark, smoky colors. Even the outdoor scene seems darker than it should be on a sunlit day. This all makes Wade seem even larger and more ominous as we see him from his victims' perspectives in several scenes. Sayles uses the lowered camera angle to shoot Buddy Deeds as well, but gives him an angelic glow with bright, white light. As if his white hat were not enough, this technique signals both the power that Buddy has inherited from Wade and his own reputation throughout the town as a heroic and fair man. Though it is clear that each scene in *Lone Star* is filtered through a contemporary political consciousness, Sayles's expert storytelling, use of lighting, and manipulated camera angles make this strategy feel like cultural genius rather than a misguided or an unintentional accident. It is more than an example of ahistorical artistic license.

In contrast to the documentary feel of Novaro's Tijuana and the rural United States countryside, *Lone Star* has the feel of a dream—a complex allegory that mirrors, but also distorts, reality just enough to make us feel both comfortable and slightly off-center. Sayles always gives viewers the feeling that every aspect of the film is carefully calculated. The fictional "Río" county and the town with the rather obvious name "Frontera," feminist theorist Amy Kaminsky points out, are in Spanish.[5] Like many places throughout the Southwest, they identify colonized spaces within the United States where Anglos continue to dominate even though the majority of citizens along the border are Mexican or Mexican American and the local culture hardly resembles mainstream USA. Thus, these names emphasize Sayles's focus on the border and its unique *mestizaje* or mixture of cultures. But they also remind us that this is in many ways occupied land.

This movie is a political one as it reveals the tyranny and malice with which a corrupt and racist system tries to enforce its legal and social boundaries, as well as protect its empire. Sayles uses one of the most common narrative motifs of the American west, the story of patrilineal heritage and power, which can only be maintained by ensuring genetic purity. The film's mystery is sustained by the desire to know—what for men has been unknowable until relatively recent times—the truth of who the father of any woman's son is.[6]

Though this has been used as a device in other films, in *Lone Star* it is particularly persuasive. It is also compelling, because Sayles complicates this disturbing lack of certainty about paternity by adding race, class, and gender to the question. In doing so, he goes beyond the traditional western film, Oedipal tales, and other storytelling rituals using the basic patrilineal plot.[7] Sayles shows us the messiness that results from human sexuality, which cannot be controlled and contained along publicly defined race and class divisions. While Sayles shows us that male power evolves and changes character over time—moving from the dictatorial tyrant to the gentler, reluctant hero—he cannot fully abandon the father/son genetic trail. It is intrinsic to his vision of how the society has been transforming itself.

Sayles tells his corrupt patriarchal story across the boundaries that divide nations, races, and classes. He is not some starry-eyed dreamer simply touting a celebratory tale about Chicano and African American achievement and acceptance in south Texas society. Sayles is not interested in replacing one fantasy with another. He wants to rid himself, the Western, and us of our delusions that we have been totally separate peoples. This provides us with a much richer understanding of life on the U.S./Mexican border as a part of our shared history—a history that is often more degenerate but all too human and much less heroic than the classic westerns that Sayles consciously imitates. In choosing this genre, Sayles updates the classic style to speak to ambivalent patriarchs across the country. With undeniable honesty he confronts the mythologizing that has characterized both westerns and Texas lore for decades.[8]

Many scholars including Kaminsky, José Limón, and Emma Pérez have taken from this an optimistic view of *Lone Star*, seeing it as a new kind of western, a more utopian vision of the future. Each seems sure that Sayles is predicting a continued blurring of the lines between races, classes, and genders—the creation of equality through desire and the ever-softening hearts and minds of historical actors. I do not doubt this possibility, but I must also keep my eye on a competing message that does not have the romantic couple riding off into the sunset to live happily ever after. Certainly the optimism, which leads Limón to describe *Lone Star* as "the emergence of an alternative socioracial order," is part of why many of us have been moved to discuss the film in the first place. The hopefulness, with which he declares we are seeing old categories and stereotypes give way because two people have found "each other in a desire that seeks to negate a conflicted history of politics and racialized sexuality," is the reason we applaud the storyteller's skills and are seduced by the film.[9] We know that Sam is not the man his father was, though it is clear the town thought they might be getting another hero when they elected Sam their sheriff on name recognition alone. We see evidence throughout the film that not only is he no Buddy Deeds, but that he does not even respect what his father was, which makes him in the eyes of the town elders, a lesser man. In a wonderfully old school Anglo Texas way, Sayles gives the following words to the outgoing mayor, Hollis, to describe Sam's masculine inadequacies. He is, we're told, "all hat and no cattle." Change is surely taking place.

I am not so sure it is the displacement of existing power relationships. I cannot agree with Limón that Sam's affair with Pilar resembles a "pure" relationship free from male-defined sexuality and any question of reproduction of the current order.[10] The protagonist after all is named Sam. No matter how different he is from the evil Charlie Wade, Sayles has given him this loaded name. It functions as a referent not only to a national patriarch, Uncle Sam, but also an ideological father for Anglo Texans closer to the border, Sam Houston. It is doubtful you could make a movie so focused on the relationship between Anglos and Chicanos in Texas and be unaware of this.

Thus *Lone Star*—as revolutionary as it is in many ways—creates mixed messages for its viewers. "The ambivalence *Lone Star* produces differs from the profound ambivalence of critical border theory," says Rosa Linda Fregoso. This is not, she contends, the *mestizaje* or border crossing described by Chicana/o theorists. "Tejana/o counter discourses are driven by a desire to disrupt social hierarchies as well as to alter the centrality of white heterosexual masculinity in the narratives of nationhood." While the film does disrupt our illusion of pureness and the ability or even desirability of guarding certain borders, it does not even attempt to displace white male lineage as the central theme. "Irrespective of its overture to multiculturalism, *Lone Star* resituates white masculinity as the mediating term that is able to cross racial and sexual boundaries while erecting the borders of its own racial purity and masculine privilege."[11]

The sticky complexity of the border that Sayles describes is the result of neocolonizers who, like their predecessors, are intent on penetrating and mixing with the bodies of the people they've irreparably harmed. While it may have been—and sometimes is in real life—wrapped in a gloss of romantic love, it cannot fully disguise who most benefits from this union in a continually racialized society. Nor can it make us forget who has had the assumed right to collect the spoils of war and to (re)create empires that continue to despise brownness in a conquered land space. In the film, as in so many U.S. cinematic narratives, "white male access to the multicultural nation takes place through the body of a brown woman."[12] Rarely do we see the opposite—the brown male body having access to the white female. Clearly this is not the story of multiculturalism that mainstream audiences want to see, no matter how often it occurs in real life. Such a scenario does not allow them to mourn the passing of their old heroes as well as the unquestioned power these larger-than-life men of the west took and were granted for so long.

In a brilliant scene, an old bartender stands before a huge mural of a cowboy on horseback roping a longhorn. (This image is reminiscent of the mural-like painting that hung in the living room of Rock Hudson's ranch house in the 1950s' movie *Giant*—another tale of boundary transgression, shifting relationships, and cultural transformation from an earlier era—also a tale of white paternal legacies and change written on brown women's bodies.) The old Texan is talking to Sheriff Sam Deeds about how the country is changing. Just as he utters the most racist remarks of the monologue, the camera shifts angles and the bartender is backlit with the glow of the neon Lone Star Beer sign, another symbol of Anglo Texas, the Texas Republic, and its separation from Mexico. (The lone star was the symbol of the Texas flag as it sought to free itself from Mexico and become an independent country. One of the most mythologized battles of the Texans against the Mexican general Santa Ana took place at the Mission Alamo in 1836.) We have no doubt that his fears are those of all Anglo Texans, that the Lone Star State is being "birthed and immigrated" out from under them.

Sayles's refusal to displace this white male perspective does not mean, however, that the film fails to disrupt the dominant narrative altogether. Sayles does show us a kind of evolution through the town fathers, all transgressors in the territory. As we move from the brutal, white supremacist sheriff Charlie Wade, to the subtler but every bit as controlling Buddy Deeds, and on to the loving but troubled son, we do see change. In Sam Deeds we are supposed to think we are seeing the new postfeminist man confronting himself as he uncovers the truth of his legacy. Yet Deeds, the sensitive son with the sad eyes, is nevertheless still a law enforcement officer and an Anglo Texan. He can walk away from the Lone Star countryside and the sheriff's badge without conceding either his skin or gender privilege. He is, after all, the hero of the film. In an era when "it isn't popular" says film critic Armond White, "to hold history responsible for anything," Sayles unflinchingly shows us that even reluctant patriarchs like Sam are held in its grip.[13]

Even if Sam steps down, an heir apparent is eager and ready to take over the kingdom. Since this newcomer is Chicano, cultural theorist José Limón sees this as an equalizing gesture, a breakdown of the traditional order in which Anglos rule over Mexican Americans. Though Sayles offers this new patriarch in the form of a Mexican American man, he is a deputy who we know is neither racially Indian in appearance, culturally Mexican, nor politically Chicano. His Mexican American status is colloquial ethnicity at best. We also see in the film that he is obsequious and self-serving. As such this gringoized version of Mexican Americanness is just imperfect enough to fulfill his role as a substitute patriarch and upholder of the existing power structure without actually becoming a hero. Here we see the historical and contemporary reality of Texas racial ambiguity in which some Mexican Americans are allowed to, and choose to, adopt an ideology of whiteness as they move up the socioeconomic ladder. Another Mexican American character, a candidate for mayor who is likely to replace the current white mayor, is similarly whitewashed. He just happens to have owned the company that worked on the Perdido land development deal. Like millions of European immigrants before them, these Mexican Americans have seemingly crossed the racial divide and melted into that great fictional mainstream pot.

But, this neowhiteness is always conditional and predicated on one's loyalty to, and active support of, the existing power structure. The deputy who would be sheriff for instance, easily sets aside his own view on the need for a new jail in order to gain favor with the town's leaders and ensure his election. This willingness to compromise, however, is only part of the equation. It is an option mostly available to those with lighter skin, no accent, and/or middle-class sensibilities, in addition to an unquestioning support for mainstream political agendas. Since Danny—played by the browner and more traditionally indigenous-looking actor—is outnumbered by these more mainstream Mexican American characters, it seems clear that Sayles is guilty of engaging in a kind of victim-blaming common to internalized dominance. It makes white imperialists look a little less culpable if it can be shown that brown folks have actively oppressed other brown folks. Thus,

Sayles is not signaling a new order so much as he is showing us how flexible the system can be and still maintain its hierarchical character. He also illustrates how easy it is to recruit agents who will act in the interest of the dominant culture.

In September 2002, syndicated columnists Patrisia Gonzales and Roberto Rodríguez responded to a *Los Angeles Times* article that took note of this phenomenon. Latinos, it seems to the mainstream press, are becoming "white." Thus, they conclude, "we" need not fear the "browning of America." Debrowning Mexicans through legal, legislative, and cultural practice has a very long history in the Southwest.[14] Designating us as white in the Treaty of Guadalupe Hidalgo—putting Caucasian or white on our birth certificates (until relatively recently) no matter the actual color of our skin, Anglicizing the names of movie stars, and pushing singers to cross over into the mainstream by using English lyrics—are all devices designed to lighten us. During the worst of the Jim Crow era and even in the post–World War II period of extreme Americanization, some Mexican Americans chose this white designation for themselves out of fear and shame. This celebration of assimilation, and the economic rewards that may come with acculturation, means the division of a people along lines determined by skin color, linguistic abilities or choices, and class positions. This is the ultimate form of a community divided against itself, because it is not white folks who will suffer from this vivisection, it is the poorest of Mexican Americans. White folks in fact will profit from this kind of diversity where the exceptional few gain access and the rest are left behind. Luckily, Sayles eventually points one of the film's most vocal proponents of this system, Mercedes, away from this collusion with whiteness.[15]

I agree with José Limón when he points out that *Lone Star*'s whiteness is not necessarily pure or singular in terms of blood or culture, but is more complicated, mixed, and ambiguous. Of course that has always been the case, assertions by self-proclaimed blue bloods to the contrary notwithstanding. But this part of our collective history has only been acknowledged publicly in relatively recent times. Old secrets have been revealed, and interracial relationships rendered less illicit than they once were. This movement toward shared culture is to be applauded. The growing socioeconomic and political power of Mexican Americans and African Americans in places like the fictional Río County is undeniable. Certainly we need to pay as much attention to class as we do to race when we examine what remains of the colonialist impulse. But, we cannot lose sight of the fact that a blurring of the lines can be just as much a strategy of the old order as it might be a move toward the open acknowledgment of mixture. The ideology of whiteness still exists, but it is not stagnant. Colonialism and its definitions of "whiteness" and "brownness" like all social orders and

constructions must change or die. Color or race in this sense is always ideological rather than biological, but this shift of the lines does not necessarily mean an end to racism. Even in the multicultural narrative, Sayles tells
us, there is no question about who has held and abused power, and who
has been most harmed by that dominance.

Shifts in demographic, economic, cultural, or environmental conditions
demand a response from any society. Though borders are crossed and lines
blurred, the intractability of whiteness as a construct (as well as patriarchy,
middle-classness, and heterosexuality) in terms of mainstream U.S. values
is reaffirmed in this film, even as it is simultaneously displaced. "Ultimately,
the narrative not only reproduces white masculine privilege, but also maintains whiteness intact, for unlike Pilar, Sam Deeds is not the product of miscegenation, of sexual contact between a white man and a brown woman.
Sam is rather the embodiment of racial purity . . . the burden of miscegenation rests on his half-sister, Pilar."[16]

Pilar alone serves as the symbol of the borderlands *mestizaje*, but since
she reveals that she can no longer have children due to her medical condition, we have no reason to hope that the multicultural, multiracial landscape Sayles describes and carefully constructs will continue. Her existing
children, after all, have a Mexican father whose absence is conspicuous
when we consider the future of Mexicans in the world Sayles has created.
Their mixture is moving away from the whiteness of their grandfather,
whereas Sam's is intact. Since inheritance in this film (and in the dominant
culture) is passed on through patriarchs, we need not worry that Pilar's
brown children will benefit from the power of the Buddy Deeds legacy.

Interestingly, neither the two office seekers (for sheriff and mayor) nor
the Chicano reporter are allowed to be sexual in the film. While it is refresh-
ing to see a film in which Mexican men do not have to be hyper-romantic
Latin lovers, we have to ask what this complete lack of sexuality (and thus
fatherhood) means in a film so concerned with the patriarchal legacy. The
film's sexuality is always mediated through white men and brown women—
Buddy and Mercedes, Sam & Pilar, the white soldier and his black fiancée.
For critic Rosa Linda Fregoso, this signals the film's "deeply colonialist and
phallocentric project."[17] Sayles's vision and Sam's hope for the future then
are not much different from Buddy's deed a few decades earlier. (Pun intended to call our attention to Buddy Deeds and the last name Sayles has
chosen for him.) Like Buddy's desire for Mercedes, Sam's desire is also projected onto the Tejana/Chicana/Mexicana body.[18] In this patriarchal tale,
they penetrate brown women's bodies just as Charlie Wade's bullet pene-
trated Eladio Cruz's body. Both are acts of patriarchal power, though some
are undoubtedly more benevolent and even consensual than are others.

Adding romance and love to the formula only serves to naturalize and normalize "white male access to brown women's bodies while simultaneously prohibiting relationships between nonwhite men and white women." Both acts proclaim the importance of paternity in this society. "By excluding and denying the history of other forms of sexual relations, namely those outside of the white-male/women-of-color paradigm, the film rearticulates and reaffirms the racist, colonialist interdiction against mixed-race unions between brown men and white women."[19]

Yet Sayles also steps outside his own perspective to make the father/daughter lineage highly significant. This strategy brings into focus the real story of sexual transgression and paternity. It also highlights the importance of who the mothers really were in that imagined West of U.S. mainstream culture. As in this story, their material reality always challenged the patriarchal order as well as the foundational assumptions and subsequent myths of ideological whiteness. While the character of Mercedes is in many ways a Malinche figure—the indigenous woman who participates in her own violation and then acts as an agent of the transgressor—the daughter Pilar is cast as the good woman. Since Mercedes has achieved social respectability largely through her restaurant, it is important to remember that the business was originally financed through her sexual connection to Sam's father Buddy. This solidifies her role as a *vendida, chingada,* or sell out, in the same way that Malintzin Tenepal was constructed as the betrayer of Mexico because of her relationship to Cortés.

Through Mercedes, Sayles dives right into the emotional frenzy at the intersection of race and class. He perfectly captures the ambivalent relationship between early twentieth-century Mexican immigrants (generally lighter-skinned and middle class in South Texas) and later migrants who are Indian and poor. While Mercedes feels and acts as their superior—and is accepted in the town as a businesswoman—she can never achieve the social status of her Anglo lover's white wife, who is described many times as "a saint." The shaming process (described in chapter 1) for all Mexican Americans and Mexican immigrants is intense in south Texas. In addition to the stigma of being brown, Mercedes may also be shamed by her well-known "secret" affair with Buddy Deeds. We see over and over, this woman trying to put emotional and political distance between herself and the Spanish-speaking "wetbacks" she employs in her restaurant. Clearly, Mercedes has had a lifetime of trying to fit in to mainstream culture in Frontera. Deriding the newer immigrants because they do not speak English and calling them derogatory names is not personal mean-spiritedness, but an imitation of the people from whom she wants acceptance. It is also the very human desire to shed the stigma from her skin, using learned behavior to place it onto someone else.

But Mercedes as much or more than anyone in this film disrupts the existing social order, even as that challenge is subtler and perhaps more subconscious than the others Sayles highlights. At the moment she decides to help the undocumented workers trying to cross the border, she leaves behind the competitive and individualistic values of "whiteness" and reverts to the traditional communal values of Mexican/Indian cultures. She does this knowing that her personal fortune, afforded by her compliance with the colonialist order, may be jeopardized by her actions. Yet as she remembers her own undocumented, immigrant history (and symbolically the history of many Mexicans in Texas), she decides to cease acting as an agent of white, patriarchal power. Ideologically, she crosses back over the border to the Mexican side, however reluctantly.

Her daughter Pilar is a teacher actively engaged in disrupting the Anglo-centric view of Texas/Mexican history—even as she does not know the full extent of her mother's or her own tragic history. This remains true for much of the film, just as it has been for much of the characters' lifetimes, a deeply buried secret. As clues to what we know will be something horrible begin to accumulate, we are not surprised when we learn that the old sheriff killed Eladio Cruz (Mercedes' husband and Pilar's supposed father) in cold blood. Yet the real mystery is something even more awful to digest. The fact that Buddy Deeds, Sam's father, has privately transgressed the boundaries he is expected to maintain in public is at the heart of this secret. It is only when the son and daughter discover the truth that they begin to understand their respective, rigid relationships with their parents.

After they have become lovers Sam, the son of Buddy Deeds, and Pilar, the daughter of Mercedes, learn that their parents' have also been lovers, and that they, Sam and Pilar, are half-brother and sister. It is then that they realize that they have unwittingly committed incest—have, because of the town's secret, transgressed one of society's firmest boundaries. Because Sayles has portrayed them as being deeply in love for many years and through many separations we must weigh our romantic desires for them to continue a life together against our revulsion that they are siblings, a social boundary we should not want them to cross—yet we do want them to be together. In addition to showing us their deeply satisfying physical love and their unbreakable emotional bond, Sayles takes another step to ensure that his audience will be sympathetic to Pilar as Sam's lover. He does so in a way that mirrors Spanish strategies for making Indian women suitable partners following the conquest. He raises her socioeconomic status to more closely equal his own. In order for this to occur, he must make her superior in a number of ways, thus she is college educated, emotionally and financially stable, as well as culturally middle class. Sayles also makes her a nonsexual mother figure until the hero claims her. For even though we know she has children, we never see any other signs of her sexual involvement outside her relationship with Sam. "How come," she says after they make love, "it always feels so right with you." Because, of course, he is not only her choice, but also ours.

In a more contemporary strategy, Sayles also makes her smart, self-sufficient, and an accepted member of the community. Her very name, Pilar Cruz (which mean "pillar" and "cross" respectively), hints at both stability and holiness. Interestingly, Sayles seems obligated to oppose this image with a white woman, Sam's ex-wife Bunny, who in one brief scene comes across as childish, emotionally unstable, self-involved, and less physically attractive than Pilar. She is also likely an alcoholic, hooked on prescription drugs, and obsessed with football. This latter addiction marks her as thoroughly Texan, but she is neither physically nor culturally a borderland or "Frontera" inhabitant. This portrait erases any unconscious or latent anxiety around miscegenation that may be present in even liberal viewers. The fact that Bunny is so thoroughly disqualified as an option for Sam in choosing a mate gives the audience permission to embrace Pilar as an acceptable substitute for this crazy white woman. While this strategy is fundamentally racist in its assumptions, it does contradict a more "predictable racial narrative" that is common in many westerns and films about the South. It does not engage in "the colonialist fantasy of white womanhood under siege."[20] Bunny is not threatened by the sexuality of brown men, or the sensuality of brown women. Her only enemy is her own craziness. The audience, then, does not expect Sam to play the hero and save her.

While Sayles goes to some lengths to make Pilar the audience's romantic choice for Sam, he cleverly leaves the future of the border region open-ended—though its white supremacist, patriarchal order is clearly in jeopardy by the end of the film. While other critics have presumed a happy ending, I would argue that it is just as possible to infer that the patriarchy is simply shifting and adjusting its tactics to a new demographic reality. I am not convinced that Sam and Pilar can decide to continue their lives together a la Roy Rogers and Dale Evans in equal partnership.

Despite essays and reviews to the contrary, which assume a ride off into the sunset for Sam and Pilar, Sayles does not make this decision for his characters or the audience. He simply explores all of the legal, masculine, capitalistic, and "familial customs" that have kept the illusionary boundaries in place and lets us guess what the future will be.[21] He does make it clear to us that these barriers have already been transgressed. This disrupts the fantasy that borders—where intimate relationships, human yearnings, and inevitable connections exist—can ever be completely policed in the real world. Yet despite the obvious fluidity at the border, Sayles refuses to completely dislodge the locus of power. He does, however, ask serious questions of it.

Sayles shows us the confusion and profound sadness that is the legacy of white patriarchs. It is the Mexican American woman Pilar who is trying to create and maintain a loving relationship with Sam and to give him a more functional family than he has ever known by including her two children (not coincidentally named Paloma, or dove symbolizing peace, and Amado, signifying love). But Sam is more ambivalent, his core more thoroughly wounded in some ways. Since the borders of his paternal estate or heritage have been brought into question, his identity is less fixed. In the final major scene, Sam and Pilar sit in front of the aging screen at an abandoned outdoor movie theater. It functions as a symbol of the 1950s and early 1960s, a period of intense Americanization in Texas with clearly defined social boundaries. The *white* screen is now damaged and the theater closed. One of the panels of the screen is missing—a dark hole disrupting its geometric perfection. Sam wants to run away from his job and the town, but Pilar seems to want to stay.

As a woman of Mexican descent growing up in Texas, she has had more time to deal with the ambiguity of living a bicultural identity and suffering the duplicity of Anglo Texans. Though Pilar is angry and shaken by the knowledge that she and Sam are brother and sister, she remains sure of who she is. She is as defiant of the old boundaries as she has ever been. Yet she wonders how they can go on as a couple. "So that's it," she asks, "we just forget the past? Forget the Alamo?"

Both José Limón and Emma Pérez have given great importance to the fact that Sayles puts these words in Pilar's mouth.[22] For them, this displacement of the reference to the Alamo from the Anglo Texan to the Chicana is symbolic of transformation. While I too think it is significant that Pilar speaks these words rather than Sam, and it points to a shift in her relationship to power, I do not think her facial expression necessarily elicits optimism. Since Sayles directed the actor, I had originally assumed he intended a conclusion far more unresolved than that. But he said in a promotional interview that he expected viewers to assume Sam and Pilar would stay together.

In playing Pilar, however, Elizabeth Peña's face expresses something I read as pain, impatience, and a moment of anguish experienced far too many times. I do not see it as resolve to stay with Sam no matter what. Also, in her voice as she utters these words (we just forget the past? Forget the Alamo?), I hear Pilar asking rhetorical questions. It is clear from their writing that Limón and Pérez hear these lines as statements.[23] Whatever the script's punctuation or the director's intentions, reception at this crucial point is highly significant to interpretation.

The differences in the way viewers hear these words can lead to a very different analysis of the film's ending. Without the question mark, they seem like statements of intention, which leads viewers and critics to assume a happy ending. Given the usual endings of U.S. films, this seems a safe assumption. But as questions, we are left to wonder what the future will be. If we think about it, Sam and Pilar cannot simply choose to forget this history and make a life together. Other people know their secret. What would her mother say, should she choose to live with Sam? Can they ignore or escape the opinions of the others in Frontera who know their real identities? Interestingly, our romantic desires may make us forget to ask such questions.

As a writer and director, Sayles has a habit of leaving his audience hopeful because of the complexity and number of questions he raises, but does not decide either the fate of his characters or the future of the society he portrays. Even as viewers may feel pointed toward a certain course of action, Sayles leaves room for doubt and speculation—even apparently when he does not consciously intend to do so. Thus an alternative reading of the ending is possible.

Because Pilar's lines sound like questions for Sam and the viewers, one wonders if Sayles could possibly have known about or read the book, *Olvidate de "el Alamo,"* by Rafael Trujillo Herrera, published in the mid-1960s. Rosa Linda Fregoso mentions the title in her article, "Recycling Colonialist Fantasies on the Texas Borderlands," as she discusses the importance of Herrera's book in overcoming the shame of sitting through history lectures in south Texas filled with anti-Mexican hatred. While acknowledging the book's uncomplicated perspective, she says that this Mexican view of the Alamo "ignited [in her] a lifelong passion for oppositional discourse and counter knowledges."[24] Fregoso, like many of us who use the word "Chicana" as both an ethnic/racial and a political marker, came of age in the late 1960s. When the knowledge of our history of oppression began to collide with the rhetoric of democracy, books like *Olvidate de "el Alamo,"* written from a Mexican perspective, were extremely influential in our identity formation as Chicanas/os.

That experience makes me assume that as a history teacher Pilar has certainly experienced knowing the difference those alternative histories can make in how we think about power relationships and our own social locations. What actress Elizabeth Peña shows me in the climatic scene is a face full of frustration at being asked to forget the secret transgressions of their personal history. But combined with the words, "forget the Alamo," Sayles makes a link between the personal pain of Peña's character and the larger history of the borderlands.

It is exactly this kind of amnesia that has been asked of all people of color throughout the decades following the civil rights movement. Common in oppositional rhetoric around affirmative action initiatives—as well as other institutional reforms designed to redress past discrimination—we are constantly told to let the history of oppression go. This disingenuous request to forget the past is disguised as a desire to move unfettered into a more equal future, as if memory was the source of inequality. It not only blames the victims of social injustice, but places an unfair emotional and psychological burden on us to keep the past a secret. Yet it is neither possible nor in our best interest for anyone to forget the violence and victimization inherent in U.S./Mexican history. "Without that memory" of who was responsible or culpable, as well as the true "complexity of social interactions" the myths of mainstream culture can only continue to be re-created.[25] Thus the social patterns that have resulted from these seductive lies will likewise continue.

As a history teacher Pilar surely knows this. She must also know, as she sits squinting into the sun and into the possible futures, that whatever she decides on a personal basis, colonization has given the "ultimate seat of decision" to the legitimate heirs of the colonizers, not to their bastard children. While Sayles certainly questions the solidity of the location of power and hints that all actors in concert have choices to make, it is not at all clear to me that an actual change has occurred or will occur. This tends to leave Pilar (and the audience) with only the "illusion of deciding" the future.[26] Yet, even this hint of a possible shift, this whiff of ambivalence rather than binaries, and this illusion of getting to decide, are intoxicating.

If anything, her recognition of this illusionary choice that is simultaneously an unfair burden, should strengthen Pilar's identity as a Chicana, though she has recently learned that her father was white. The acting and directing at this point in the film make me believe Pilar is at the very least wondering whether or not she can live as a Chicana in love with a white man in a racist society—something many Mexican American women have had to consider. (This is very similar to the choice Halle Berry's character must make at the end of the film *Monster's Ball*.) In this sense, Pilar does have social agency and a very real decision to make, but this does not necessarily guarantee social equality. In many ways, this is the story of America's political future and we are in Sam and Pilar's position (to one degree or another).

A director's choice of images creates a hypernarrative in which the visual scenes manipulate our attention to, and feelings about, certain characters, relationships, and spaces. This is why they must be read critically. How we internalize or respond to the messages conveyed by the filmmakers' techniques must also be analyzed and interpreted. It seems funny that we should have to learn how to read these texts, but we are often most vulnerable to information when we are being entertained, and popular culture greatly influences public discourse on any number of topics. Alan Stone has said that we are not simply unconscious products of our history. In fact, he says, who we are has much more to do with the stories we choose to tell about ourselves, our families, our various communities, regions, and nations.[27] To have filmmakers unafraid to show main characters as less than noble representatives of U.S. mainstream culture, and to even hint at future equality in a serious way is downright revolutionary.

Sayles gives us the sensitive Sam in opposition to the tyrant Charlie Wade, and the sympathetic but forbidden couple contrasted by the benevolent but still dictatorial sheriff Buddy Deeds. The thoroughly Anglo, yet astute, Sayles leaves me with some romantic hope for Sam Deeds—who may be the alter ego of Sayles himself. Clearly Sayles has produced something more substantial than we are used to seeing from most U.S. filmmakers, but that has always been his greatest gift. While I maintain my wariness and reserve the right to be cynical, I wish to make it clear that I have great respect for Sayles's artistry as a filmmaker. His talent for bringing complex ideas to the screen and making viewers think about our social constructs and our varying relationships to power is brilliant and necessary. Whatever my criticism, ultimately I am grateful to Sayles for opening these conversations and raising questions that most filmmakers will not or cannot approach. I hope that he will continue to do so, and that other artists will follow this brave path despite the financial limitations of the media and the desires of mainstream audiences who simply want to be entertained and reassured by happy endings.

Sayles has found a new way of telling the story, but has he displaced the rhetoric of supremacy? In the end, I'm not sure it matters. Perhaps the trying is what is important. White folks with the kind of political consciousness Sayles demonstrates in much of his work often feel alienated from their own cultures. Because such visionaries can be separated from those they love by their work, they often feel alone, in exile from those still frozen in the normalizing rhetoric and methods of white supremacies. In contrast, people who rise to political consciousness out of oppressed groups join a global community of revolutionary thinkers and activists who have been employing what Chéla Sandoval calls "the methodology of the oppressed" for a very long time—even as they may separate from their home cultures. One of the reasons John Sayles garners so much attention is because he is a kind of lone hero among filmmakers, and progressive people identify with his projects and characters. Whatever his faults and inabilities to step outside his straight, white, male (read: colonizer) identity, he has clearly made a commitment to deconstructing myths and reinventing signs. As such, he is a welcome ally.

El jardín del Edén

While I have lived the majority of my life away from south Texas, those early years made the borderland spaces depicted in *Lone Star* and *El jardín del Edén* feel remarkably familiar. Through both experience and family stories I recognize the culture that is a mixture of both nations but more than the sum of its two parts. I know about the legality of the border because every time we cross now, we are questioned relentlessly, and it has become increasingly difficult for family members from Mexico to visit us. But what I remember most about south Texas were the social boundaries between cultures, races, nationalities, and classes—boundaries so carefully guarded, protected, and maintained in public, yet daily transgressed in private. I remember small towns with three Catholic churches—one black, one white, and the largest one Mexican. A lot has changed since the 1950s and 1960s, but many of these lines still exist just under the surface of polite society and the law. But a small scratch of trouble or the burn of alcohol in cantankerous bodies can expose these boundaries in a heartbeat. And a quick glance at the socioeconomic situation will tell you that Chicanas/os are still overrepresented among the working poor. De facto segregation still exists in housing and education. That certain look from an Anglo Texas woman that I experience to this day that reminds me of my place in her eyes and makes clear that some boundaries still exist, even as many Chicanas/os have succeeded in ways their parents could only imagine.

I know this ever-present irony of the border. Because I was light-skinned, I often had privileges many of my siblings and cousins did not. White storeowners let me spend my pennies on candy while darker-skinned kids were chased out of the shops. Yet in other settings, Anglo Texans left no doubt that I was Mexican and not welcome. I carry wounds from blonde-haired, blue-eyed kids who played with us in kindergarten and spit on us by the time we hit eighth grade. The memory of the white men who would come to our side of town with money or gentle promises at night, then brutally ignore the Mexican women in the light of day, still provoke fury in me. And today, there is the guilt in knowing that with my U.S. citizenship and Ph.D. in hand I can cross the literal and figurative borders relatively easily, while my cousins *en las colonias del valle y del otro lado* cannot.

In *El jardín del Edén*, Novaro demonstrates her attitude toward this ironic existence with both humor and pernicious seriousness. In the same way that Sayles shoots his film from his own national perspective on the U.S. side of the border, Mexican filmmaker María Novaro sets most of the action of her film in Tijuana. Though both clearly mean to make a statement about the border as a unique space of exchange and mixture, each begins from a different vantage point, with Sayles rooted in the United States looking south and Novaro solidly in Mexico looking north. As a filmmaker, Sayles has often stepped out of this U.S. perspective and makes an effort in *Lone Star* to represent other viewpoints as he gives voice to African American experience, as well as Native American and Mexican opinions (backed up by history) on U.S. society. Novaro's only concession to perspectives other than Mexican is her empathetic portrayal of the Chicana character, Liz.

In an unintentionally sequential prediction, and in contrast to Sayles's decline of male power, Novaro shows us the ascendancy of the white female as the new imperialist. The white male in Novaro's production—when he appears at all—is depressed, artistic, settled into a self-chosen marginality in Mexico, and incapable of affecting a dominant pose. Thus both filmmakers foreshadow the continuation of hierarchical social structure through new enforcers, Chicano in *Lone Star* and white female in *El jardin del Edén*. Like Sayles has done with his most dominant patriarch, Novaro often lowers the camera gaze to shoot Jane, the new imperialist, from below.

While common in films emphasizing the power of patriarchal figures, this technique has traditionally signaled the evilness of a woman rather than her role as the major protagonist. As the filmmaker's intention merges with the audience's socially conditioned response to this image, women shot from below seem to exhibit an unnatural and frightening desire to dominate, whereas it seems normal to shoot the most powerful man from this angle. Novaro disrupts this gender norm to deliver Jane as a substitute for the overpowering male in more traditional films.

Though her perspective is fixed, Novaro alternates her camera time between those for whom the border barely exists and those locked on the Mexican side of the fence. In contrast to Jane as the freewheeling individual and representative of imperialist culture, she turns her lens on a village where undeniably poor Mexicans are camped next to the border. It is a transient place, yet we see people building social networks, cooking food for their families, and creating businesses to support themselves as they wait for their chance to scurry across. Though temporary residents, these people nevertheless establish communal structures. Selling food to passersby, they erect signs for their transitory enterprises. With great irony and endearing humor, one reads "Always on Vacation." Another food stand is self-consciously labeled "El ilegal." Of course, there is also a more directly political and confrontational sign painted on the border fence itself that says "If the Berlin wall came down, why not this one?" This acknowledges the similar history of the U.S./Mexican border as a space divided by war and enforced by governments unmoved by the needs and desires of the peoples split apart by the line. With these written messages, as well as the very existence of this ever-changing "community," Novaro challenges the entire border-spanning economic system. She makes a mockery of the concepts of individual choice and free trade—to which NAFTA is only rhetorically linked in the service of certain political and financial agendas.

The people who wait in Novaro's village are provided a kind of entertainment as they watch those new to the border-crossing game try to outrun the U.S. agents. They cheer and yell encouragement to their *compadres* as if they are at a soccer game. Novaro's border patrol agents, the real transgressors in this ancient space, find entertainment also as they watch the kids on the Mexican side play baseball. We see these uniformed soldiers in the United States' war on immigrants give each other high-fives when one of the players gets a good hit. Yet Novaro makes clear that these same jovial figures could in the next twenty-four hours use their SUVs to run down these Mexican boys and shoot them in the back as they try to enter the United States.

One of the failures of works that emphasize too much the permeability of the border is that they often lack a strong critique of the ways in which it is concrete for some people. Those that celebrate it and affirm it as a space for *mestizaje* and ambiguity tend to deflect our concern for the material consequences for history's victims in the processes of transgression and mixture, even if that is not their intention. A young woman from Guatemala recently told me that she couldn't read Anzaldúa or Cherríe Moraga because she feels "choked" by them. Given her own history and experience with repressive governments and undocumented migration, she feels betrayed by the ease with which they approach their complex identities. For this young woman, borders are places of danger, where one's relationship to power is not in the least ambiguous. Mestizaje as a concept is neither empowering nor useful. It is the memory of violence and the rape of brown women.

The dangers for the "community" Novaro creates are similarly concrete and unambiguous. They are well known to its old timers and completely underestimated by the rural people who have come from Mexico's interior for a chance to cross. Yet all of Novaro's Mexican characters are aware that it is more than mere metaphor in their lives. Because this has been part of the history of so many families, they know this act goes beyond who they are as individuals. Migration to the United States is a process that affects everyone close to the actor as well as the larger nation. In the present, this is often demonstrated through her character, Felipe, the Mexican peasant who is desperate to cross the border. Novaro also represents the effects of past migrations, as well as the colonization that made Mexicans U.S. citizens after 1848. We see them in the Mexican women's responses to Liz, a Chicana working in Tijuana. The desire of these women to help Liz understand her own Mexicanness, even as they express their frustration with her *pocha* ways, reminds me of the sentiments expressed by Lorna Dee Cervantes in her poem, "Oaxaca, 1974."[28] In the poem, as in the film, we see that the women of Mexico do not blame the Chicana for her lack of Spanish and cultural fluency, but the historical circumstances that have separated her from Mexico.

Some critics still view Chicanas/os in much the same way as did Octavio Paz, as *pochos* who have discarded our Mexicanness in favor of an outlaw identity. But Novaro avoids such harsh judgments, showing us instead her sensitivity to Liz's acute pain as she confronts her own linguistic and cultural inadequacy in Mexico. A woman of Mexican descent brought up in the United States, Liz is deeply anguished. Novaro shows the audience that this is a genuine sense of loss, not a romantic longing for a nonexistent homeland. Through film clips and photographs we see that what preoccupies Liz is Chicanisma, not Mexicanness. Twice, scenes from Guillermo Gómez Peña's *Border Brujo* interrupt the film's action, focusing our attention on Liz's emotional response to another Chicana who is trying to deal with being brown, but feeling white because of her acculturation.

This layering of images and audiences, watching viewers look at images, is a constant in Novaro's film. Like Sayles's flashbacks, this technique helps to manage our response to certain events and dialogues. During one scene, Jane and Liz look through a book of Graciela Iturbide's photographs and Jane seems to see her friend Liz in one of the photos. This repetition of reflexivity—of looking at images—is overt and intentional. Thus, it commands us to pay attention to it and reflect on its meaning. Liz especially immerses herself in photographs, video clips, and paintings. An enormous mural of Frida Kahlo's eyes appears to be watching the reunion of Liz and her white friend Jane in Tijuana. Kahlo's own mixed heritage and identity ambivalence together with her clear political and cultural allegiance to Mexico seems a fitting background for this encounter. In another scene Kahlo's famous painting, "The Two Fridas," serves as the inspiration for a photography shoot in which Liz and Margarita Luna (who look remarkably alike) pose together. (In this painting, the two Frida's are joined at the heart by a mutual network of blood vessels among other things.) Through her physical resemblance to Margarita as well as through the links depicted in Kahlo's painting, Novaro marks Liz as part of Mexico. In contrast to the moving camera when Liz and Jane occupy the frame together, Novaro holds the camera on Liz and Margarita for several seconds imitating the stillness of a painting. These opposing techniques make Liz appear nervous in the company of her gringa friend, yet eternally calm with the woman from Mexico. Thus, Liz's connection to the nation and culture is solidified through her relationships to Mexican women, rather than merely being based on her ethnicity or her romanticized longing for a homeland.

Novaro displaces the critique of Chicanas/os romanticizing and eroticizing Mexico, by taking it from Liz and putting it onto Jane, the gringa character who constantly demonstrates that she understands neither Liz as a Chicana, nor Mexico as a functioning society—though she claims to love both. Novaro uses backlighting, filters, and slow motion to show us the way in which Jane's vision romanticizes and objectifies both men and women in Mexico. We see her lustful gaze aimed at Margarita, the woman Jane talks her brother into hiring as a maid, as well as a young bird vendor toward the end of the film. Novaro also uses it when Jane first sees Felipe, the Mexican migrant who will become her lover. Though he has actually appeared earlier in the film, Novaro's romantically blurry lens makes us feel that he is only now being introduced to us, and we participate in Jane's objectification of Felipe. Novaro here sends a message to her more self-reflexive and conscious viewers, making us squirm. We do not like having to see Felipe in this way, from the perspective of the transgressor Jane, who throughout the film, plays out the role of the ugly American.

While Sayles shows us that the colonizer changes in form if not in substance over time, Novaro's character Jane never learns. Even as she causes one catastrophe after another, she continues on her entitled way, transgressing many personal boundaries. In scene after scene Jane violates the spaces and sensitivities of Mexican and Chicana characters though she is unaware of her transgression. In one scene she imposes on the sanctity and private mourning of a culturally distinct funeral in a rural Mexican village on the U.S. side of the border. Marching unself-consciously into the middle of the service and handing money to a grieving Mexican woman she has never met, she completely disrupts the ritual grieving of the family. Similarly, Jane clumsily interferes in any number of Mexican lives as she deludes herself into thinking she is helping them.

There is no doubt in *Lone Star* that Sayles means to use his characters to rid us of our illusions about our separateness as nations, races, cultures, and classes—thus the sanctity of borders is challenged. Novaro is more heavy-handed than Sayles. While she clearly wants us to see that Mexican and U.S. mainstream cultures transcend the political demarcation between the two countries, she uses Jane to incinerate any fantasy we may have about the dislocation of power. When Novaro discusses the propensity of the colonizer to view the colonized with desire, it is not done through a tale of undying love, star-crossed lovers, or adult sexuality. She wants her audience to see what it means to travel to Mexico wearing our U.S. middle-classness. Like a spiky new pair of high heels on a sandy beach, it is inappropriate.

Yet, Kaminsky, a specialist in Latin American literature, states in an analysis of the film that "it is hard . . . not to like Jane, even as . . . we are annoyed, irritated, and even angered by her." For me it is not in the least difficult to hate Jane. I can scarcely encompass my contempt for Jane in mere words. Her actions call up so many people like her in my own history— people who have invaded my family's life, people who have unknowingly hurt me in various ways because they cannot see beyond their limited perspective. People who cannot wait to tell me of their latest trip to Playa del Carmen, or how much they loved Mexico after vacationing in Cancun and can't wait to go back. Students who have gone to Latin America to study Spanish over the summer and come home thinking they are authorities on Latino cultures. Or those who become Chicano studies majors because they've fallen in love with Mexico in general or just one particular Mexican man or woman. As if these literal or figurative invasions of the Mexican body give them some right to claim the nation or culture as their own, to continue to act out their desires for brownness and try to make friends with me. Such relationships are never forged on the human need to make real connections or the genuine desire to know the individual qualities of another person. They arise out of a selfish hunger to consume difference.

From the minute Jane appears in Novaro's narrative, I recognize her and her intentions, and I hate them even if Kaminsky cannot. As a woman of Mexican descent, I've had far too many encounters with Jane, each one connected in my soul with more than five hundred years of transgression. Novaro, I think, shares this sentiment. She gives her viewers visual clues to Jane's insensitivity and its meaning beyond this one white woman, some of them quite elaborate. We know from the title to pay attention as Novaro pans the landscape for repeated references to Edén/Eden. Showing us, for instance, this motif represented on two hotel signs: "El jardín del Edén" in Tijuana and "The Garden of Eden" on the U.S. side of the border. These names span the linguistic and legal demarcation to symbolize the wholeness of a space violently divided and insensitively transgressed. Now, we are asked to accept this reuniting of the borderland space through commerce, to see this commercial spanning of the legal line as a substitute for what has been lost to Mexicans who once traversed this space freely for thousands of years. Novaro's Mexican and Chicana characters represent the Mexican cultures that persist on both sides of the line. Jane represents the border spanning commerce that exploits Mexicans and the ease with which capital so easily transcends international boundaries. Perhaps this space once was a kind of paradise or has the potential to be a multicultural garden, but the capital Jane represents has nullified its utopian possibilities.

In addition, we hear Jane remark as she and Liz look at Iturbide's photographs, "these women must live in Paradise." But Novaro has already shown us that this is not paradise for the poor of Mexico and she shows us Jane's distance from Mexican and border culture when her camera lingers knowingly on Jane's copy of the text *Paradise Lost.* In this and other cases, Novaro intensifies our view of Jane as *la güera suprema.* From the Mexican perspective she brings all of Jane's seeming naivete into focus not as good intentions gone awry, but as transgression and "colonialist fantasy."[29] Jane is never fully immersed in the gritty reality of Tijuana or the dark desperation of having to wait for a chance to cross the border in fear. She has the privilege to buy a car in Mexico and smuggle Felipe across in the trunk. She surrounds herself with the intensity of travel and adventure—accumulating, collecting, and distributing people like commodities. Jane indulges in the flamboyant sensations of local color and difference. But she is always at a safe distance from both danger and the truth of her social location. The quality of her relationship with any one of the Mexicans she encounters is traded for the sensational quantity of the people with whom she temporarily interacts. In this way, she exemplifies not only the historical explorer/conqueror but also the postmodern neocolonializer.[30]

Novaro's Jane is like the man who excuses any manner of insult by proclaiming that he didn't mean any harm, or certain crimes against a woman's body by saying, "I did it because I loved her—I didn't mean to hurt her." She resembles the conquerors who thought forcing Christianity on Indians would bring them enlightenment. Kaminsky calls Jane's love affair with the Mexican peasant Felipe "simultaneously sexually charged and thoroughly innocent."[31] But I see it as a metaphor for the same old colonizer's desire to invade, fundamentally alter, and penetrate Indian land, culture, and bodies. Like many invaders before her, Jane takes advantage of the generous spirits she encounters and their willingness to live a fully human existence with others even though she is not one of them. It symbolizes the hunger to claim or exert ownership over that which cannot in any spiritual or emotional sense be owned—the irresistible urge of the patriarchal master (even if it is through a female representative in this case) to turn everything and everyone into a controlled object. Such desire has often resulted in taking possession of the one being objectified and is accompanied by the uncontrollable fear of losing what is owned.[32]

Audience members who have internalized dominance can perceive the objectifying desire displayed by Jane as a benign and even comic social ineptitude. In mainstream films, making someone like Jane the "Ugly American" makes dominant culture viewers feel comfortable because they can so easily distance themselves from this over-the-top cliché. But in Novaro's hands, this portrait is less cliché and more accusation toward U.S. liberals who practice a kind of multiculturalism that leads them to enter Mexico without any useful knowledge of history or the political and social forces harming Mexican people. "All domination," said Paulo Freire, "involves invasion—at times physical and overt, at times camouflaged, with invader assuming the role of a helping friend."[33]

Even if we were to view the coupling of Jane and Felipe without a historical lens, Novaro's cinematic narrative tells us that Jane's relationship to power is much different than is Felipe's—they are not equals. Jane has a kind of freedom in the world—bought by her skin color, class position, and citizenship—that Felipe will never attain. But she also has a psychological blindness that causes her to miss things Felipe readily perceives. Jane is a border-crosser who inhabits Mexican spaces and invades Mexican lives for a short time. As she enters into Mexican public culture, her image and the things she does are observed and remembered by the Mexican people, even as her own memory of her actions is distorted by what she cannot see. What is missing is Jane's ability to understand what she is experiencing, to perceive the objects of her lustful gaze as speaking, feeling, thinking subjects capable of seeing her. Unless Jane can understand who she is to Mexicans, and thus perceive something beyond her own subject position, the knowledge she might have gained as a result of her experiences can never really be available to her. Thus, these people she claims to love remain forever outside her intellectual grasp.[34]

Sayles at least made an attempt to equalize his lovers by making Pilar the more educated of the two and showing her as a financially and emotionally independent woman. Throughout the film, there is evidence that Sam is capable of seeing himself and his preceding patriarchs through Mexican eyes. If anything should give us hope for an equal and truly multicultural future, it is Sam's ability to perceive how white male dominance looks from the subordinate position. But in Novaro's film, Jane clearly represents the colonialists' gaze and pose without this consciousness. Felipe is the object of not just sexual desire, but also the need for the exotic Other. Their national, racial, and class positions outweigh the gender imbalance that might otherwise have given Felipe more social power based just on his masculinity. Thus I do not think that Novaro wants us to see this relationship as "innocent." Yet neither does she want to leave us with the impression that Felipe is merely a victim of Jane and what she represents. Jane's attempts to objectify Felipe are never entirely successful.

Felipe, despite his sexual relationship with Jane, finally cannot abide her intrusive behavior. He is outraged by her inability to understand the culture she has been privileged enough to witness during the funeral ritual.

Previously enamored of Jane, he sees through her Good Samaritan facade and confronts her. Demonstrating his ability to make his own decisions and to take control of his life—as well as act on behalf of other Mexicans— he yells at Jane in an effort to confront her social clumsiness. Her stagnant knowledge of the world and her desire to impose her own cultural values on others become a poison he refuses to swallow. Felipe cannot make her see that just being there, witnessing this family's and community's grieving process is a gift—a gift Jane hasn't the slightest ability to perceive, let alone repay. This is true not because she is individually dense, but because she has so thoroughly internalized the power and privilege her race, nationality, and class have provided.

Though he has little or no formal education, it is Felipe who understands that Jane's brand of cultural invasion and patronizing behavior help to maintain inequality—that her "parochial view of reality" is not only the result of colonization but also an extension of the conquest.[35] He leaves her because he knows her good intentions really imply "superiority" more than they do generosity, as well as her assumed "inferiority" of those attending the funeral more than they do benevolence.

Jane's privilege prevents her from understanding Felipe's outrage. Despite her good intentions and her romantic love for all things Mexican, she glides through the border landscapes like a snail leaving a trail of sweet slime wherever she goes. When I first realized that Jane was going to seduce Felipe with her little blonde self, I was worried. I thought this was going to be part of the cinematic tradition in which Anglo women get to show their superiority over men of color. But Novaro makes Felipe morally superior and smarter than Jane when, despite the economic, legal, and romantic benefits of being with her, Felipe walks away. His dignity is affirmed when he refuses to forgive Jane for her complete immersion in a U.S. middle-class worldview. He knows she can never really be a good ally to Mexican people.

In both films, the link between a firm understanding of one's subject position and the ability to love other people and share in their lives plays an important part in the narrative. In the last scenes of El jardín del Edén, Liz, and the Mexican women, Juana and her niece Serena, are together contentedly watching their children play baseball. Jane, the gringa, is absent because she must continue to search for herself, to find some substance or reason for being. She cannot love herself because she cannot see herself as she appears to the rest of the world. She tries to rectify this by traveling through Mexico and following the exotic objects of her desire, (which of course, ensures that she will never find her true self).

Novaro presents lovable images of Mexican women in opposition to the solitary thoughtless white woman, Jane. Dispensing with the patriarchal narrative completely, Novaro portrays love and happiness as the result of Mexican, matrilineal family relationships in which she includes Liz. Jane, though she clearly thinks she belongs, is soundly excluded through her own behavior, assumptions, and transgressions. Though Sam is completely present in the climatic scene of *Lone Star*, it is Pilar who is given the task of deciding how to deal with their predicament and how to heal the wounds of history.

Thus, in both films we see that despite their relative socioeconomic and political freedom and dominance, it is the Anglo characters who have yet to develop a solid sense of self. It is their ambivalence and clumsiness that complicates life along the border for both Mexican nationals and Chicanos. Yet, it is brown women who are asked to pick up the pieces and to restore some normalcy after the emotional tornado of colonialist desires has exited the landscape.

Novaro's female Mexican eye is less generous toward notions of a multicultural society than is Sayles. In theorizing white consciousness, Chéla Sandoval discusses Franz Fanon's notion of an open door of consciousness that could be "not only a location of access and departure," but also "a site of crossing, transition, translocation, and metamorphosis where identity alters and is mutated."[36] Surely this is the metaphorical site Sayles was hoping to construct. Novaro seems to be saying that while Chicanas may be capable of opening this door of consciousness, the Janes of the world are not. To some viewers, however, this is a more realistic, if discouraging and cynical, vision than is Sayles's portrayal of Sam Deeds for whom that door may be open.

Jane's door of consciousness is firmly locked. Like both Presidents Bush, she speaks just enough Spanish to be annoying. As my grandmother used to warn us after encounters with well-meaning white folks, *"no te creas de un gringo que habla español."* (Don't trust a white person who speaks Spanish.) I guess she intuitively understood all those years ago that these smiling faces would more than likely become our transgressors—our Jane, our Buddy Deeds. It was a warning to us to develop an acute sensitivity to the colonialist gaze, the dominant pose, the white mask, a caution about the way in which, despite good intentions, some people were born and raised to build, protect, and subsequently transgress boundaries as their desires for the other beckoned. My grandmother never read Barthes or Fanon, but she knew something about internalized dominance.[37]

Though Jane is far less ambiguous than is Sam Deeds, both Novaro and Sayles ask us to reevaluate the patriarchs or their agents as well as the social rules they construct. Parallel messages exist in these films. Novaro and Sayles show us that those people most restricted by the U.S./Mexican border are in the best position to understand perfectly its reality. In some ways,

Novaro seeks to simplify the border's meaning as a symbol of power—who has it and who doesn't. She tells us that the person who can slip easily from one side to the other due to national and economic privilege can never fully understand how concrete it can be. Sayles offers us an unexpected and more genuinely complex vision of race, culture, history, and social conflict in this region. Yet he also tells us that those with the most power least understand the border. We are dishonest, he seems to impart, if we think we can control human imperatives. And, as he has in other films, Sayles demonstrates his uncanny knowledge that those who stand guard are often more serious transgressors than those they are trying to keep out.

Novaro's film pays attention to theories about the borderland as a place of ambiguity and mixture, a liminal space that while dangerous can nevertheless be crossed. But she does not imagine the border as open in a way that invites trespassers. Novaro seems to understand that celebrations of mestizaje and declarations of rampant border crossing—once taken over by mainstream desires for the other—can become rhetorical disguises for the same old imperialist intentions. Discursive tricks by neocolonialists who still want to control, penetrate, seduce, and suck dry the energy and vitality of poor, but always exotic, brown folks. This kind of talk about border crossing is as useful to Mexicans and Chicanas/os as the mission system was to the Indians. Conquered or colonized citizens cannot be integrated because they are forever objectified and seen by the Janes of the world as inferiors in need of help.

If we give ourselves over to an obsession with the many ways the borderland space is crossed, complex and ambiguous, we will lose the ability to see it from any other perspective. This leaves us in Jane's position, loaded with good intentions but incapable of being good allies for those who daily confront concrete and violent boundaries. "Ironically," speculation about the disappearance of national borders and the realities of globalization are "frequently carried out in a [language] that only facilitates the further erosion of public [knowledge and awareness]."[38] The importance of films like *Lone Star* and *El jardín del Edén* may be found not only in their extraordinary content, but also in their ability to reach audiences that an academic analysis cannot.

CHAPTER 5

The Virtues of Conflict

*Challenging Dominant Culture
and White Feminist Theory*

In analyzing María Novaro's film, *El jardín del Edén,* I began to think about the social milieu within the university and the boundaries that divide colleagues from different social, racial, class, and ethnic locations. In part this has to do with the film itself and the way in which my response to one of the major characters mimicked my feelings in regard to some colleagues on my own campus. The setting in which I first viewed the film also inspired me to make the leap from film analysis to exploring the relative sociopolitical positions of women in a contested space where theory regularly collides with material reality—where intuition and experience push up against textual knowledge and expertise—and where idealistic rhetoric smashes into subconscious oppression and learned behaviors.

I began my discussion of Novaro's work in the previous chapter, but want to focus here on two aspects of the film. First, the Chicana character Liz's struggle to express and deal with her border-straddling reality, and second, the white woman Jane's failure to understand Mexican and Chicana experience despite some very intimate connections to people in both cultures. Both themes are relevant to the conflicts between working-class women of color in women's studies classes and departments with a primarily white senior faculty.

In the spring of 1997, the women's studies department at the University of Minnesota—with a generous grant from the McKnight Foundation—ran an experimental course called the "Chicana/Latina Quarter." Though I was still a graduate student, I cotaught this course with Amy Kaminsky.

Students wishing to participate registered for twelve to fifteen credits, focusing their entire quarter under this general rubric. The course was interdisciplinary in nature, with a combination of literature, history, film, and cultural studies. Students met formally for ten hours spread over four days each week. In addition, they attended films and special events. With the exception of their participation in a larger class three hours a week (also attended by people not part of the Chicana/Latina quarter), the students attended discussions and workshops in a room set aside just for them. They all had keys to the room and could hang out there whenever they liked. They spent the first week or so decorating it to reflect their personalities and diverse backgrounds. Some funds for this came from the grant, but they also brought in personal items. There were no desks. Instead, we brought in sofas and chairs, Mexican blankets, soft pillows, and rugs for those more comfortable on the floor. Food and drink seemed ever present. The required readings were made available in the room, as well as supplemental articles and books. Posters, snapshots, and plants gave the room color and a less institutional feel. A boom box allowed for background noise and dance music whenever the mood struck.

In this relaxed environment over which the students felt some sense of ownership, we discussed films and assigned readings, listened to guest speakers, and wrote poetry with workshop leaders Carmen Ábrego and Pat Mora. On one of the most emotional days of the quarter, we brought in our mothers and other caregivers for a session called "Celebrating Our Mothers/Celebrating Ourselves." Some of the students read pieces they had written all beginning with the phrase, "Mother, I always meant to tell you. . . ." Throughout the quarter, we experienced the sheer joy of putting Chicanas and Latinas at the center of the discussion for such extended periods of time. But we also dealt with conflicts that threatened our sense of well-being.

We had seventeen women and one Chicano in the course. Latinas were more than half the class. Several of these women were both Chicana and Puerto Rican. The other women of color included: two Native American women, one African American woman, and one woman who was Navajo and African American, as well as one woman from Colombia. Two white women also took the course. The man left the course before it was finished due to unforeseen circumstances. This too was painful for a variety of reasons. He had really enjoyed the class and the friendships he made, but voluntarily left for the sake of the larger group. While the course was in many ways the most satisfying of my career, it was also the most frustrating. It was intensely emotional with periods of extreme closeness as well as moments of confrontation and alienation. We loved, laughed, screamed, and sobbed—and not incidentally, learned a great deal.

Jacqueline Zita, chair of the department, had proposed and planned the quarter by committee with very little input from me. The funding agency made possible guest speakers and a related film festival, visiting scholars, a short residency for the Puerto Rican company *Teatro Pregones* from New York, well-known Chicana writers to conduct workshops, and a three-day field trip to an out-of-state conference focusing on Latinas. It was only after the funding had been secured and much of the quarter planned that I was brought on board. Not unpredictably, this led to some difficult debates and embarrassing conflicts. But, it was in this setting that I first viewed María Novaro's *El jardín del Edén*, blissfully surrounded by women of color.

Rumor has it that Mexican audiences did not like this film. If this is true, I suspect that one reason might be because Mexican nationals had nothing in common with two of the film's major characters. They might also have harbored more than a little anger toward one of them. For the women of color watching it in Minnesota in a predominantly white institution, it had much to offer as it explored the question of Chicana identity and validated many of their experiences with white women. Like the women in Novaro's film, we too had varying social locations—spoke to each other across many borders—and met in a space where illusion and reality collided.

In 1989, Eliana Ortega and Nancy Saporta Sternbach began their introduction to *Breaking Boundaries: Latina Writers and Critical Readings*, disputing the established reading of ethnic literature as a search for identity. We Latinas, they argued, know who we are. The proverbial search for the Self really involves looking for a way to express or articulate our reality, our worldview, and our experience. It is not a questioning of our deepest selves so much as it is a questioning of the way we are seen in relationship to the norms and universals of the dominant culture, as well as those of our "home" cultures, which feel both foreign and familiar to us. We want to talk about what it means to feel constantly off center and to express the extent to which this disequilibrium is a hard way to live—though I would also argue that it can be an exciting and strong life at the same time. In some cases it is a search for an adequate or new language, a new method for explaining how it feels to be in skin (literally and figuratively) deemed alien nearly everywhere we go. Unfortunately, we rarely get the opportunity to delve very deeply into this kind of questioning in serious dialogue with other women of color generally or among Chicanas specifically, especially in predominantly white institutions. In that setting, our inventiveness and exploration of new languages, methods, and theories will always be stifled by listeners neither sensitive nor intuitive enough to understand our identities beyond the colloquial expression of them.

Historically oppressed peoples often seem in a constant struggle for inclusion and against invisibility. But sometimes we must also fight for *exclu-*

sivity—fight for a space that is both communal and to some extent separate from members of the mainstream in order to grow on our own terms. This is a necessity "for those whose daily practice involves not only crossing borders but also setting territorial limits that sanction a public space for progressive action and self-reflection within an increasingly hostile and inhumane environment."[1] While we can never fully escape the dominant culture, we can be with each other in a way that is not possible when oppressive intrusions abound. From the beginning of the Chicana/Latina quarter, the students longed to fulfill the promise and possibility of a course so presumptuously named, that of creating a Chicana/Latina space they owned and defined, a place to discuss the long unsaid and ask the hard questions around identity politics of each other—a private conversation in which to face the contradictions.

Their first truly rebellious act came early in the term. The students asked Kaminsky not to come to their daily discussions. To her credit, she agreed to stay away except when guest speakers were scheduled. She also continued to teach the portion of the course attended by students not participating in the quarter. As the messenger of this request, I hoped that she would not take it personally, but would understand it as a reflection of the students' need to discuss the issues brought up in the readings and films without the intrusion of what they saw as the dominant culture and "white feminist theory."

They did not like having their experiences, ideas, reflections, and questions labeled or filtered through academic language. Kaminsky's intention, of course, was to help them understand how what they were thinking and saying fit into feminist discourse. But the students perceived this as a critique of their expressiveness, as a devaluing of their ideas, and as a preference for a language that made them uncomfortable. Instead of feeling celebrated for finding a new way to talk about their experiences, test their ideas, and reflect on meaning, they felt put down for not being able to translate what they were saying into Lacanian, postmodern, Gramcian, or Foucauldian terms. They felt shamed for not knowing (or caring) about the work of Butler, Kolodny, Irigary, Spivak, or Sedgwick. They were doubly shamed by not knowing the work of the Latin American scholars with whom Kaminsky was so familiar. And, they were angry about having their interpretations of Latina poetry disputed by someone they saw as outside the experience.

They did not mind arguing about meaning among themselves or with me. But their expectations of the course, which had promised to put them at the center, empowered them to do as much as they could to make the space their own. It gave them permission to discover that they felt oppressed by Kaminsky's presence, not because of who she is as a person, but because of her very different relationship to power. There was, of course, no intent on Kaminsky's part to shame the students. She was merely trying to return to them in an organized form what they were saying, to challenge them, and to motivate them to begin their own organizing—to substitute rigorous argument for mere opinion.[2] Nevertheless, she honored their request and stepped back. Toward the end of the course, some of the most vocal students were able to work with Kaminsky one-on-one in a way they might not have been able or willing to do if she had not complied with their initial desire for some measure of self-segregation. Once this had been accomplished, discussions proceeded to a depth few of them had ever experienced in the classroom.

While most of the students had read Gloria Anzaldúa's *Borderlands/La Frontera*, we were able to move beyond talking about it as rare gift—a remarkable way of using language and autoethnography to explain Chicana, Mestiza, or borderland experience. We were able to stop defending its shortcomings and exploiting its use in the development of a political and personal identity. As we discussed its historical context, we were able to look at its possible limitations without being afraid that our criticisms would be used against Anzaldúa specifically and Chicana feminist theory generally.

We were also able to talk about the way in which all revolutionary texts are eventually co-opted, exploited, and drained of meaning by the larger culture. Once useful new language then becomes part of the sociolect and moves out of the control of the community that created it. The fix it once provided is diluted as its ideas spread to a mainstream audience who may never have read the original text—or the book itself becomes a "classic." It is then taught by instructors who understand little of its social context, are insensitive to much of its cultural significance, and do not really know its historical function in the group's identity or political development. Thus, they cannot possibly explain its depth or meaning for the present and future. Or the text may be claimed as a transgressive or postmodern expression, and thus universally applicable. The originality and specific subjectivity of the author is forgotten. Then, its unique style is imitated, and the original text loses its value. In this way the mainstream continues to create the need for identity politics, as well as highlight the need for more women of color as professors in the classroom who share with students certain cultural understandings and historical experiences. Anything less feels intrusive.

Though Mexican audiences may not have appreciated Novaro's *El jardín del Edén,* the participants in the Chicana/Latina quarter loved it precisely because it spoke to many of these issues and others that provoked intense emotional responses during discussions. (Ironically, it was Kaminsky who brought the film to the class.) The students and I responded immediately to the thick cultural layers colliding in the borderland space of Novaro's Tijuana, and quickly focused on Liz, the Chicana with whom we identified in many ways. We also took notice of Jane, Liz's gringa friend, and she became the target for much of our anger around the intrusion of mainstream culture into nearly every space we inhabit.

Liz is drawn to Mexico, but both she and the Mexican women she encounters recognize that the extent of her Mexicanness is limited. Novaro shows us that while the Mexican women's struggle is primarily economic (though it is illustrated in personal terms), the Chicana's conflict is largely internal and reflective. Her level of acculturation to U.S. mainstream society and away from Mexico embarrasses everyone. But the white woman who is her friend seems not to notice this estrangement and difference of experience or culture.

One of the most fascinating aspects of *El jardín del Edén* is that Novaro sees the border as both a fluid space, enigmatic and easily crossed, as well as a concrete wall or a material symbol of violence and injustice. In the movie, the words El jardín del Edén and The Garden of Eden appear on signs naming different hotels on each side of the border, symbolizing a cultural sameness within the border region while using language to simultaneously signal a sharp divide between two cultures. Novaro's character Liz, who is organizing a mixed-media show of Mexican American art in Tijuana, represents the Chicana's struggle to express and deal with her cultural mixture. We also see through Jane, for whom the border barely exists, the dominant culture's ability to transcend the border without shifting social locations.

In one of the films most poignant moments, a Chicana on one of Liz's videotapes is confessing her ambivalence about her apparent acculturation, her loss of language and tradition. She tries to justify this disappearing Mexicanness, to find some peace from the national culture that shadows her constantly, to apologize for having gone through the process of "Americanization." This process, as the Latina and Native American students recognized, often happens outside any conscious choice we might have made. Clearly it is a subject about which the film's Chicana has spoken many times. So much so that she discusses the topic relatively free of emotion. Then the interviewer asks her to think about her grandfather. The Chicana looks away, imagining his face. "Think about your grandfather. Tell him. Tell him, 'grandfather, sometimes I feel white.'" The Chicana dissolves into her uncontrollable sadness sobbing with the agony of being forced to forget who she is and the emotional burden of being unable to do so—the simultaneous forces that constantly churn in Chicana/o stomachs. We see this scene as a film clip, but as Novaro's camera pulls back we also witness Liz watching it, confronting the same inner turmoil. This scene had great impact on the students and was especially meaningful to those women claiming indigenous identities.

The lifelong influence of language usage on Chicanas was another topic that played a significant role in both class discussions and Novaro's film. Though Liz speaks Spanish more competently than her white friend Jane, she does so with more reluctance and shame. Constantly scolded by the Mexican woman who takes care of her daughter for not being able to pronounce the child's name correctly, Liz collapses into her own tearful moment of realization as she confesses to Jane the extent of her sinful acculturation. She has given her daughter a beautiful Mexican name, Guadalupe. But as products of the United States neither of them can ever linguistically own it. Their tongues are tattooed with their citizenship and cultural ambivalence even if their faces are not.

Through her character Liz, Novaro demonstrates that the Chicana/o connection to Mexico is something more than a nationalist romanticization of a place that no longer exists. For many of us, Mexico symbolizes a palpable relationship to our unacculturated relatives, friends, and acquaintances—those people who taught and still teach us a great deal about being Mexican even when we do not realize we are learning it. It also represents a desire for a homeland since we do not feel totally at home in the United States. It also symbolizes a culture we might not even realize we miss. (¡Qué lástima!)

Jane, the white friend who is unaware and unself-conscious throughout the film, understands none of this. She sees her Chicana friend and the Mexican women she encounters as one in the same—exotic alien creatures always available and open to her friendship and in need of help only a gringa can provide. Jane's lack of understanding is made explicit in a scene where she introduces Liz to a waitress in a rural Mexican restaurant saying, "this is my friend, she's Mexican too." The Chicana and the Mexican women face each other in an uncomfortable silence, not knowing what to say. Both finally stare at the floor. The waitress has to move past Liz in the narrow space between the tables to carry dishes back to the kitchen. The two women move together to trade places, dancing in a small circle of embarrassment, each knowing that Liz is and is not Mexican. For these two women the border is what Chicana poet Gina Valdés describes as "a bolted door without walls."[3]

Jane, always with the best of intentions, is unaware of their bruises, unaware of the injuries she inflicts. In scene after scene we witness the intrusive nature of her desire to be part of Mexico—the relative ease with which she crosses the border and disobeys the rules of both Mexican and U.S. society when neither Chicana nor Mexican characters can do so. Her arrogance does not rise up out of ego or vanity, nor does it grow out of a conscious desire to do harm. Her romantic vision and naiveté are by-products of privilege and power, as well as a whole set of assumptions based on U.S. middle-class values. In discussing Fanon's work, Rosa Linda Fregoso talks about his take on well-intentioned white folks. "Dominant Euro-American ways of thinking are not ordered with any intention to hurt or anger the colonized. The peculiarity, however, of their order for making meaning is that it is just this *absence* of wish, this lack of interest, this indifference, this automatic manner of 'classifying,' 'imprisoning,' and 'primitivizing' that injures colonized and colonizer alike."[4] Jane's failure to see herself as an oppressor makes it impossible for her stop intruding in private spaces. Her desire for the life of the Other renders her unable to think critically about her own social location—in much the same way that many well-intentioned white folks will talk about race and ethnicity as if they are not racially marked.

In watching Jane, who is some combination of perky cheerleader, missionary, and latter day hippy traveler, I am reminded of a speech delivered by Ivan Illich in 1968, at the Conference on Inter-American Student Projects in Cuernavaca. Illich, known for his opposition to any and all North American "do-gooders" in Latin America did not congratulate the students who had volunteered to spend the summer working in Mexico. He began by reminding them that voluntary powerlessness or poverty were not the same things as actual subjugation or economic vulnerability.[5] Like those students, choosing to spend the summer in Mexico, Jane had privilege she neither recognized nor comprehended.

In discussions, it became clear that we had all had encounters with intrusive "Janes." While this is true for most people of color on a daily basis, the students eagerly shared more blatant examples following their viewing of the film. Each had someone who reminded them of Jane, or some experience with her style of insensitivity. A young Chicana photographer talked about entering her work in a local juried exhibit and her anger over some of the photographs and artists chosen for the show. CreArte, the sponsoring organization and home of the exhibit, is funded and run as a Latino arts organization in the inner city. Yet as the photographs were being installed, it became obvious that the work of mainstream photographers would dominate the show.

As part of the exhibit, the gallery held an artists' discussion, which I attended. Many of those participating questioned the non-Latino photographers about their motives and the propriety of some of the pictures they had taken, especially those of indigenous dancers in sacred ritual. There were also questions about shots taken at a child's funeral of a family the photographer did not know. The mainstream exhibitors seemed shocked by this line of questioning and did not understand the objections raised by people in the Chicano/Latino community. Some of them took the questions seriously and listened politely, though they tensed with discomfort, others laughed and tried to move on. It was clear that even those willing to listen never quite understood that what we were questioning was their right to make objects of people without interrogating differences in power and privilege. They could not grasp the concept of violation, and felt secure in their role as artists documenting "what fascinated" them and "what [not who] they loved."

Some of the photographers just dismissed our concerns, made jokes, and refused to participate in the discussion. None of them understood they were trespassers, because they assured themselves they had only the best of intentions and thought they were contributing something valuable to the community. Yet none of them thought enough of their subjects to ask for permission to take, or display, the pictures. (A fact, which they disclosed without a hint of shame.) They dismissed the questioners as radicals and turned for approval to the curator. Trying to appease both sides of the argument, he remained diplomatically the man in the middle—a strategy that bestowed tacit permission for this kind of intrusive fetishizing of ethnicity.

Like these photographers, Jane argues that she is making a contribution to the community—that the people's need outweighs the impropriety of her actions. Illich called people like Jane, who "pretentiously imposed" themselves on the poor, "benevolent invaders of Mexico and vacationing salesmen of the U.S. middle-class lifestyle." This he said was the only way of life they would ever truly know.[6]

As the film ends, we see Jane romantically gazing at a young Mexican woman walking through a dusty, crowded Tijuana street with small cages strapped together on her back. The entire pack, with its many pairs of live birds, is as large or larger than the woman herself. We know from Jane's previous actions, as well as the film technique, that she is already planning some way to tamper with this young woman's life. Novaro clearly wants us to feel dread as we witness this new awakening of Jane's fascination. Making use of backlighting, lens filters, and slow motion, Novaro shows us the bird vendor through Jane's dreamy eyes. As this precious vision moves through the street, we remember all of Jane's indelicate presumptions, and are left with the sinking feeling that her impending infringement on this woman's life will also become part of the spiritual trash she leaves behind on her journey through "exotic" Mexico. Unconscious of how the United States has shaped her, Jane seems to think that everyone everywhere can capitalize on, or has equal access to, the democratic ideals of equal opportunity and free enterprise. In her estimation, they just need a gringa to show them how.

"Next to money and guns," Illich said, "the third largest North American export is the U.S. idealist."[7] It is this idealist who goes out into the world to convince people of the benefits of being befriended by people of the

United States. But, this seduction in the form of help is a little like selling your soul to the devil, because at some point you will be called upon to politically support your friends' actions. While Novaro's film illustrates this on a personal level, it can be seen as a metaphor for help in the form of institutional aid and economic development programs, which once accepted become expectations to protect the alliances between dictators, representatives of the elite classes, and the U.S. government. More than once I have heard people ask with genuine confusion, "Why do these countries hate us so much when we give them so much money?" Like Jane, they believe it their duty as Americans to share some part of their bounty with those less fortunate, but fail to understand how U.S. dominance contributes to or causes that inequality. They do not ask questions about how much of their foreign aid is really military spending, whether or not the poor actually benefit from it, or how much of it is simply used to build infrastructures that make global commerce possible. Without this consciousness, the only thing development money is likely to buy is the right to trespass and to create chaos in the lives of underprivileged Latin Americans—just as Jane did and continued to do even after the Mexicans she encountered tried to tell her she was unwelcome.

What remains closed to the Janes of the world, the *gueras*, the "do-gooders," is what lies beyond art, literature, music, dance, food, and those brown exotic faces. While Jane moves easily (as do many scholars) across the legal border, she cannot cross the line between the way she sees the world or feels about our relative places in it, and the way others see and feel. She cannot understand notions of privacy or modesty that differ from her own, cannot sense divergent conceptions of love and sin, rules in relationship to age, sex, and kinship. Nor can she grasp the conversational patterns in specific social contexts, what is appropriate, logical, or valid in another culture—cannot for one minute conceive of the danger, inhumanity, and violence that occurs in the lives of the oppressed. Since she cannot understand their pain, she cannot really be part of their joy and triumph, or moments of self-discovery and generous love.

For these and other reasons, the students of color in the Chicana/Latina quarter felt they needed to talk to each other without the intrusion of a Jane. While it seemed to some that this request for exclusion was based on race, and at one point they were accused of being anti-Semitic, having white skin privilege was only part of the picture. Throughout the term they struggled to articulate the difference between being white and being an intruder like Jane. They also tried to separate race and class, to see them as different, but sometimes overlapping, categories. In the midst of this discussion, the visit of a well-known anthropologist turned into an excruciating experience for all of us. It brought out the worst in some of us, divided us, made us question our beliefs around identity, and elicited many tears. I have no doubt that some of us are still thinking about the questions that arose—sifting through our emotions, conclusions, behaviors, ideals, and lingering doubts.

Happy to be with so many women of color, and confident that we had achieved a kind of cohesion rarely experienced in the academy, we settled smugly into a period of infatuation with our exclusivity. What we had failed to consider was how deeply we might be affected by our class, racial, religious, sexual orientation, regional, skin color, and age differences among other things. Nor had we taken seriously the complexity of racial identity in a Caribbean context and how that might be different from the way in which Mexicans, Mexican Americans, and certainly Native Americans think about race. The romance of solidarity ended with the visit of Ruth Behar, author of *Translated Woman*.

Having read the book, conflict was in the air even before her arrival. It only escalated once she appeared, and the group never fully recovered from the two visits she finally made to the classroom (though she had been scheduled for a ten-day residency). I would never have assigned the book, nor made Behar one of the guest speakers for this particular course— though I might have welcomed her in another context. But as I said previously, this decision was made before I joined the project. I would have predicted that her work would be controversial with this audience. Yet, given the often-unpredictable virtues of conflict, some good did come of it despite the pain for us as a group and as individuals. It became the source for much theoretical soul-searching. Though I am sure that Behar wishes she had never set foot on our campus, the students and I were forced to question our assumptions around race, class, ethnicity, and gender and to ask deeper questions about oppressed/oppressor categories, and learn new ways to articulate our positions.

For the Mexican, some of the Chicana, and the Native American students a healthy skepticism and learned cynical attitude toward anthropology accompanied them on their journey through Behar's telling of "Esperanza's" story in *Translated Woman*. They wanted to know who Behar was before they would accept her as the teller of this Mexican woman's life. Because Behar is generously open about her own background, this information was easily available, but it was not kindly received. To the Native Americans, for whom blood quantum has historically been an important marker of Indianness as well as one's tribal affiliation, Behar did not meet the criteria for claiming a Latina identity. This was also important to the Mexican and Chicana students, as was the second major concern expressed by the Native Americans, the extent or limitations of her cultural ties. Since we were told that Behar's family had immigrated to Cuba during World War II, and had subsequently moved to the United States when she was only five years old, the students felt that her cultural ties to the island were tenuous at best. It was, however, these things in combination rather than either blood or culture alone that made these students question Behar's Latina identity and thus in their minds, the appropriateness of her telling the Mexican woman's story.

Most of the Puerto Rican students were less critical of Behar's choosing to self-identify as Latina. Indeed the Puerto Rican actors visiting the class, who were staging a play based on *Translated Woman* thought it was ludicrous to question this identity on the basis of blood and culture. Having known Behar for some time, they insisted that she was Latina in every way that was important to them, which included her ability to speak Spanish. This was a less important marker for the Chicanas since so many Mexican Americans do not speak Spanish, but for the Mexicans this added significance to her claim. One of the Native Americans pointed out that in her tribe even non-Indians (in terms of blood and cultural history) might be considered Indian if they had enough ties to the community. In fact, the ultimate deciding factor was being known and vouched for by known members of the community. Thus for her, these Puerto Ricans accepting Behar as Latina was enough to make the claim legitimate.

Though there were many unanswered questions, some students remained convinced that Behar was not Latina, but Jewish. It was clear that some saw these as mutually exclusive categories, and that rather than seeing Jewishness as a religious affiliation, which is practiced throughout the world, they saw it as ethnicity and to some extent a racial category. This led to accusations of anti-Semitism. But for most, it was not conscious anti-Semitism, but an attempt to articulate what it meant to be Latina by identifying what it was not. It was not whiteness, not upper classness without brown skin, not a temporary move by one's parents to an island in the Caribbean, and not Jewishness *if* it was devoid of a Latin American cultural context. Through discussion we identified many Latinas who are also Jewish in an effort to affirm that one could be both, and to recognize the similarity between unconscious anti-Semitism and unconscious racism. As each of these categories picked up more and more qualifiers it became obvious how slippery definitions of insiders and outsiders can be. Yet, the students' inability to articulate and succinctly describe the unequal power relationships they knew existed between themselves, Behar, and the Mexican peasant woman of her biography, intensified their frustration.

Vicariously experiencing a feeling of betrayal, one of the Mexican students felt that Behar had misused the *comadre* relationship she had developed with the woman. With angry tears in her eyes, she said, "I just don't know how you could do that." The student explained her feelings that in the context of such intimacy it was unforgivable that the anthropologist had become a kind of Jane for "Esperanza." Worse, she had exposed her to ridicule in her own community after the woman made it clear she did not want her neighbors to know that she was talking to the U.S. scholar. Though the publisher chose the material for the cover, it was Behar's photograph of "Esperanza" that appeared on it. This made Esperanza's true identity recognizable to the small community where she lived—the family, friends, neighbors, and enemies she expressly wished to keep from knowing about the book. Behar did not improve her image with the students of color when she gave a public lecture on campus discussing her relationship with her Afro-Cuban nanny. Though she had left the island at the age of five, Behar had returned and entered a new relationship with this woman. The subtitle of the talk was, "Jewish Daughter and Black Mother after the Cuban Revolution."

Students continued to raise questions about the nature of anthropology and a tradition of building scholarly careers and reputations on the backs of subjects who do not subsequently benefit from this work. It became clear in Behar's answers to these questions that Esperanza's life in her village, because of the things she revealed and the subsequent discovery of her identity, probably became slightly worse than it had been before the release of the book. This inability or unwillingness to protect Esperanza only added credibility to the arguments of the students who continued to question Behar's self-identification. They felt that a Latina scholar would not have betrayed her subject the way they thought Behar did. But others were quick to point out that simply being Latina/o did not mean you would not do this kind of ethnography. Though the process was excruciating for everyone, this arguing over identity among the women of color was appalling to the two white students. They were not prepared to witness such antagonism among people they subconsciously saw as a cohesive group. It had been simple for all of us—they were white, and we were nonwhite. As often happens in classrooms, mainstream students are shocked to discover that people of color and people of similar ethnic and racial groups can fight among themselves over skin color, class issues, and who might be excluded from anyone's definition of a given identity.

After Behar's departure, many of the harsh judgments were to some extent mitigated by continued discussion of the issues raised during her visits. The conversation shifted from Behar to the students' frustrations, fears, anxieties, sureness, and doubts around their own identities. In this way Behar was the catalyst that pushed them to develop more complex ways of thinking about identity, shifting positionality, exclusion, and inclusion. Out of this conflict, new understandings—and questions—emerged. While many theories, ideas, and opinions were tested, we did not all come to the same solid conclusions.

One of the issues that continued to trouble us had to do with the usefulness of scholarship in the lives of the disenfranchised, as well as the responsibilities of the scholar to protect their own communities. Though all of the women of color in the class hated the character Jane, we felt uneasy as we recognized the way she might be us as we studied and defined our own communities. We were terrified of the ways in which we might have internalized domiance. If it is true that we despise others the most when we see something in them that reminds us of what we dislike in ourselves, then this could explain why we took such delight in Novaro's unwavering portrait of this intruder. Jane is not just an ugly American, she is what we fear we might become as we continue to operate in the mainstream.

Part of our aversion to high theory and academic language comes from this fear. Often my opposition to theoretical constructs and the jargon academics create is assumed to be a defense. People assume I don't like it because I don't understand it, but the truth is I fear it. Not because it is difficult, but because I fear it will turn me into Jane—it will separate me from the people to whom I feel I belong. More important, I believe it is often part of the rhetoric of supremacy that "structures and naturalizes the unjust relations" that exist between the oppressor and the oppressed.[8] Thus, I fear its insidious potential to render me incapable of recognizing Jane, incapable of being able to feel the affects of different relationships to power on a daily basis from the subordinate perspective.

Many of the students voiced this ambivalence about scholarly language and work. Novaro's film offered them, as U.S. Latinas, an alternative to Jane. When we feel a genuine connection to the people then we must—as the Chicana Liz does—supplicate ourselves to their wisdom. We should look to them for clues on how to act, speak, and behave and not arrogantly assume we know best. Novaro's Liz is not trying to sort out what it means to be a Chicana alone, but what it means to be one in relationship to a familial or communal group of Mexican people. She does her work setting up the mixed-media art show, which is completely alien to the Mexican working people with whom she interacts. Yet she also makes every effort to figure out how she belongs to this Mexican context and how best to fit in. Unlike Jane, Liz is not interested in simply adding some adventure to her daily life, but in becoming part of something larger than herself. She understands that her relationship to Mexico is deep, but also tenuous. This dual vision is what keeps her from making foolish declarations about her identity.

Jane, on the other hand, constantly overestimates herself in relationship to Mexico. The fact that Jane eats food cooked by a young Indian woman, is the best of friends with a Chicana, makes love to a Mexican migrant, and then sneaks him across the border in the trunk of her car, only renders her life a little more interesting—it does not alter the real struggles of any these people. It does not change the fact that thousands of migrants are beaten senseless, robbed, raped, or killed trying to cross the border. It does not alter the socioeconomic position of the single mothers in the film, the photographer, the housekeeper, nor the bird vendor. Yet, Jane believes she has helped each of the Mexicans she encounters. And though she meets people along the way who tell her to go to hell with her good intentions, Jane remains oblivious to just how much she remains outside Mexican culture and society.

Conversely, the Chicana Liz—who also enjoys a U.S. middle-class lifestyle—understands all too well that she cannot impose herself on Mexico, help its people one by one, or intrude on their rituals. This insight is hers because she understands and feels the pain of her *pocha* existence. She also deals daily with her friend Jane's unaware, commonsense, subtle, self-righteous acts of racism. Thus she retains her sensitivity to the difficulties of crossing boundaries and the realities of differing socioeconomic and political locations. She identifies with the Mexican women even as she realizes their true differences. Unlike Jane, Liz cannot reduce the Mexican women or herself to sameness even as she might understand both Chicanas and Mexican women as victims of oppression. Like the student who so palpably felt the betrayal of "Esperanza," Liz cannot indulge in the dominant culture's process of exoticizing or objectifying Mexicans and thus distancing herself from the Other.

What U.S. idealism buys women like Jane, and has often allowed anthropologists, is the right to trespass and create chaos in the lives of underprivileged people. By contrast, the Chicana cannot access this "right" even though she too is a U.S. citizen. This makes it possible for Liz to understand that in relationship to the Mexican women she encounters, it is her life that is chaotic and culturally underprivileged, whereas Jane would never see this emptiness in herself. She is too busy romanticizing poverty. Liz also sees that while it is she who is visiting Mexico, it is the Mexican women who enter her psychological space by chastising her for her inability to speak Spanish or to pronounce words correctly or to care for her child in a traditional way. They fill Liz with anxiety about what she has lost by being a child of the United States.

Jane, on the other hand, gets to keep the illusion that she has successfully crossed a cultural border because she is never criticized for the way she speaks Spanish, though it is laughable throughout the film. While Liz actually speaks better Spanish, the Mexican women constantly make her aware that they consider her *pocha* tongue unacceptable. They humor Jane because they expect nothing from her. They know she will never be fully conscious of their lives or experiences in the world. But they do have hope for the Chicana. Clearly, they see themselves as her figurative mothers, albeit nagging ones, whereas they are polite strangers to Jane.

Jane can never become part of the culture that tantalizes her. She is locked in a worldview that does not question the construction of whiteness as dominant and brownness as subordinate. While she knows she wants to help on an individual basis, it never occurs to her to go to Washington to confront and try to change a government that supports capitalism worldwide. Those of us like Liz—who have grown up as *mestizas,* who have lived with cultural ambiguity, and who have had great difficulty crossing many borders—know that this is not the liberating metaphor white folks imagine it to be. Even as we confront the mixture that exists in our very bodies, we Chicanas can never forget that mestizaje, border crossing, and hybridity are also the history of the rape of brown women. And, at some level, many white women have always participated in this most horrible of transgressions even when they have been well-intentioned and claimed to love us. Viewed from this perspective, Jane's actions and understandings of social justice turn into a public spectacle of her missionary mentality.

While many Chicanas/os may identify most closely with the Chicana whose identity comes under close scrutiny in Mexico, the behavior of Jane can inspire us to ask hard questions of ourselves. Those of us who are highly functioning in the dominant culture must wonder how much we have in common with Jane. How many of us work or vacation in Mexico and "love" its people but have no idea how to genuinely interact with the poor on either side of the border? As our class positions change, we must pay attention to the smokescreens that prevent us from recognizing our own power and privilege and make us ineffective as agents of social change. In light of my experience in the classroom during the Chicana/Latina quarter and our questioning of Behar's Latina identity, we must remain vigilant for the ways we have been infected with internalized dominance, the ways we might set up norms that exclude rather than include. We must police ourselves for good intentions that actually support an oppressive system or prevent people from naming and inventing themselves in opposition to the dominant ideology.

Films like Novaro's remind me that I will never be finished with this topic. Just when I think I've spent enough time thinking about our shifting positions, there it is again, like a red cape being waved in front of a bull. I snort and paw the ground because I am tired of looking at it—weary of it taunting me, teasing me, daring me to charge right in and make a fool of myself—challenging me to bring the question down to earth. And I always do, even though I learned my lesson long ago, that this target is illusive. It is symbolic of much deeper challenges and more complex puzzles for all of us. Just once, I wish the bull could win a decisive victory and get it all figured out.

CHAPTER 6

Donde hay amor, hay dolor
Where There Is Love, There Is Pain

The urge to create or maintain community is related to the way we perceive it. Yearning for connection can sometimes be a signal that such an experience is no longer being lived, but has lapsed into memory. When our sense of community is constantly threatened with annihilation by a preeminent force outside it, we feel our solid grounding slipping away. This fear of loss and the longing for community may come from an emotional and/or political recognition of the significance of feeling connected. When we become afraid, what has been denied us, taken for granted, or seemed unimportant for so long, a feeling that we can depend on one another, may suddenly seem key to our survival. In the cultural production of Chicana writers we see this longing and sense of urgency, as well as both new and old ways of thinking about community and our connections to others. It is in part what Chéla Sandoval has called in much of her work "the methodology of the oppressed." The desire to identify, celebrate, or create community—as well as socially conscious coalitions—is very much a part of a political revitalization cycle.

This occurs in response to socioeconomic conditions at various points in history and follows some predictable patterns toward social reform. It can involve relatively small numbers of people at the local level or it can swell to encompass huge portions of various populations around the world. Since it is a cycle, it can be repeated at all levels in large and small ways, and individuals often experience some form of it on their own or out of sync with an activist group. While I am writing about how it relates to Chicanas/os specifically, the major elements of this movement can be applied to many groups and situations. While the formation of coalitions

145

is an important stage of this cycle, it is important to look at the cycle in its entirety to understand the reason why coalitions break down.

For Chicanas/os, one of the most important aspects of the revitalization cycle has involved the redefinition, reclamation, and reinvention of ethnic identity. While this group identity is not entirely a conscious manipulation of the explicit or learned knowledge of Mexican history and culture within the United States, political desires have certainly played a large part in its formation. As Dennis Valdés pointed out to me, subjective response and material conditions are often mutually reinforcing. The awareness of one's ethnicity happens in conjunction with an "Other," and our thinking about ethnic identity is in dialectical relationship to that Other. This is only part of what it means to be Chicana/o. The way we feel or experience, express, or emotionally understand our ethnicity, like faith, is based more on affective responses to day-to-day experience than on scientific evidence or cold logic, and to the extent this is true, it may be thought of as an essential part of who we are. This does not mean there is something in our genetic makeup that tells us we are Mexican. However, it does mean that we *experience* our ethnicity as if we are born with it. That "essence" subconsciously responds to, as well as produces, material culture. It propels us toward a community that is Mexican at its heart, if not in deed. Thus, our ethnic village is not simply the presence of our creative imagination.[1]

Our desire for community is not the same hunger that is present in mainstream U.S. culture. The United States and its prevalent mythmakers have taken full advantage of scaring the population about some outside, catastrophic threat for decades. But they still remember their days as pioneers and remain fondly attached to the idea of this nation as a grand experiment unlike any other. Investing heavily in individualism and whiteness (rather than any of several European ethnic origins), the mainstream has been left with no community of its own. Because mainstream culture has become largely organized around consumerism—the combination of shopping malls and giant corporations has made this a relatively similar experience around the country—even regionally based identities are giving way to a rhetorically common culture without an agreed-upon history. The ability to form a common national identity has worked for some people, but is illusionary for others. Part of the fantasy of a shared national community is created through declarations of being the most powerful nation in the world, the pretense that no race or class divisions exist, and sentimental appeals to loyalty. These often come in media images of an emotional response to the manufactured symbols of freedom—flags, eagles, and U.S. soldiers. Attached to the self-proclaimed "one nation under God" is the idea that "we" are a society separate from and above the rest of the world, but still a champion and patriarch of democracy everywhere—conflicting ideas to be sure.[2]

But the "search for a distinctively American 'national character,'" has taken the country down "many blind alleys," burying the lofty idea of transcendent boundaries beneath a heavy layer of "chauvinism."[3] Rather than accepting or celebrating ambiguity, difference, and chaos, those in power have worked toward cohesion and unity, toward nameable subcategories and distinct boundaries between us and the rest of the world. (Of course this is an exclusionary device in practice, that only keeps *people* out, and boundaries disappear when it comes to commerce.) Throughout the various debates over identity and the politics of ethnicity, there has been an underlying middle-class dream of stability, homogeneous life, and a common culture.

Secure in their hard-won positions of power and privilege, defenders and beneficiaries of the status quo want to relax and enjoy their prosperity—not worry about an enemy within. Yet the country continues to find itself in crisis as the world economy shifts. Many people resent the increasing gap between the haves and have-nots. As the poor and disenfranchised in this country begin to identify with the people in other nations whose resources and labor are being exploited in the global economy, we may be on the verge of another revitalization cycle, just as the reforms of the last major cycle are being dismantled.

Traditionalists, who do not enjoy the energy of new challenges to existing relationships to power, desperately seek a unified (read: homogeneous) nation—though they are careful to salute (read: dilute) diversity. This is in response to discordant voices, but it nevertheless maintains the power and privilege of the core. Though American ascendancy is primarily economic (and there can be no such thing as a national community on that basis), capital still depends on the popular imagination and sentiment to promote its explicit cultural values and its covert expansionism. This is essential to keeping the middle class from joining forces with the working class, working poor, and the destitute citizens who no longer figure into government statistics. "There is a kind of monotony to the regularity of schemes, phrases, or theories produced by successive generations to justify" the lurid reality of American economic and political dominance in the world. "Beliefs, visions, and daydreams" about America are necessary to marketing us as a great and benevolent nation.[4] The relatively recent daydream of a common culture in response to fear and the reality of a fragmented society is the desire to maintain a "community" that never really existed.

One could argue that the Chicana/o attempt to maintain and create community is just as flawed—just as based on something that never existed—just as much an illusion as is a common U.S. culture. After all, great diversity exists within the Mexican American "community" as well. These differences are based on history, origin, class, gender, immigration status, region, sexual orientation, age, and linguistic abilities among other things.

Chicana/o culture in Los Angeles is much different from Chicana/o culture in south Texas. And within these regions, class differences abound. What about those of us in Minnesota? *¡Hijole, primo!* We're a whole different kind of Mexican altogether! So, why is our attempt to identify with a particular community different from an investment in whiteness? Unlike the mainstream, our desire and longing grows out of shared histories, similar experiences with racism and classism, traditional rituals, and being indigenous to the Americas—not out of a sense of superiority. Nor does it arise out of either false individualism or false universals. Neither is it engendered by commerce. But—like the mainstream—our desire to feel connected is also fueled by fear. Many things in our own country threaten our physical and cultural existence every day.

Chicanas require a space, both physical and imagined, in which we are able to express our ethnicity in all its dimensions—a multifaceted identity in dialogic relationship to others, not in competition with them. In this chapter I want to discuss the reason for the (re)creation and maintenance of a Chicana ethnic and racial identity. As I look at the process of social change, I want to show why it is cyclical, as well as why and how we keep entering the revitalization cycle. I also discuss our alliances and the similarities we share with other groups in our day-to-day experiences with oppression. This necessarily includes a discussion of the oppressive elements in society that create and maintain inequality and strife—as well as encourage horizontal hostility between oppressed groups—rather than inviting commitments to group action. Rhetoric to the contrary, this society and its institutions do not in practice, tolerate or accept difference, though they will easily celebrate the illusion of difference in public and self-congratulatory displays.

The Third Culture

Prior to World War II and the gains of various civil rights movements, we as a country simply took for granted the existence of different cultural groups. We assumed, correctly, that contact between groups would change the social behavior of each in some way. Yet, even as the world began to "shrink" and European immigrants assumed that assimilation was inevitable for anyone living in this land space, some groups remained outside the mainstream. In addition to the mechanisms of exclusion—racist practices in housing, employment, education, and the justice system—came the realization and puzzling reality that for some people the need to express ethnic identity and racial difference was not going to disappear. Even as the global economy has further eroded nationalist isolation, Mexican Americans continue to re-create an ethnicity that is some combination of Mexican and U.S. mainstream, but more than simply the sum of those two bases. For many, loyalty to a community outside the mainstream has survived migration, mainstream education, cultural imperialism, exposure to mainstream popular culture, and other assimilation pressures.

Researchers Keefe and Padilla found in their study of ethnic identity that "ties to family and community were strongest among those respondents who were in the best position to break away, that is, to the more acculturated and/or upwardly mobile . . . this stands in contrast to popular conceptions of the more able and acculturated members of an ethnic group fleeing en masse to join mainstream society."[5] It is also counterintuitive to those who assume it is only the poor and most recently immigrated who remain committed to an ethnic identity primarily as a function of class position and language skills. In fact, first generation immigrants may be surprisingly eager to shed their Mexican identities, especially as they are shamed by mainstream perceptions that to be Mexican equals being poor, uneducated, and likely to commit crimes. For the children of these immigrants and for Chicanas/os, even many generations removed from the immigration experience, the choice to maintain an ethnic loyalty and the reality of living in the United States opens us to the absorption and innovation of a blended culture. But, this "third way of life," which possesses "many unique features," is not "simply an amalgamation of Mexican and American cultures."[6]

One of the problems with studying ethnicity is that the word, and the concept it signifies, includes many dimensions—even as it has a specific, material referent.[7] Ethnicity, for Chicanas, is not just a name, a history, a language, or learned behaviors, but also that emotional and spiritual part of the Self that seems most mysterious and carries such force in our lives. And because, it is exactly that part of us—the heart of us—that remains most invisible to outsiders and difficult to explain, our humanness (and everything that includes) is often negated and we are reduced to stereotypes.[8] Though we are born with much to learn and choose from as we develop an ethnic identity, this task can be especially difficult for women. Chicanas live in a world where the dominant culture wants to ignore, or see as inconsequential, our specific experience. Even when that is not true, we are presented with many more male than female models of what it means to be Mexican American. We are taught our history from a male perspective. We grow up in two cultures that devalue and trivialize what is perceived and defined as feminine. Of course we may also be socially controlled by the devotion and adoration with which certain feminine traits are revered. Though many Chicana writers have described their experiences, sought to articulate what it means to be a Mexican American woman, tried to recover or imagine a female history, and to problematize traditional feminity, masculine voices are far more often afforded greater prestige in community organizations.[9]

In his approach to the work of Maxine Hong Kingston, Michael Fischer discusses the bewildering experience of constructing an ethnic identity or finding a voice in a context where no previous or acceptable example exists. For Chicanas in the last decades of the twentieth century, this process has included discovering or creating what Anzaldúa described as a "*mestiza* consciousness" in her book *Borderlands/La Frontera*, and Ana Castillo called "*Xicanisma*," in *Massacre of the Dreamers*. This construction of identity also benefited from writings by Cherríe Moraga, Carla Trujillo, and Sandra Cisneros among others. All of these writers served extremely important functions at critical points in our historical development and, despite masculinist critiques to the contrary, will continue to speak to particular aspects of our experience. Though some in the next generation of Chicanas may be more open to Michele Serros's more ambivalent definition of what it means to be an ethnic Other in *Chicana Falsa*, it is clear that these texts share some common ideas. All of them involve defining ourselves through complexity and combinations. Each articulates "images that are neither" Mexican nor Anglo American—distinctly female, but not submissive, sexual but not "bad," out from under but not on top.[10] Most also posit identities that are in some ways culturally traditional, yet also anti-homophobic.

Natasha López articulates the difficulty of naming an identity with little or no precedent in her poem, "Trying to be Dyke and Chicana." She begins with "Dyk-ana" and "Dyk-icana," but after going through possible aspects of this identity, as well as the problems each choice poses, López settles on "Chyk-ana."[11] This is closer to Chicana, but still makes clear that sexual orientation cannot be separated from ethnicity. I do not think of poems that describe this kind of process as a "search for identity" in the conventional sense, or as many literary critics define it, so much as it is a desire to find expression for what exists. It is the voice we know we have—the dual spirit voice that is concrete/diaphanous, multifaceted/simple, indigenous/European, female/male, brown/white—the voice that has wanted to speak for centuries.[12]

> Today I speak their languages, both English and Spanish, but
> I am neither, nor do I want to be . . . I am Chicana.[13]

The "Ethnicity School"

Attempts to nullify a strategy of resistance and a demand for social justice based on ethnic origin and historical oppression arose in the late 1980s in what scholar Alan Wald calls the "ethnicity school" of thought. This was an extension of Glazer and Moynihan's definition of ethnics as "special interest groups." Wald tells us that cultural critics, like Werner Sollors, Mary V. Dearborn, and William Beolhower, wrote about ethnicity as a primary category in which race was incidental. This made it easy to include white ethnics as categories for comparison.[14] Discounting race in this way led to descriptions of the way poor white immigrants faced initial discrimination, assimilated into the mainstream, worked hard, and rose above the social locations where they experienced prejudice. The underlying, mean-spirited message was always that it was only a refusal to adapt mainstream manners, behaviors, and values that kept certain ethnic groups from achieving socioeconomic equality. Its major flaw as an analytical device, of course, is in its failing to understand several important factors.[15]

First, that race (and the history of racism) has everything to do with social hierarchy, systematic exclusion and oppression, as well as opportunity.[16] The Irish may indeed have experienced some discrimination when they first arrived in the United States, but let's not pretend that the children of those immigrants continued to suffer that experience either to the degree or for the hundreds of years that Native Americans, African Americans, or Mexican Americans have. Second, that group identity and ethnic loyalty—based on the experience of being nonwhite—are necessary survival skills for people of color (literally and metaphorically speaking). When no such thing is forthcoming from the dominant group, we must seek opportunities for leadership, social connections, intellectual validation, and psychological support among other things from within our own group. This does not encourage us to seek assimilation. The ethnicity school's theoretical stand also ignores the fact that the extent to which one may make a free and rational choice to assimilate may depend heavily on skin color, class, social location, or some combination of these factors. To some extent, as race and ethnicity overlap, our identities may be conferred upon us. The closer we resemble U.S. stereotypes of what a typical member of our group is supposed to look like, the less able we are to transcend that identity. Finally, and perhaps most important, in a political sense the ethnicity school writers make no room for the possibility that people might choose not to assimilate for cultural and ideological reasons, and that they have every right not to do so without being penalized in a supposedly free and open society that values diversity. While acculturation to some extent may coexist with the choice not to wholly assimilate, it is wrong to insist that everyone adopt mainstream values and behaviors in order to participate as an equal.

While contesting elitism, patriarchy, and eurocentrisim, these ethnicity school writers ignore the power differences and specific experiences with discrimination that are based on skin color and class. These differences exist between ethnic groups in the United States and within the groups themselves. Like Glazer and Moynihan a decade earlier, the ethnicity school scholars view the socioeconomic system as something individuals *choose* to enter. Unfortunately, they fail to recognize or report that there is a correlation to be made between white ethnics and their abilities to more easily enter the workforce or institutions, just as there is a correlation between the lack of economic opportunity and race. We must also take into account the fusion of race and class in this society. White ethnics, once they lose their accent, learn certain behaviors, and dress in the "right" clothes, can hide both their class and ethnic origins. In this way they avoid discriminatory hostility toward society's least affluent members. But nonwhites, no matter how perfectly they speak English or rid themselves of any accents, how they behave, or what clothes they put on, may still fail to escape this class bias. When they do, their ability to be seen as something other than lower class often correlates with light skin color. Those who think of race as secondary to ethnicity, class as unimportant, and ethnicity as merely symbolic are speaking the language of privilege and internalized dominance. In doing so, they reveal an ignorance of their own socially, economically, and racially based position or identity, from which they cannot imagine a different relationship to power. Such people, in their own best interest, ignore the extent to which the oppressed have needed to cling to and preserve some alternative culture where they will not be viewed with such little consciousness.[17]

Ethnicity school writers make no attempt to analyze historical developments that have been the direct result of racial difference. Many also fail to adequately address the different origins of various ethnic groups, or differences based on race in determining traditional occupations, religions, cultural values, and historical experiences in a U.S. context.[18] The failure to take the social upheaval—as well as the specifically racialized ethnic assertiveness—that inspired the revitalization movements of the 1960s seriously produces this liberal, yet benign, definition of ethnicity and cultural process. Obviously such scholars still hope for or believe in what Suzanne Oboler refers to as "organic assimilation."[19] This is something that is thought to occur as the inevitable result of living in the presence of a dominant culture despite skin color or personal group loyalties. Thus, no critique of unequal power relations based on race takes place.[20] While it is true that assimilation and acculturation do happen through day-to-day contact between groups, it can only be thought of as an organic process to the degree to which no coercion is involved. But the pressures to adopt U.S. mainstream values and behaviors are enormous and come to us through schools, the media, popular culture, and certainly employers. Despite rhetorical claims about valuing diversity, the social norms are firmly in place and we are all expected to conform. We are told what masks or faces to wear if we want to fit in. To disguise our difference, we often must bury our home cultures and hide our family and friends. We are excluded if we do not comply. The promise of inclusion carries with it the expectation of conformation. No provisions are made for those who *cannot* comply.[21]

While some mainstream folks understand the struggle of marginalized people to be included in the socioeconomic and political life of the nation, few recognize or respond to our efforts to broaden the very definition of what it means to be "American." Fewer still, understand our desire to be included with our racialized, ethnic identities and cultures as equal to whiteness. Almost no one wants to hear about our opposition to the five hundred–year "whitening" of the Americas.

The desire to create a constantly evolving third culture is in many ways antinationalist. In the spirit of our ancestors that desire accepts acculturation but denies assimilation. Its various manifestations change as necessary over time. In its current form it is a politically motivated response to ongoing discrimination and the new forms of economic imperialism that go beyond this one nation and its government. While our natural allies in other nations are being exploited by the global economy, marketing has made use of our images and taken notice of our population increases to the extent that they represent possible markets. But many Mexican Americans (as well as other Latinos) do not easily fit into, or remain in, the prescribed boundaries of traditional music, quaintness, folkloric rituals, and exotic food that are demanded by marketable constructions of diversity. Sometimes we exhibit beliefs, values, and behaviors that go beyond the accepted "colorful" characteristics ascribed to subordinate populations. Despite claims by cultural studies scholars that ethnicity in today's world is largely symbolic, it continues to be an intensely significant part of Chicana/o identity. This is because it is not based on Mexicanness (in either a national or a cultural sense) alone, but also on a racial and class identity that is different in a U.S. context. Working on a project about ethnic identity and awareness, researchers Keefe and Padilla found, through statistical analysis of responses from four generations of informants, that "perceived discrimination is a major contributory force in the maintenance of ethnic loyalty."[22] While it is true that as Mexican Americans we may encounter discrimination based on a number of characteristics, including national origin, language proficiency, and cultural behaviors, surely race and class are also significant categories on which this perception is based.

Revitalization

Fortunately, many scholars have an approach that is the antithesis of the ethnicity school writers and their idea that one model of ethnic assimilation fits all. Their approach pays full attention to the attempted genocide of Native Americans, slavery, conquest, and the racially based hierarchies created to justify compulsory labor, theft of land, and the exploitation of people and resources during colonization and beyond. It also recognizes how these historical forms of oppression evolved and changed through the years to ensure the exclusionary and discriminatory practices of today—many of which still depend on race as a marker. Unlike more benign approaches to ethnicity, the theoretical positions Chéla Sandoval describes in her work see the social construction of race in specific time periods as crucial to an analysis of ethnic identity issues in the present.[23] Such theorists argue against the ludicrous notion that people of color can be compared to white ethnics. They see the dangers inherent in defining everyone as part of an ethnic group, with these groups in equal competition with others, and how this functions to support the current, racially based hierarchies.

The most obvious way in which Chicana/o writers and scholars counter the notion that we are analogous to Italian, Irish, or Polish immigrants is to foreground our origins on this continent. This includes our racial heritage—our indigenous past and present. Even though many of us have embraced our *mestizaje* (mixed blood), a politically conscious Chicana/o identity is still based on the notion that we are indigenous to this land space. In this way we resist the idea that we are immigrants, we make a connection between ideological skin color and the soul, and we identify with a specific racialized body.[24]

"I've looked for you For your body
Your soul Brown like mine"[25]

Reclaiming a mythic past rooted in the concepts of indigenous America—whether or not it is romanticized—is part of the group's movement toward self-definition and away from victimization and devaluation. The emphasis on racial identity in Chicana/o culture certainly has its foundation in the biological and historical reality of Mexico and the United States, but it is also a strategic/radical position that separates us from the experience of European immigrants. It challenges the notion that race is incidental to the way the country structures its national identity with hegemonic rather than diverse notions of a "shared" culture or "building community."

The contemporary focus on indigenous ancestors and the continuing confluence of race and ethnicity is a sane response to the reality of living in a particular sociohistorical environment fundamentally shaped by color classification. This part of Chicano ethnic identity represents a new cultural construct that is more than the sum of its parts, with referents in two nations—as being Indian resists the dominant culture in both Mexico and the United States. This third culture with indigenous roots is an identity specific to this group, geographical location, and historical context. The incorporation of Mexico's northern territory into the United States was the result of a catastrophic series of events that made us neither wholly Mexican nor U.S. American. We have continued to be socially, culturally, and in some cases economically, brown (as race and class are conflated in U.S. culture)—yet legally we have always been labeled white. It is this brownness as an ideological position in which we are investing politically (because of, and simultaneously without regard to, our actual skin color). As an ethnic enclave, we have been expected to assimilate, but have continually been seen by the larger society as inherently different from (and inferior to) European Americans on the basis of race (in addition to assumed nationality) in a process that continues to evolve and is evident in anti-immigrant hostility in the last half of the twentieth century and into the twenty-first.[26]

Much in the same way that we have reclaimed labels once derogatory and injected them with pride, many Chicanas/os have ceased to see our difference and separation from the mainstream in negative or shameful terms. Unlike earlier generations who sought to escape the stigma of being Mexican by totally assimilating, we not only accept our exclusion from the mainstream, we embrace it. We want equality and justice, but we do not want to discard our difference, nor surrender our "home" space to live in a "shared culture" constructed without our needs or desires in mind. We do not want to share an imaginary space with people who want to deny us our unique experience and heritage out of ignorance, fear, hatred, ethnocentrism, or all of the above and more. What terrifies the mainstream is exactly what excites our dreams and gives meaning to endurance. Bernice Zamora in her poem, "Sin Titulo" (untitled), captures the breathless possibilities of the persistence of ethnic identity as the best political strategy. She does so with four extraordinary words, "What if we survive?"[27]

The creation of a third culture, tied to its Mexican roots but aware of its contemporary location in the United States, is a process responsive to both the subjective reality of the individual and the socioeconomic and political position of the community. As loyal as Chicanas/os are to a Mexican ethnic identity, we must always remember that the national state we inhabit is part of the First World (even though many of us may occupy Third World–like status within it). We are citizens, born on the U.S. side of an unequal, socioeconomic border. While businesses can relocate freely to the other side, people are not free to move to the United States. To remain totally identified with Mexican nationals is to co-opt their experience, which we are not morally entitled to do. Though we may feel at the visceral level connected to it, and it may be part of our family's history or reality, it is not our experience. To some degree, growing up in the United States and becoming acculturated means that the Mexican culture of the Chicana/o political and romantic imagination—especially what remains from the early movement—probably does not exist. *(Donde hay amor, hay dolor.)* This is very difficult for most of us to admit or accept. We are people born into irony and contradiction. To feel such loyalty to a nation space that in many ways we do not know and a homeland that often does not recognize us when we visit is truly about love and pain.

Yet paradoxically, Mexico and the Mexican experience is never far from us. While the socioeconomic differences between the two nations cannot be ignored, many Mexican Americans are neither acculturated nor unrecognizable in Mexico. Many on the U.S. side of the border live in abject poverty, do not speak English, continue to live in traditional Mexican homes. Poor communities along the border are still called *colonias*—a label befitting the socioeconomic reality of the people and their continuing, colonized status. This means that for Mexicans and poor Mexican Americans, the day-to-day life is relatively the same in both countries (though Mexican Americans may have some privilege based on their citizenship alone). Borderland culture transcends the legal demarcation in many ways. As the number of Mexican immigrants and Mexican American births increases the population in the United States, the legal border may still divide the two countries but the line becomes more and more indistinct in terms of culture. Even in cities and some rural areas far from the border, the great influx of migrants from Mexico—as a result of the global economy—has revitalized the cultures of established Mexican American neighborhoods.

Nevertheless, our awareness of certain material differences in a global sense, social locations, and the Mexican government's collaborative role in the exploitation of Mexico by the United States are some factors that necessitate a third, distinct culture for Chicanas/os. While we remain culturally loyal to Mexico, we understand that a government of elitists, whose fortunes depend on the interests of transnational corporations at the expense of the people, is the same enemy wherever it exists.

Gender and Ethnicity

For Chicanas, male scholars who construct ethnic identity without considering gender gloss over certain realities in much the same way that the ethnicity school writers ignore race. The racial components of Chicana ethnicity cannot be separated from gender, for they are all crucial to our contextual experience, and thus the subjectivity, of women. Analyzing the process of developing an ethnic identity must include the way in which race and ethnicity are encoded in constructions of gender, and gender is encoded in constructions of race and ethnicity.[28]

Growing up Mexican American often includes warnings about behaviors that are seen as things accepted in "gringo" households but not in ours. We can be ostracized in our homes and communities for doing things categorized as *"Chicabacha,"* or *"Chicangla"* (a Chicana who acts like an Anglo woman). Men can practice most of the behaviors that inspire such labeling without censure, because they are often seen as part of the public space. Such behaviors are only negative if pursued by women—being too assertive or rebellious, speaking loudly or abrasively, being angry, going out unescorted, going into certain bars, leaving our parents' home if unmarried, or becoming politically involved among other things The independence of *mujeres de fuerza* (strong women) is an insult to patriarchal culture. To be in public spaces alone is to be looking for a man, which a "good" woman would not do. Or worse, is the implication that you *do not need* a man. *¡Qué escandoloso!*[29]

As women, we are sometimes confronted by Anglo males who expect us to live up to the stereotypes of the "hot-blooded" Latin women embedded in their socially constructed imaginations. This is compounded by internalized dominance that makes them see us as racially and socioeconomically inferior women to which they not only have free access, but can abuse or exploit without negative sanctions. In many cases this kind of racialized objectification means they can act in ways toward us that they would find morally objectionable with white women. This hypersexual image of Latinas is in direct opposition to the expectations of traditional culture, which demands the purity of "good" Mexican women and sees *gringas* as too sexually liberated. (Both stereotypes reflect patriarchal desire to control female sexuality.) In some families, we are blamed for any violation of the sexual propriety code, whether or not we actively participated. In most families there is pressure to marry, yet in motherhood we continue to be idealized as nonsexual beings.[30] Though class variations exist, Mexican culture—like other patriarchal constructions—sees the woman's body as one source of the family's honor. This is solely her burden. Bernice Zamora illustrates the double standard of morality that plagues us in her poem, "Pueblo 1950." In recalling the reaction to her first kiss, she writes, "My mother said shame on you / my teacher said shame on you / and / I said shame on me / and nobody said a word to you."[31]

Rooted in the upper classes, the authority of all men is expected to derive from this ideology, which translates into the society-wide subordination of women of all races and classes.[32] Thus gender must be considered in looking at the prevalent modes of oppression as they operate simultaneously with the revitalization process. Profound social change depends on our willingness to break down certain traditional relationships based on power differentials, as well as our ability to conceptualize and respond to diversity in less destructive ways than the colonizers' culture has taught us. Like other writers actively deconstructing patriarchal constructions, Sandra Cisneros, in *The House on Mango Street*, shows that maintaining our ethnic identities (which she signifies through the name "Esperanza"), does not include accepting the subordination of women.

> My great-grandmother. I would've liked to have known her, a wild horse of a woman, so wild she wouldn't marry until my great-grandfather threw a sack over her head and carried her off. Just like that, as if she were a fancy chandelier. That's the way he did it.
>
> And the story goes she never forgave him. She looked out the window all her life, the way so many women sit their sadness on an elbow . . . Esperanza. I have inherited her name, but I don't want to inherit her place by the window.[33]

If we do not want to inherit the systems that oppress us, it is important to understand the cyclic and self-perpetuating nature of revitalization movements—where they are effective and where they are weak. We must also pay attention to the way in which the basic concepts of the cycle may apply to various groups at different points in our histories. The cycle's importance to Chicanas/os is located in both our individual subjectivity and in our communal struggle against oppression. As Mexican Americans we are countering the assimilation pressures as well as the systematic oppression that persistently plagues us. As women, we are trying to recover the female principle, to (re)create the balance and equality destroyed by patriarchy.

The Cycle

As a cycle without directional flow, there is no real beginning or end to this revitalization process—though at various points in history we can trace its rise and fall by tying it to specific events. Neither is there a distinct, sequential transition from one point to the next. Groups often repeat the cycle through years of conflict between dominant and subordinate cultures. This cycle can be adjusted and applied to individuals as well as groups since younger members of any society or movement must learn their history in order to understand their contemporary relationships to power. This often means that the individual will relive the cycle as she or he studies the group's socioeconomic, historical, and political development. Thus smaller enclaves or individuals may go through it in or out of sync with a larger group. But, in order to talk about or conceptualize this social process, it is necessary to delineate certain phases of it. To do this, I will begin by borrowing educator James Banks's general model of ethnic revitalization, with some revisions.[34] I also owe much to Suzanne Pharr's work on the common elements of oppression in her book, *Homophobia: A Weapon of Sexism*.[35] In looking at the general cycle I also point out how the prevalent modes of imperialism operate, as well as how they act in tandem to maintain the dominant culture and neutralize revitalization movements.

I want to reiterate the fluid nature of this as a dynamic and cyclical process, though I will be listing these phases in a sequence to create a model for quick reference.

- A history of oppression exists simultaneously with an institutionalized democracy. This may or may not be accompanied by institutional and socioeconomic power being held in the hands of a small, elite class. The group holding power and privilege uses all means of socialization and the media to establish and enforce the society's norms.
- Anger rises in direct response to the contradiction between rhetorical freedom and the reality of oppression. Inability or unwillingness to assimilate to the established norms and false universals creates interest in active resistance.
- In establishing a resistant identity, those who have been marginalized experience rising expectations of equality and inclusion. In these early stages, many call on the ideals already stated in a liberal defense of democracy.
- Realization that the exclusion of certain persons from the foundational documents of the dominant society means an ongoing struggle for inclusion.
- Political positions are declared, protests take place, and there is a revitalization of group cohesiveness.
- Controversy quickly polarizes public opinion. This, combined with the inflexibility within groups, leads to the isolation of marginalized groups. During this phase, social problems and inequalities are ascribed to single causes or sources. Essentialism rises within the group and stereotyping increases from conservative defenders of the status quo.
- An increasing backlash from those defending their privilege and power rises. Media outlets help to disseminate rhetoric that neutralizes or trivializes radical arguments and demands. Conservative elites name themselves defenders of tradition.
- In response to the conservative attack, meaningful dialogues between oppressed groups begin to take place. Diverse historical information becomes known and theoretical sophistication increases. Coalitions between groups are created.
- The philosophical and rhetorical backlash emphasizes foundational membership as a marker of authority on what is best for the society. Policing agencies and institutions begin to infiltrate resistant organizations and isolate activists from one another.
- Through activist work, coalitions, and diverse scholarship, polarization decreases and multiple explanations for the cause and source

of oppression develop. Conservatives increasingly blame the victims of oppression for the social ills of the society. Those in power make a simultaneous attempt to minimize the perception of inequality so as to quiet activism.

- Some elements of the demanded reforms are institutionalized. Token inclusion is gained, and some strides are made toward increasing diversity at the institutional level. While resources for the conservative backlash are unlimited, groups demanding inclusion must fight over scarce resources.

- Resistance to the instituted reforms becomes more organized. Internalized oppression and horizontal hostility rise in response to the tokenized nature of inclusion, the persistence of false universals and stereotypes, and the myth of scarcity.

- Conservatives feel threatened by a changing society. Tactics to suppress coalition politics intensify. Organized groups begin to lobby for the repeal of reforms. Coalitions begin to break down as multiple issues make a clear focus diffuse and difficult to sustain. Energy for a large movement is drained by having to defend the previous reforms.

- Many of the original concerns are invalidated by organized attacks from conservatives and by conservative or moderate voices within the resistant movement. Antireform groups are successful in eliminating or diluting the most profound changes.

- Oppressed groups begin again to point out the contradiction between liberal democratic ideals and the history of oppression.[36]

It should be pointed out that during all phases of this model, people with power control the justice system. Violence and the threat of violence toward anyone not complying with the system exist throughout the revitalization process. The following expansion of this basic outline will make the cycle historically specific to Chicanas/os as a group. It looks at the way we have moved through the past four decades in a process begun in the 1950s, but including many more public participants in late 1960s and early 1970s. I have tried to give the reader specific examples of what happens in certain phases of the revitalization cycle, but I am not writing a history text. In addition, it has been my intention to write generally enough so that readers can call up more specific historical facts and fit them into the model—or think of other events, movements, and groups for whom the general model might be applicable. I have included information about the changes in the nature of the cycle as it is repeated because some shifting due to historical specificity is inevitable. I will also suggest, with the help of Chicana writers, points at which the cycle may be broken and oppressive mechanisms may be subverted, or at the very least, countered by more substantial and longer lasting coalitions.

As the larger society asserts its dominance over us through various modes of imperialism, it forces us to face our Otherness, to stop denying the emotional residue of trauma and shame, and to actively resist the workings of power. It does little good for us to work toward assimilation and shared culture when the social norms are set by a hegemonic society that does not know or care who we really are. It has historically excluded us as a people through the prevalent modes of imperialism and has the power to redefine the terms for inclusion at any point. This is so because the disenfranchised do not control the means of production, the government, the media, the justice system, or educational institutions.[37]

Democratic Ideology versus History of Oppression

A history of oppression against many peoples exists simultaneously in the United States with an institutionalized ideology of freedom and equality. This situation dictates the socioeconomic reality of Mexican Americans, as well as influences the way we perceive the world and respond to it. Much of our social experience in this nation is forced upon us. As we come to understand that we are U.S. citizens either through coercion—through war, social violence, and political conquest—or having to become economic refugees, we begin to question our continued exploitation. As we study history, we see that the dehumanizing practices of the colonizers continue in the present, albeit in more highly sophisticated ways. This history of oppression coexists with U.S. liberal democratic rhetoric.[38]

As we contemplate the contradiction between the promise and the reality of America, we come to realize that racial hatred, the exploitation of our labor and resources, discrimination, and exclusion have been part of the pattern of behavior throughout American colonial history.[39] For Chicanas this racially based marginalization overlaps with subjugation on the basis of gender, which has historically existed inside as well as outside our community. This sexist oppression has existed simultaneously with not only liberal democracy, but also Marxism and rebellious calls for civil rights based on race.

We learn this history of oppression from many sources. Much of it is experiential and personal. It lives in our families and is transmitted orally by relatives or communal storytellers—*abuelitas, tías, madrinas, or las chismosas*. Other forms of public discourse are also available in the barrios and in the fields. Even after we individually leave these sites, many of them continue to be "in both symbol and reality the heart of the ethnic community."[40]

This may include kitchen table conversations, as the telling of family histories, a passionate activity in many families and extended kinship groups.[41] We also collect history from community center events and songs—from corridos and ballads to spoken word and hip hop—as well as murals and public performances.[42] Religious, community, political, and labor leaders also transmit important pieces of our history. The visual and print media can also be sources. Seldom does it come to us through public K–12 schools. Since one of the primary functions of public education is teaching its youngest members to be good citizens of mainstream society and obedient subjects of the nation, only one worldview can be taught. This is true even when information on other cultures is included in token fashion. Thus, schools generally disseminate middle-class U.S. culture, history, and values. The inclusion of information about specific ethnic or racial groups rarely contains any class analysis or interrogation of unequal power relationships, except as they might have occurred in the past. Thus no link will be made between past and present forms of discrimination or contemporary social locations. Those hungry for alternative information will be forced to find it elsewhere. Chicana/o writers, scholars, and activists may have access to all of the above sources, but they are also reading and creating academic theory as well as rewriting history from a Chicana/o perspective. While all Mexican Americans may learn something from this work, access to it varies widely depending on individual desire, class, levels of education, and economic access among other things. Yet, the vast majority of us—whatever our social location or source of information—realize the incongruity between our oppression or current status as a group, and the stated ideals of the institutionalized democracy in which we live. Like many people of color, our history is littered with institutionalized discrimination in terms of education, housing, health care, and socioeconomic opportunity, as well as institutionalized and socially accepted violence against us.[43]

Rising Expectations

Throughout Mexican American history it has been essential that leaders be available and willing to articulate the gap between democratic or pluralist ideology and the reality of our socioeconomic and civil rights status. These people have risen from a variety of social locations, political affiliations, and socioeconomic arenas. Many such women and men have come out of the labor movement, sparked by conflicts in mining, manufacturing, food preparation, farm work, and garment industries during peak periods of labor unrest.[44] Other leaders have risen in the community through religious or social service organizations and legal aid groups.[45] While each of these Mexican American leaders or activists has been moved by a specific event or circumstance in a given time period, they have had something in common. Each knew that there existed in the United States an unequal social structure that was accompanied by a democratic, liberal ideology. This created in them the desire to achieve or make the dominant culture live up to its professed ideals. Following World War II and into the 1950s and 1960s, Mexican American men newly educated under the GI Bill and other Chicano veterans who had fought to ensure democracy, began to speak out about the reality of the discrimination they faced. Each humiliation only increased the anger they felt. Male scholars and community members of both genders began to disseminate information about our history and the development of the nation. This combination of knowledge and experience led to ethnic and social protest, as it had done in the African American community, around education and civil rights issues, especially in Texas and California.[46] It did not, of course, immediately lead to a critique of gender oppression, despite the fact that women continued to raise the question.[47]

As more information spread into communities, neighborhood houses, and work sites, more people began to organize and strive toward basic civil rights. Mexican Americans began to accept and champion the concept of democratic pluralism as a serious possibility, which we had not previously experienced. The enthusiasm and energy of these early efforts, limited support from sympathetic members of the dominant group, and gaining a visible public platform led to rising expectations of social justice. As a renewed self-interest in our origins and a need to reclaim lost traditions and social practices as a resistant strategy surfaced, more people looked into our history of oppression in a systematic way.[48]

For Chicanas/os in the late 1960s and early 1970s, primary leadership came out of the efforts to unionize farm labor, newly educated Chicanos in universities and colleges, land grant struggles, and political battles for office in cities and towns with large Mexican American populations. This part of the process included an attempt to downplay inherent social differences among Mexican Americans. Emphasis was placed on deliberate and direct racial or ethnic oppression as the cause of our marginalization. Community diversity in terms of class, race, gender, geographic location, education, levels of acculturation, and assimilation were ignored in an effort to create solidarity. Strategically, it was preferable for spokespeople to appear to represent a united, homogeneous group. Into the early 1960s, the ideology of developing Mexican American scholarship and its discourse went relatively unchallenged in the larger society.[49]

By the mid-1960s, many Mexican American activists had begun to validate our lived experience (though in largely male terms). Activists reclaimed the word "Chicano" to signify our identity. Once a derogatory descriptor

used in reference to newly arrived or rural immigrants who were unaccul-
terated and out of place in urban environments, "Chicano" took on new
meanings. Scholars and activists located the word in the Nahuatl language,
affirming our indigenous heritage. For Chicanas/os this meant embracing
our status as "Other" and calling attention to it as a means of self-affirmation.
It also signaled a declaration of our unity and a refusal to be separated by
national origin, regional, or class differences. Pride came out of and grew
into a sense of belonging to a group. This represented a psychological development as well as a political one in that it was an identity antithetical to
the effects of historic trauma (which I discussed earlier). Literature
through the 1960s and into the 1970s was dominated by angry testimonials
about personal experiences with injustice, resistant Marxist narratives,
protest poetry, and Chicano autobiographical writing. As has often been
the case for colonized populations or political expatriates, writers were extremely important in the project of validating Chicano culture and identity, as well as the revitalization of indigenous and Mexican culture. But
Mexican Americans were not exiles living on foreign soil. Some scholars
have referred to us instead as, "internal exiles."

The idea of the Mexican American community as an "internal colony"
grew out of Latin American scholarship.[50] Largely referring to social location theory it saw Chicanos as a racial group exploited and controlled
through a variety of institutionalized mechanisms. It was combined with a
Marxist economic perspective connecting capitalism to the development
of communities that served as reserve labor pools. The internal colony
model met with criticism because its class analysis lacked substance and it
went outside accepted or canonical scholarship. It did not really describe
the historical reality of the Southwest and could not act as a solid ideology.
Nevertheless, it shattered the illusion of assimilation and democratic pluralism for many Mexicans and Mexican Americans. It made clear that we,
and other racialized and marginalized groups, were being deliberately kept
in a position of subjugation and used to keep workers' wages low, whereas
assimilation generally worked for white ethnics.

Student and labor union activists began Chicano-centered protests
aimed at popularizing a developing ideology and championing various
causes. Much as their predecessors had done in the battle to free Mexico
from European rule, these new rebels expressed pride in our native heritage. Political rhetoric and protest art rejuvenated traditional symbols
from Mexico's ancient past. They became part of the popular culture in
Mexican American neighborhoods gracing calendars, candles, T-shirts,
and murals. Aztec warriors and male deities, especially war gods, romanticized images of muscled, indigenous men carrying lighter-skinned Aztec
maidens from danger, images heavy with eagles and jaguars appeared

throughout the neighborhoods. These indigenous symbols also appeared in comic book form. In keeping with the dynamic nature of an emerging third culture, these traditional icons found their way into expressions of *Chicanismo* as new symbols were created using the old motifs.[51] They were a part of our collective past. As Marcela Lucero-Trujillo has pointed out, the reclamation of Aztec symbols functioned as a unifying mechanism among the diverse segments of the Mexican American community—not all of whom wanted to identify with radical college students, were Catholic, Spanish-speaking, or phenotypically similar.[52]

But the multifarious nature of Mexican American experience could not be hidden forever. Beneath the beauty of Quetzal feathers and the Fifth Sun, Chicanas felt the need to resurrect specifically female symbols and archetypes.[53] Our purpose was twofold: to reclaim or highlight a rich Mexican cultural legacy particularly relevant to women, and to (re)define their meaning in ways that were not sexist. Malinche and Guadalupe, the earth goddesses, Coatlicue and Tonantzín, as well as La Llorona, represented the *indigenisma* we sought, but it had to be divested of its patriarchal gloss before it could be transplanted into our contemporary lives. Our purpose would expand as we began to deal with historic trauma, feeling the need to recover the feminine principle and the nurturing possibilities of our figurative foremothers. Writers like Anzaldúa and Ana Castillo made it clear that this was an attempt to heal the split between female and male, and to balance the masculine in order to create a healthy social context. As Marina Rivera writes in these selected lines from her poem "Mestiza," we needed someone (a mother) with the capacity to truly know us. "If all the rest misunderstand / you will understand me, mother / with a heart made of trodden earth."[54]

Uncomplicated Explanations

Polarization occurred between Chicanos and more conservative Mexican Americans—between certain leaders of the movement and Chicana feminists—and between Chicanas/os and the dominant culture as we sought to reject our "U.S. citizen" identity and articulate, (re)create, and declare our ethnic or Mexican identity. While this was more about cultural loyalty than nationalism or an attempt to politically cede from the union, Brown Power protests were nevertheless met with state-supported police and military action.[55] Public speakers offered polemic, uncomplicated explanations and causes for our marginal status. They gave voice to our intense emotions about political injustice. As artist Judy Baca says, "I had all these feelings but no place to hang them. The *Movimiento* gave me a place to focus them and affirm the fact that I wasn't crazy."[56]

Many Chicano activists in the community wanted to acknowledge and to legitimize racism and ethnocentrism as the major or only source of oppression of our people. Scholars and labor leaders were generally inclined to focus on class as the primary source, seeing some connection between Chicanos within the U.S. system of capitalism, and Mexicans, as well as other Third World peoples, as subjects of multinational corporations.[57]

Backlash

Conservative members of the dominant society felt besieged by demands for equality and social justice. Many opposed any shift in the dominant/subordinate paradigm. Becoming spokespeople for white privilege, these people supported the status quo and mainstream ideals. (Though they protected the interests of the powerful, their rhetoric appealed to the middle-class and/or all members of the hegemonic population who felt threatened by any challenge to authority.)[58] Mainstream response to radical rhetoric was simplistic in the early stages. Arguments from conservatives insisted that the United States was a democracy and that no laws needed to be enacted to enforce the principles of the Constitution and the Bill of Rights.

When young Chicanas/os encountered this kind of hostile backlash, the importance of the past became even more crucial to maintaining a sense of pride and purpose. Understanding not only our own history but also that of other groups told us that we were not alone. What we were experiencing— the violent efforts to subdue protest as well as the resistance itself—had occurred previously in histories between enslaved or indigenous people and their imperialist colonizers. This knowledge did not immediately lead to coalitions. The desire to maintain a separate ethnic identity was in part preservation of the core Self, which was constantly under attack by the hegemonic machinery of the colonial empire. This only increased with the conservative backlash to calls for social justice and equality. Initial responses to mainstream hostility contained statements about our essential sameness as a group of like human beings. This sped up the adoption and codification of a nationalist Chicano ideology, canonization of certain pieces of literature, and a constructed identity that grew out of both the real and the imagined culture.[59]

As the protests and the backlash continued, dominant culture critics set themselves up as guardians of the "American" way of life. In public forums they blamed the larger civil rights movements and public protests for disrupting the smooth operation of "the great society." Such critics believed that the political resistance itself was responsible for any perceived exclusion. Protesters were vilified and labeled troublemakers. Major issues and challenges were neutralized by mass media attacks on personalities, rhetorical styles, methods of protest, and the choices activists made about clothing. All of these commentaries trivialized or obscured the legitimate reasons for the defiance.[60]

Despite the backlash, political awareness continued to increase community-wide. Housing projects and barrio businesses sprouted political murals filled with indigenous symbols and representations of native ritual and Latin American heroes. To the extent it was possible, young Chicanos continued to reject Euro-American values and philosophies. Mexican images and ideas found their way from popular culture into museums, literature, and classrooms. Radio stations in major markets in the Southwest—as well as larger metropolitan areas in the rest of the country—began to broadcast special programs geared toward Hispanic communities. Disc jockeys began to speak the living language of the barrio and to voice publicly the concerns of the community. Going beyond the early simplicity of protest poems and polemics, new anthologies were compiled, giving multiple voices to Chicana/o experience. Throughout this process, Chicanas/os as political organizers, and Mexican Americans as a group, became more and more visible to the mainstream.[61]

This, combined with increasing numbers of Mexican immigrants and Central American refugees, inspired conservative rhetoric to grow more vehement and dismissive. Local and small presses with limited distribution capabilities published most movement and radical literature. But major publishers eager to fill the growing demand for information on the "ethnic" experience released some creative literature and a few histories meeting conventional scholarly norms. In the mid-1970s, Richard Rodríguez's autobiographical *Hunger of Memory* was released. In contrast to Chicano movement literature, it favored assimilation, discounted Mexican heritage as a viable public culture, and spoke out against bilingual education. Originally published by Godine and then Bantam Books—major publishers with enormous distribution channels—it found its way into classrooms and became for the mainstream, the essential Chicano experience. Both the right and liberals within the mainstream embraced the book. Chicano activists and leftist scholars responded with a hostile rejection of the book, renewed emphasis on language retention, and the institutionalization of bilingual programs.

Coalition and Complexity

In addition to the availability of more information about "minorities" by the mid-1980s, thoughtful dialogues with other oppressed groups and sympathetic members of the mainstream increased our awareness of imperialist strategies. Self-reflection and study of social mechanisms engendered more sophisticated theorizing around relevant issues. Out of this discourse came a more complex and insightful explanation for inequality, as well as suggestions for change. Eventually sources other than race or class were acknowledged—though sometimes begrudgingly—as methods of creating unequal and inferior status. Patterns and models of behavior began to be recognized across cultures. Dialogues with African Americans and Native Americans created *alliances and coalitions* for both men and women in the Mexican American activist community.[62]

Solidarity among Chicano activists (both male and female) remained relatively strong, but not without challenge. As the diversity of experience within the community began to find its voice, issues became more complicated. Many of the issues central to the Chicano movement generally were equally appreciated and endorsed by women. We too wanted self-determination, but we wanted it both as Mexican Americans and as women. We saw the need for emphasizing our indigenous roots, but we wanted to recognize women leaders and role models as well as male ones. No argument came from women in regard to the desirability of having movement champions coming out of the community (as opposed to those completely assimilated, though that became increasingly hard to determine)—but we wanted women to be equally sought out. While some objected, many women were not adverse to confrontational political tactics and participated in the most heated and direct attacks on institutions and politicians. We too "felt a strong sense of urgency for immediate social change."[63] Yet the fact remained that Chicanas—lesbian or straight—were virtually invisible to the more publically acknowledged planners and scholars in the early stages of developing Chicano theory and history. This, among other things, made obvious the reality that race or ethnicity could not be separated from gender and sexual identity as sources of oppression for women of color. Because Chicanas do not become women solely on the basis of biology, but also through socialization processes in a variety of cultural locations, we could not transcend our need for an ethnically specific, woman-centered method of resistance. Despite our fierce bond with the men in our communities, we could not overlook the symmetry of, or the confederations between, aristocratic and folk patriarchs—both of whom had the capacity to be unaware of our experience.[64]

Similarly, Chicana lesbians had to create theory grounded in Mexican American lesbian experience. Positioned through the same simultaneously occurring forces of class, race, gender, and competing ideologies as straight women, lesbians also had to deal with socialization through systematic heterosexuality. This meant paying attention to, and attempting to illuminate, the collusion between heterosexual women and men. Subject to different kinds of shaming and rejection within as well as outside the community, lesbian Chicanas had to live with "double negatives," being unwilling *and* unable to fulfill the expectations for Mexican American women in terms of sexual behavior, religious practice, and traditional childrearing, as well as social and sexual subjugation by men. While many heterosexual Chicanas challenged the same values in different ways, this was seen as a choice on their part, which could conceivably be changed. But lesbians threatened patriarchal control precisely because there was little hope (however delusional some individuals might have been) that conforming to traditional expectations would be possible.[65] In a sense, Chicana lesbians have been cast as the ultimate Malinches.

One of the early voices on the Chicana feminist scene, Cherríe Moraga has gone through a sifting, sorting, or fine-tuning process in terms of her ethnic identity. But her lesbian identity was strong, articulate, and complex from the beginning of her published writing. She gave us a voice that was defiant and loving, playful and deadly serious, experimental and solid. In a direct, sexual, earthy short story called "La Ofrenda," Moraga painted a picture of a rough, on-the-edge segment of Chicana dyke life, which was nevertheless filled with love, fear, and loss.[66] The narrative voice told the story of her relationship with Tiny—the homegirl to whom everyone else looked for guidance. It also contained a swipe at the Chicanos who defined the early ideology of the movement, respecting the political involvement itself, but challenging both male authority and the strict boundaries between heterosexual and homosexual behavior.

> "Lolita Lebrón," that's what they used to call me at Cha Cha's. Of course, they didn't even know who Lolita was until I came in with the story of her with the guys and the guns taking on the whole pinche U.S. Congress. They'd say, "Hey Lolita, how goes the revolution?" An then they'd all start busting up and I'd take it cuz I knew they loved me, even respected what I was doing. Or maybe it was only Tiny who respected me, and all the others had to treat me right cuz of her. Tiny used to say her contribution to La Causa was to keep the girlfriends of the Machos happy while they were being too revolutionary to screw.[67]

Like Moraga, we realized that few of us belonged to a group, or were marginalized from a society, based on a single set of characteristics or some essential sameness. We knew we existed between many polarized positions—sometimes spanning the distance between contradictory discourses and cultural practices.[68] Chicanas grew increasingly frustrated with having to choose between important loyalties. The mainstream women's movement, undergoing a revitalization cycle of its own, had generally not included the experiences of women of color or poor women in its early theorizing of gender.[69] While this changed throughout the 1980s, and continues to be less true, the "years of exclusion" in Chicano and feminist theory "have had a serious impact" far beyond temporary invisibility.[70] It is similar to the lack of foundational inclusion of Mexican Americans, African Americans, Native Americans, Asian Americans, and women of all races and ethnicities in the original documents that made the United States a nation. It means that basic ideas, views, ways of learning, and passing on knowledge, as well as history, have evolved without regard for the perceptions of, and lives of, Chicanas.[71]

Consequently, much of the theoretical work had to try to adjust existing masculinist or mainstream feminist discourse to include Chicanas. In some cases, women's issues were merely added—one course in Chicano studies programs, one chapter in Chicano histories, one essay in an anthology, one speech at conferences, and so forth. This is a little like erecting a multilevel building with no ramps or elevators and then telling handicapped people they're free to move in. You can add certain provisions later, but there will always be counters too high, inaccessible closet rods, no way to get a wheelchair into the shower, and so on. By its very design it excludes the reality and experience of the people who must live with it. Obviously it would be better for the disabled to design and erect a new building of their own.[72] This reconstructive task fell to the early Chicana writers, some of whom would be vilified by Chicano criticism.

While early movement texts are historically important, they provide a good example of why Chicanas began to resist and critique certain aspects of traditional culture. For us, Chicana feminism was not a choice between disciplines, or between white women and brown men. It was a response to inequality in both locations. The simple add-on approach could not take the place of a Chicana/*Xicana*-centered consciousness that had to be present in any method we would use. The patriarchs in our own community, as well as those in the dominant culture could not be seen as outside class, gender, or racial hierarchies because a fundamentally masculine agenda was congenitally linked to the formation of such categories as well as existing hierarchical arrangements. Unfortunately, we knew from experience that many Chicanos and white women seemed all too willing to replicate these models.[73]

In recognizing that "all aspects of reality are gendered, and that the experience of gender changes according to race, class . . . and sexuality," Chicanas had to initiate a revitalization cycle of their own.[74] The basic characteristics of the cycle remained the same, the difference is that Chicanas went through the process simultaneously in varying social arenas around intersecting and overlapping sources of oppression.

Chicanas of varying sexual orientations began to create and develop history, theory, and methods that centered on our experiences and emanated from our perspectives. Since it was impossible for these women to separate ethnicity, race, and class from gender and sexual orientation, conventional objectivist history and strict Marxist approaches were not entirely useful. Still, many scholars steeped in Marxist theory continued to insist that the "revolution" would not occur if we wasted energy considering "women's issues."[75] For models and colleagues we looked to African American and Native American women writers, some radical white feminists, Spanish and Latin American feminists, as well as early Mexican American women writers. But, we also looked into Greater Mexican history for rebellious female ancestors, precursors to contemporary Chicana feminists, noting that organized feminist activities at the local, national, and international levels had taken place in Mexico since the early 1900s.[76]

With the new methods and theories developed by Chicana writers, a more complex explanation for our subordinate positions developed and tenuous coalitions were formed. Race, ethnicity, gender, and class in some combination were legitimated as broad sources of Mexican American oppression, and these were seen in conjunction with other forms of discrimination inside and outside the group. Locating these multiple sources of inequality and injustice—intersecting, overlapping, and acting simultaneously—as well as the formation of coalitions and alliances, meant that the extreme polarization was reduced. Though it is true that tension still existed, we could see that the common elements of oppression formed a highly complex matrix through which people were filtered and categorized on a hierarchical scale.

Stolen Language

We must recognize that the hierarchies against which we struggle are constructed, even though they are often characterized as naturally occurring. But the dominant society constantly creates new models for dominance and subordinance, or redefines the meaning and function of the old ones. To remain enforcible, the many ways of determining divisions between "us" and "them" need to be (re)constructed, secured, and maintained, or they may be deconstructed, neutralized, and left to decay—depending on what is best for those in power.[77] Many strategies are employed against those who challenge power and privilege. One of them is to take over the resistant language, redefine it, and use it against its originators.

In the late 1970s and into the Reagan-Bush era, defenders of the status quo—many still unhappy with the U.S. failure to win the war in Vietnam—launched rhetorical and theoretical attacks against the ideas of all groups wanting social change. They desperately tried to maintain or re-build "American" ideals, social and academic conventions, and cultural traditions. Desperate to regain their sense of unquestioned authority and recapture whatever privilege they felt they had lost, the backlash against the revitalized political identities of marginal groups intensified. Covert operations in support of the dominant regime searched for ways to diffuse public support for widespread social transformation. Developed by mar-ginal groups, protest language and concepts were stolen by the main-stream. Co-opting the left's rhetorical strategies changed the original meanings of words, catch-phrases, and concepts in ways that blamed victims for their own oppression. The charge of "reverse-racism" is a classic exam-ple. Since racism (as is the case with all "isms") is the combination of dis-crimination or bias *plus power*, and the victims of oppression do not have power, reverse racism cannot exist. Yet, the whole concept had such cache with the mainstream who were looking for someone to blame for their declining real income, that it proved an effective tool in conservative rhetoric. The few adjustments that had already occurred were held up as the cause of existing social ills, and conservatives predicted that any more change would result in the dissolution of the society as a whole. True trans-formation—as well as the economic resources for change—continued to be scarce.[78]

Instituting Reforms and the Power of Imperialism

Nevertheless, logical and well-supported arguments demonstrating the moral correctness of suggested social or legislative changes began to have an affect on the public at large. As a result, some elements of the demanded reforms were instituted.[79] An increase in bilingual education programs, curriculum changes bringing Chicana/o culture and experience into pub-lic classrooms, the election of more Mexican Americans to legislative of-fices, and affirmative action, were all examples of institutional modification. Chicano studies departments—as well as Women's Studies, Afro American Studies, and Native American Studies departments and programs—became part of university life. Affirmative action policies were put into place and grant monies were allocated for developing programs addressing the needs of specific populations, as well as increasing the diversity of public institu-tions. Formulated in other phases, these reforms were concrete steps toward closing the gap between the reality of oppression and the ideologies of dem-ocratic pluralism and equal opportunity.[80]

Inspired by these successes, or because of the promise they offered, other marginalized groups began to voice their own grievances as they sought more encompassing results of the previous dialogue—just as Chicanos had been inspired by the struggles and successes of African American social justice movements in the early stages of the revitalization cycle.[81] Groups similarly oppressed, and newly politicized Mexican Americans began to borrow the rhetoric and language of liberation from earlier struggles as they entered their own cycles. They too began to critique and demand change within various liberation movements—just as Chicanas had resisted the masculine rhetoric of the early Chicano movement.

While Chicanas and other women of color continued to question the mainstream feminist movement about its propensity to collapse all women's experience into rhetoric that really only described white women, Chicana activists persevered in their critique of Chicano theoretical constructs, and Chicana writers were detailing our history, experience, and identity processes. In addition to contributing to both mainstream and Chicano collections, anthologies created by Moraga, Anzaldúa, Alarcón, Trujillo, and Rebolledo among others, gathered together work by an amazing number of Chicana writers in a variety of genres throughout the 1980s and into the 1990s.[82]

At this point, contributors to the dominant discourse began to develop social science studies and researched texts intended for popular distribution showing that the failure of Chicanas/os and other oppressed groups to achieve educationally and succeed economically could be attributed to our ethnically or culturally inherited social characteristics, as well as our failure to assimilate. Conservatives began to recruit assimilated and equally conservative Mexican American representatives and incorporate them into mainstream institutions and media sources. Cautionary tales that replicated the Horatio Alger myth, like Linda Chavez's book, *Out of the Barrio*, were printed by mass-market publishing houses, and full assimilation continued to be encouraged and applauded.

But the price of admission to mainstream culture was extreme, and meant suppressing so much of ourselves—a clear "violation of the spirit."[83] María Herrera-Sobek articulated the dangers of acculturation and conditional or token acceptance by the mainstream in her poem, "My All-American Son." In it, she remarked on America's love/hate relationship with color. While it relishes the brown skin of blondes who have gotten tan on the beach, it fears and hates what Herrera-Sobek calls "earth brown," the color of indigenous people and many Mexican immigrants. Even so, her son, who spoke perfect English and struggled with Spanish, seemed to slip in and out of mainstream culture with his dignity and pride intact. But this does not ease the mother's fear; she understands his mercurial position. "One false move / And he'll be / Ejected / Rejected / Put in 'his place.'"[84]

Those Chicanos who blatantly or publicly refused to submit to such assimilation were cast as troublemakers. It soon became clear to mainstream leaders that the rapidly increasing population of Spanish-surnamed citizens, and the discontent of not only Mexicans but other Latinos as well, needed to be "rounded up" to make us easier to identify and thus susceptible to normalizing strategies. During the Nixon administration, we were subsumed under the word "Hispanic," stripping all of us of our unique cultures and denying Mexican Americans our indigenous origins.[85] This label—which gained in popularity during the Reagan-Bush years—cast us as "foreign" to the United States and the Western Hemisphere. It is a name without history or social context—antithetical to our reality. "Hispanic" allowed elite (and largely light-skinned) Cubans—traditional allies or managers of the corporate interests who fled Castro's communist revolution—to be co-opted and used as representatives of "the Hispanic community."[86] In this capacity they could act as a model of assimilation. Since they treasured their refuge from socialism, and thus extolled the virtues of U.S. democracy, they also served as model Hispanic citizens. Leftist women and men among both Mexican Americans and Puerto Ricans rejected this Cuban perspective and the term "Hispanic."

Increased numbers of women scholars continued to experience sexism and homophobia within the community and within activist organizations. They sustained a serious critique of Chicano ideology, theory, methods of protest, and exclusionary practices. This fostered animosity from previous leaders who saw themselves as the original innovators of the Chicano social justice movement. Resentment often caused tension that could not be resolved. Rather than see themselves as purveyors of a dominant/subordinate paradigm, such leaders charged their (largely female) critics with cultural and political treason. Caught up in unhealthy responses due to internalized oppression, we sometimes acted out of the shame-based behaviors I described in an earlier chapter. Many unnecessarily vicious (and sometimes personal) attacks were launched due to horizontal hostility and internalized dominance. We found ourselves re-creating the hierarchies we had all learned and as a group, had trouble seeing beyond our differences. We lost sight of the virtue and strength that might come out of complexity and pluralism *within* Chicano ideology or through alliances across race, class, and gender divisions. This happened not because we disbelieved the possibility, but because we were responding to the cultural imperatives of a competitive society and because we got caught up in our anger and defensiveness. Some leaders and participants felt that the critiques would dilute the revolutionary potential of the movement they assumed were guaranteed if we kept a unified front. But that unification meant capitulation for anyone who disagreed with any aspect of their narrowly defined ideology, strategies, solutions, or ultimate goals. It also meant that all charges of sexism or homophobia within the movement be silenced.[87]

Respected for their experience and initiative in *El Movimiento*, leaders used their positions to demand a continued focus on race and class, eschewing possible alliances with other groups and knowing they could depend on a certain amount of loyalty and support from within the ranks. As women writers began to articulate their early experiences within the movement, we learned that these leaders had initially and continued to take advantage of their powerful reputations in their personal relationships as well.[88]

In Bernice Zamora's poem, "Notes from a Chicana 'Coed,'" we hear the narrative voice of a young woman describing her relationship with a graduate student involved in Chicano politics. She is told by the man, "It's the gringo who oppresses you, Babe." Yet it is clear from the poem that he has used the woman sexually, though he is married and has five children. It is also clear that the narrator, a single mother who has worked two jobs to put herself through school and feed her kids, feels less than sympathetic when the man talks about himself as bearing "the brunt of the gringo's oppression." The Chicano who has reaped the financial rewards of a patriarchal system not available to women objects to the woman's feminist challenges. "Don't give me that / Women's Lib trip," he tells the narrative voice, "that only divides us / and we have to work / together for the movimiento." At the end of the stanza, he insists it is the white man who is our oppressor— silencing any accusation against him as a patriarch.[89]

In the next stanza, the narrative voice makes clear her understanding of who her oppressor is, and she calls his game. In the last stanza she expresses the frustration of having to think simultaneously of both sources of oppression in her life, adjusting her position accordingly. Marcela Lucero-Trujillo expresses similar impatience with Chicano sexism in her poem "Machismo Is Part of Our Culture," a phrase the man in her poem uses to justify his mistreatment of Chicanas. Like Zamora, Lucero-Trujillo calls attention to the hypocrisy of the man's exaggerated *Chicanismo* (or nationalistic political position) and his simultaneous sexual association with white women. But as the narrative voice points out, he cannot use culture as an excuse to mistreat his white lovers. Interestingly, Lucero-Trujillo does not blame the sexism on traditional Mexican culture, but on the lack thereof. She makes it clear that the Chicano her narrator addresses has only a shallow understanding of that culture. Thus, the machismo he seeks to display is not a Mexican or Chicano cultural expression, but sexism learned in a mainstream context. As such, it is a mutation of Mexican machismo, developed in the United States—both in the barrios and among middle-class, acculturated Mexican American men. While not saying that one form of sexism is better than another, the narrator tries to point out that this appeal to tradition cannot work on a Chicana who not only knows the culture, but rejects mistreatment under any circumstances. She also tells Chicanos that being thought less worthy of respect than white women is the ultimate betrayal.[90]

As the rage and frustration of these and other women's voices was understood, and new generations of Chicanas/os entered the fray, many more began to express the idea that the old rhetorical and activist devices had lost their effectiveness. New organizations, initiated and run by women, began to articulate the concerns of women, serve as places of refuge for Chicanas frustrated by continuing sexism within the movement, and valuing the ideas, activism, and scholarship of women.[91] Nevertheless, the original leaders of the movement—still seen and respected as elders—were supported by a wide range of voices. Some of these were young scholars of both genders and others were veterans. Even some early challengers to male hierarchy in the movement returned to early nationalist ideology. Others tried to ignore the questions of gender and sexual identity altogether by remaining primarily involved in traditional labor union struggles, immigration law, and the relatively new issues being raised by NAFTA and the global economy. Every day there seemed to be new policies profoundly affecting domestic workers, international laborers, and Mexico's economy. Organized attacks on bilingual programs, welfare rights, and healthcare benefits began to appear, and the movement continued to diversify. Some saw the maintenance and return to nationalist ideology as a movement away from critical thinking and a denial of the complexity of issues, as well as the continued reification of patriarchy. Others chose their positions according to audience and the particular battle being fought. Some writers, like Cherríe Moraga, found usable aspects of the early ideology and incorporated them in her own revitalized sense of being a *lesbiana* of color.[92] Others of us became immersed in academic jargon and theoretical constructions. Many women were still trying to hold firm to our ethnic and racial identities, yet clinging just as fiercely to our feminist positions.[93]

While testimony and an emphasis on a specific cultural past were still important, writers began to see their experiences in comparison with Third World populations around the globe. Chicana feminist writers developed a strong, public voice.[94] Negative responses to feminist critiques of the masculine, nationalist movement and homophobia pushed some Chicanas into alliances with white feminists, and/or other women of color—straight and lesbian—and out of specifically Chicano politics almost entirely. But men in the movement who were responsive to criticism and progressive in their thinking about complex social paradigms began to produce thoughtful interpretations and insightful analyses that included women and other marginalized people from the beginning. They began to question not only the construction of femininity and masculinity, but gay and lesbian identities as well. This only increased the already intricate theoretical inquiries into every facet of our lives.

The Breakdown

Under the weight of the by-now powerful opposition to various pieces of civil rights legislation—as well as feminist reforms—some coalitions began to fall apart. Women of color walked out of the National Women's Studies Association's annual conference in the early 1990s. Some of the most vocal Chicanas began to boycott the National Association of Chicana and Chicano studies conferences. The professionalization of ethnic studies departments took many scholars out of activist organizations, and the struggle over scarce resources plagued most groups in and out of the academy. Because of the perceived threats to white power and privilege, some groups became particular targets of an increasingly vocal and well-organized backlash. It did not take long for conservatives to begin to capitalize on the tensions within activist communities.

The focus of the early movement became diffuse and much of the original fervor was lost. Philosophical, ideological, and methodological differences led to fights within and between oppressed groups. Some of these arguments began to fill public discourse. Any opportunity to exaggerate these differences was seized upon by the mainstream press and used by conservatives to cultivate further squabbling. As unity broke down, and the ability of leaders to bring large numbers of people together for a sustained protest decreased, the backlash against reformers only picked up energy. Like vultures waiting for the dying movement of bodies to take their last breaths, conservatives and moderates went in for the kill. Well-funded centers and institutes for the dissemination of conservative ideas to the public were established. Reactionary media figures rose to prominence, spouting oppressive language and ideas that would not have been allowed in more socially conscious times. Once they had won the hearts and minds of the middle class, the most important changes in the social structure were attacked and some were eliminated. Others lost their effectiveness, and the dominant group's position was reinforced.[95] This happened because the ideals of inclusion and the rhetoric of diversity were popularly adopted long before real or fundamental social and legal transformation took place.

The focus of public discourse and scholarship, rather than fighting to discontinue the existence of traditional, hierarchical structures, began to center on the divisiveness and conflict on the left. As multiculturalism became part of widespread public discourse, institutions were already starting to back out of earlier promises, cutting off funds for such programs even as they publicly praised the efforts and claimed to be committed to diversity.

Many leftist scholars got caught up in the culture wars, or seduced by the promise of postmodernism. Oppression became a tainted word in serious scholarship. Focus shifted from particular ethnic groups to generalized and non-specific differences. "Multiculturalism" ceased to signify multiple cultures in a pluralistic society and came to be a euphemism for the old "melting pot" theory, or the machinery of assimilation. Consequently, it had to be assailed by the very people in whose interest it was initiated.[96]

In contrast to the disharmony on the left, the conservative movement seemed to coalesce, growing ever more passionate, sophisticated, and forceful. Throughout the 1980s and for most of the 1990s, increased numbers of marginalized people began to inhabit previously exclusive arenas. Though these people were not included in sufficient quantities to actually threaten the status quo, the dominant group feared this possibility to a much greater degree than was warranted. Members of the dominant group exaggerated the effects of various reforms and cultural shifts. They used middle-class fears to mount wholesale attacks on immigrants (documented and undocumented), the poor, liberal journalists and scholars, single mothers, and anyone else who did not fit the image they projected of an idealized "American."[97] (After September 11, this would come wrapped in rhetorical appeals to national security as well as loyalty to the "American way of life.") Using readily available legislative and media support, conservatives turned moderates away from reform by trivializing or falsely portraying oppressed groups. Hostility toward immigrants and reformers diverted public attention away from government support for corporate policies and failed responsibilities, as well as expanding the global economy. The dismantling of welfare, the denial of social services, and English-only agendas grew out of this climate of acrimony and fear, garnering increasing support among states, and more recently, at the federal level.[98]

Supporters of the status quo had access to popular media outlets, a history of political organizing, a ready reserve of intellectuals, and networks of influence. They knew how to take up and use any disagreement within the marginalized group to neutralize its strength and dismantle its solidarity. They turned expressions of newfound pride in ethnic identity into an opportunity to critique the "balkanization" of America—propagating fear in both mainstream audiences and those Mexican Americans who still favored assimilation or desired inclusion rather than marginalization. But, this fear was largely articulated by white men, who may or may not have been "innocently unaware of [their] own biases."[99] What had once been a barely noticed ethnic group in terms of national politics, suddenly became a threat to U.S. unity. Mexican Americans—at times romanticized or considered quaint, at other times ignored, mistreated, and labeled as a social problem—became a national liability as politically aware Chicanas/os refused to accept an inferior, second-class status. By casting us as a threat to a unified culture in an attempt to silence us, or force us into compliance, they betrayed the very ideals of democratic pluralism so foundational to this nation. Clearly, more than just cultural changes were at stake.

Fighting over scarce resources and semantic differences produced more horizontal hostility, anger, and competition. This did not necessarily occur out of the mere recognition of differences within and among groups, nor was it the result of developing more complex theories about oppression. It was the combination of socioeconomic dependence, internalized oppression, and internalized dominance. New questions did indeed dilute the focus and intensity of all movements. But this did not happen because the new demands were less worthy or incorrect, but because we failed to stay committed to certain coalitions and alliances as troubles arose. In some cases we misdirected our fury and frustration at one another. Healthy disagreement was impossible between members of groups who had common historic or experiential trauma, had failed to resolve their emotional turmoil, and had internalized the shame engendered in mainstream social spaces. We had, in effect, been trained by a racist, sexist, classist, and homophobic society to suspect the worst of one another. We had also been taught destructive ways of dealing with our anger and the fine art of constructing hierarchies. While some coalitions did hold and many people remained committed to working across differences, this was often more successful in informal, unorganized, and noninstitutional settings. (In racially mixed and nontraditional families, or housing projects, poor neighborhoods, and on some work sites—rather than in political organizations, social service agencies, arts groups, universities, or labor unions where some money existed to be fought over.) In mainsteam locations the internal fighting over resources was compounded by ongoing oppression and the stress of inhabiting uncomfortable social spaces.[100]

Many coalition members were dispirited by having to constantly defend initiatives from charges of reverse discrimination. The myth of scarcity became more meaningful as the budgets for diversity and multicultural programming began to dry up. Encouraged by successful discursive attacks on tokenism, affirmative action, and other efforts to diversify institutions, plaintiffs and lawyers began legal battles supported financially by conservative foundations against major universities. Ironically, they used civil rights laws and language to protect the interests of white clients. Public voices started to focus their critiques on changes in the law and society they saw as being too rapid, too extreme, unfair, and unnecessary. These changes, they thought, made it possible for members of the historically marginalized groups to oppress the dominant group or obtain unfair advantages.[101]

Mainstream pundits successfully redefined horizontal hostility as racism by one oppressed group against another, breaking down empathy between subordinate populations *and* relieving the dominant group of its guilt and personal responsibility. ("Why should we be expected to free ourselves of racism when they can't even get along with each other?") This took away the concept of racism being prejudice *plus power*, leaving it open for reconstruction as something that "naturally" occurs when humans encounter difference. It also located the source of racism in the individual actor rather than in institutionalized and socially constructed systems of power.[102]

Traditionalists used public forums to speak as reformers at the same time that they reaffirmed the status quo. "Affirmative action" became synonymous with "less qualified" and "reverse discrimination." Martin Luther King, Jr.'s, famous "I Have a Dream" speech, in which he hoped that one day people would be "judged by the content of their character, rather than the color of their skin" was transformed into anti-affirmative action oratory. (This ignored the fact that his dream of equality had not yet been achieved, that people of color were still routinely excluded, and that methods of redress are still required to ensure equal representation.) "Diversity" and "multiculturalism," once popularized and put into mass usage, became almost meaningless. They often signaled tokenism, or wholesale inclusion of everyone and everything, with no clear political agenda or intent. Once rich in possibilities, these ideas often came out of the homogenizing process with as much substance as spit on a hot sidewalk.[103] You can see it, but does it serve any purpose?

Realizing the provincialism of paying homage to diverse cultures without studying imperialism or the construction of whiteness as an ideology led many of the original champions of multiculturalism to abandon it as a vehicle for transformation. Conservatives received with glee the criticisms of multiculturalism from the left and attacked curriculum changes with unrestrained vigor. Fence-sitters failed to understand that liberal and radical scholars and critics were not opposed to the basic concepts of pluralism, diversity, or multiculturalism, but to the ineffectual manner in which these concepts had been interpreted and instituted by mainstream organizations.

The simultaneous occurrence of conservative backlash, mainstream shifts toward the protection of white power and privilege, and the breakdown of political alliances created new alienation and the desire to be protected from seeming chaos. This caused some individuals to withdraw from movements and activist organizations altogether. In the United States, the difference between the major political parties had narrowed and the country had shifted to the right in its fear of profound and lasting social transformation. This made the underclass more vulnerable to things like the dissolution of support services, increased harassment from law enforcement agencies, and increased legislation in favor of the interests of capital, generating a wider gap between the socioeconomic status of the elite and the poor.[104]

This brings the process back to the point where freedom and equality exist as ideals, but the history and reality of oppression continue. We enter a new cycle of political revitalization as the dissolution of reforms triggers an increase in polemical responses. Some radicals have begun to see postmodern fragmentation theories and the liberal critiques of nationalism as less than useful. Cherríe Moraga, the self-declared "white girl gone brown," in her book, *The Last Generation,* uses highly politicized and polarized language straight out of early activist discourse. (Yet, she continues to rethink gender, sexuality, and nationalism.)[105]

Disillusionment accompanies this new cycle, and the tone is perceptively less open to diverse views and some kinds of coalition. The rising importance of the global economy and the increased militarization around the world, as well as the return of hard-line, conservative ideologues to Washington coincides with the rise of a new peace movement. Militant student organizations languishing in the 1980s are reborn in new forms. Angry texts from the late 1960s and early 1970s (usually misogynist and/or homophobic) have been recycled, and newly created imitations are cropping up. Not surprisingly, they have been released by major publishers who stand to profit from the revival of this early activist literature, as well as from the debate that is occurring between Chicana and Chicano scholars around gender and sexual orientation issues.[106] What those of us who have been through this cycle may lose sight of is the merit and purpose of those original voices. While it is necessary for us to critique this literature, it is incumbent upon us to remember and point out the valuable role these innovative texts played in our historical development and personal processing. We must also keep in mind how they may stimulate and inspire those Mexican Americans who are just now developing a resistant consciousness—for whom the revitalization cycle has just begun. We must let them go through the process with enough guidance to push them into their own critical thinking, but not so much negativity that we silence them. Shedding their own white masks, discovering their brown hearts, and coming to recognize how they have been hurt and shamed in an oppressive society earns them the right to process this information at their own pace then to join a revitalization cycle in this particular time and space. These new Chicana/o activists will figure out their own path.

New Visions

As I said previously, the revitalization cycle is repetitive and nonlinear. It is also contextual. Geography, time period, and social location may all influence our position in the cycle or the usefulness of returning to any phase.

Elements from each stage may exist separately and simultaneously with any other stage, or people may get stuck in one phase and never move on, especially in small clusters of individuals. There will always be groups that form around single issues and never stray from their original focus or broaden their view. It may be necessary for an individual, or the group, to return to certain phases in response to the particular kind of backlash we face at any time. As Chicanas/os go through healing processes, they may need to repeat the cycle with a new consciousness. Because of heterosexism in most cultures, many people politically aware in other categories, still have not entered or conceptualized a cycle based on sexual orientation. To do so might come to mean acquiring a more flexible identity and the ability to recognize the relationship between various forms of oppression and the extent to which we are forced to choose one half of a binary pair over the other.[107] At some level we must know that we cannot expect equality unless all forms of discrimination are eliminated at the institutional and systematic levels, *and* we stop performing them in our personal lives.

Eliminating all forms of oppression is an ideal that no single person can hope to achieve—nor can we expect complete agreement. But a cultural shift does not insist on total cooperation, it only requires the force of strong coalitions willing to work around and respect differences for a larger goal. It also means dumping distrust and paranoia, accepting that the people who should be our allies really are, even though we may have differences and make mistakes. Once we begin to see ourselves as part of a larger community seeking transformation, we have no excuse for continuing to act solely on our sense of alienation. After the revolution, Lucha Corpi tells us in *Delia's Song*, "That's when the real struggle begins."[108] That is when we must fight to maintain connections, stay with complexity, work our way through our differences and the despair that comes with defeats along the way. Given human nature, even the successes can sometimes wreak havoc in organizations. With outright suppression, we often bond in our mutual frustration and anger, but neither of these emotions can sustain a movement. "The challenge" to coalition building, Caryn McTighe Musil says, "is to hold on simultaneously to these two contradictory truths . . . we are the same and we are different."[109] Gloria Anzaldúa, recognizing this, sees total unity as a utopian myth, but she nevertheless envisions a social movement in which "affinity" groups can gather together.[110]

By making cycles and cultural process obvious, we can show newly conscious Mexican American women not only the development of Chicana feminism, but the way the repetition of the cycle gives reformers another chance. We can also show them the residue of earlier battles, the changes that remained however intense the backlash. When we look at history, it is true that we see repetition. Yet some reform is maintained, knowledge gained, and evidence does exist of widespread cultural shifts. We must also use the cycle to illustrate the unceasing imperialist agenda, and the danger in thinking that we have come far enough. Using the basic model, we can point out convergent and divergent thinking among people of similarly oppressed groups, and talk about our "overlapping communities of struggle."[111] This makes possible conceptualizing ways of creating lasting coalitions, maintaining momentum, and thus increasing the effectiveness of the cycle toward truly profound social transformation.

One of the ways we might strengthen alliances with other oppressed peoples is to build a foundation from which we can, without judgment, listen to other peoples' perspectives and experienced realities. This can only be accomplished if we have a solid sense of ourselves and a firm political understanding of our position in the world. It also means shedding our learned competitiveness and the kind of individualism that leads to isolation from others. We must develop a sense of trust in a larger vision and assume that disagreeing over the details is healthy and to be expected. It means we have much to learn from others, not that we need to withdraw.[112] "Constructive solidarity requires pride in oneself." This is true because "pride carries with it an indignation against the abuse of any human being, including oneself, and a vast resource for perseverance and righteous struggle . . . pride contradicts both internalized oppression and internalized domination."[113]

Because the person in the subordinate position almost always knows much more about the dominant person's experience than vice versa, everyone interested in coalition work must agree to the necessity of traditionally excluded voices setting the tone during discussions. In some cases this may also include letting those same people set the agenda for activist projects. When disagreements occur within the group, it might mean assuming that those who are subject to certain types of oppression are the experts on that experience. As such, those who are in the dominant position should capitulate to their judgment. Any group declarations must reflect the major concerns of all members. When articulating the history and experience of oppression, setting up guidelines or structuring organizations, and determining resistance tactics, the dominant members must defer to the traditionally marginalized voices. Otherwise, Anzaldúa reminds us, "the group will automatically operate under" dominant "assumptions . . . definitions . . . strategies."[114]

Though we know that it is impossible to view one form of oppression in isolation because they are all connected by their common origin in the imperialist impulse, we rarely grasp the significance of how these variations act in harmony to limit, control, and destroy countless lives inside and outside our identified communities. Most people involved in social justice work can identify many of the ways in which human action—based on binary thinking—damages the earth. But few of us are willing to think about the ways in which that dreaded binary thinking may actually help us to maintain coalitions. For historically specific groups, this might mean that our racialized, ethnic, gendered, or sexualized identities must remain opposite a mainstream "us," but in a regulated way. As long as we understand it as a strategy—and thus keep it from turning us into unreasonable demagogues—it may help us to weather our differences with other progressives and keep our resistant focus on the power brokers. Understanding it as a political strategy may also help us to delineate this use of it from true acts of internalized dominance. We could then deal with the guilt or denial that keeps us from taking responsibility for the ways we, our community, or our institutions have acted oppressively in the lives of others. This kind of guilt and denial blocks us from challenging the kinds of dominance that benefit us personally.[115] Thus we must work to eliminate it from our lives.

To be effective, the struggle for social justice cannot be a provincial battle though it may begin that way in the early stages of a revitalization cycle. Thus we are morally obligated to understand not only our own difficulty, but the plight of similarly oppressed peoples. While it may be impossible to know all of the historical details or political demands and parameters of another group, we can easily see in their experience certain elements of oppression that we share. While we may cling to our own groups for a variety of reasons, including a feeling of home-like safety and not having to constantly explain our worldview, we must always know that our fight is not unique, nor more worthy than that of another oppressed group. As single group perspectives and isolation in regional or national landscapes give way to global views, fallacies present in U.S. proclamations of democratic pluralism become even more obvious. The ominous universe of transnational corporations require us to understand the political ideology of this country, of capitalism, and the imperialist impulses inherent in the most powerful. It also requires complex conceptualizations. The pervasiveness of exclusionary practices worldwide provides evidence that we must act and think in a variety of locations simultaneously—that we must develop the ability to understand multilevel historical contexts and political processes.

While we may have conflicts with other Latinos over scarce resources, class differences, and tensions caused by internalized hostilities, it remains important for Chicanas/os to know the history of exploitation and dominance in the relationship between the United States and Latin America, not just Mexico. As members of an oppressed group, we already have the tools to understand how power works in unequal relationships. This knowledge, which is both academically and viscerally learned, seems basic to meeting the demands of analyzing race, class, gender, and sexual orientation issues—personally, locally, or globally. While we may be better equipped to understand them in a U.S. context and to find allies in similarly oppressed communities within this country, we cannot ignore the position of "our" nation in a world context. We must know the meaning and the effect of being subjugated by imperialism even as we understand our privilege and power in the world as U.S. citizens. If we, as Chicanas, ask Chicanos, white women, or elite Latinos from other countries to think about internalized oppression and power differentials, then we must be prepared to do so also.[116]

Those of us in the academy must resist the institutional pressures that separate us from our communities. Lucha Corpi's Delia tells us that private entrance into mainstream culture does not mean the end of our struggle as a people. "I belong to a privileged class now. I have a doctorate—whatever that means. Chicanos can't afford not to be ruled by their ghosts. We're like ants who carry their dead on their shoulders."[117] Perhaps we need to (re)imagine things like multiculturalism—despite mainstream or institutional ineptness in implementing the concept—in order to make this a better environment for students and faculty of color.

We must also devote some time to organizations and groups outside the academy. Working in service to our ideals and actively supporting resistance efforts can be beneficial to the spirit. It brings meaning to our lives, puts us in contact with dynamic people, and increases our knowledge of other people's experience. In addition to fulfilling our need to respond to oppression, activism involves us in a moral quest, keeps us from isolating ourselves as it pushes us toward groups less alienating than the dominant culture, and teaches us to confront and challenge those who exert unjust authority over us.[118] The revitalization of our political spirit and resistant identities can be an emotional catharsis. It can give us the energy to continue to swim against the tide lest we all drown in arrogance, unearned power, selfishness, and greed.

While it is certainly a political necessity that we continue to struggle against injustice, we should not be afraid to think or talk about it as fundamental to human psychological development. We all have an emotional need to feel connected to the past as well as to a community—to be part of a collective action in service to others. It is this need that propels us toward anger and protest when we realize the contradiction between the history of oppression and liberal democratic ideals. It is then that we begin to understand our personal pain as part of a communal process. In some ways, the tensions for each generation as they enter the cycle parallel the struggles of the previous ages. The newly politicized must critique and as necessary change the existing models that are the legacy of earlier movements. But they must not get so caught up in this that they lose sight of a genuinely revolutionary vision. Until a fundamental and profound transformation occurs, the frustration caused by inequality will be rekindled and the cycle begun anew. Limited modifications may give us hope, but they alone will not erase the grief and rage of oppressed groups nor provide deliverance for the oppressors.

Within the community, the dissimilarity in perspectives between Chicanas and Chicanos, lesbians and straight women, or gays and heterosexual men means that we will select different cultural symbols and traditions to have meaning in our lives. We may be moved to revise history in our own way, and find different ways to protest and work toward change. It is likely we will focus the primary part of our resistance efforts on particular issues. In fact, it is neither desirable nor strategically sound for all of us to be doing exactly the same resistance work, but having a focus should not inhibit coalitions or solidarity when such things are required.[119] The ability to make connections is often difficult, but we must behave as if we know it is absolutely possible and necessary. We have to do it despite the hardship and real dangers involved. Such a commitment increases our capacity to perpetually incorporate new voices, to critically think about and acknowledge questions and challenges as they arise, and to refocus on a larger vision. An awareness of each other and constant sorting out or choosing between strategies is crucial so we can create solidarity but not deny difference. Communication and coalition are necessary to keep our views flexible enough to prevent us from locking into incorrect premises and opinions that are no longer viable.[120]

While some theoretical shifts simply reflect the academy's voracious appetite for new language (but not necessarily new concepts), we should embrace the need new scholars have to question and challenge old models and methods. In working toward a broader view for Chicana/o scholarship and creativity, we cannot become so rigid that we exclude new voices. If we can agree that we are headed in the same general direction—away from the normalizing mechanisms and imperialist impulses of an oppressive society—then perhaps we could come to view our disagreements in a different way. Perhaps we could begin to see that arguments within our selected groups and coalitions are not battles we must win, but lovely dances we do to deepen our political relationships.

Notes

Chapter 1

1. Rosemary Catacalos, "(There Has To Be) Something More than Everything," *Daughters of the Fifth Sun: A Collection of Latina Fiction and Poetry,* ed. Bryce Milligan, Mary Guerrero Mulligan, and Angela de Hoyas (New York: Riverhead Books, 1995), 58.

2. Demetria Martínez, "The Conquest," in *Chicana (W)rites on Word and Film,* ed. María Herrera-Sobek and Helena María Viramontes (Berkeley: Third Woman, 1995).

3. Melba Vasquez, for instance, tells us that "a person who is subjected to a great deal of racist treatment can be afflicted by powerlessness, learned helplessness, depression, anxiety, and even post-traumatic stress disorder." Melba J. T. Vasquez, "Latinas," in *Women of Color: Integrating Ethnic and Gender Identities in Psychotherapy,* ed. Lillian Comas-Díaz and Beverly Greene (New York: Guilford, 1994), 343. These symptoms, of course, can also result from repeated exposure to a variety of oppressive mechanisms. See also Elena Avila, "La Llorona Has Found Her Children," in *Chicano Studies: Critical Connection between Research and Community,* ed. Teresa Córdova (National Association for Chicano Studies, 1992) on the effect of trauma on individuals in our community. A psychiatric nurse and *curandera,* Avila uses her knowledge of psychology and her culturally based healing practices and ceremonies to work with patients suffering from PTSD. Manuel Ramirez, III, has written articles and a text titled *Multicultural/Multiracial Psychology: Mestizo Perspectives in Personality and Mental Health* (Northvale, NJ: Jason Aronson, Inc., 1998), that also touch on the subject of how history and contemporary racism combine to shape the Mexican American psyche. Published in 1995, Eduardo and Bonnie Duran's book, *Native American Post-Colonial Psychology,* includes an extensive section on post-traumatic stress disorder experienced by Native Americans and how it is passed on to succeeding generations. Eduardo Duran and Bonnie Duran, *Native American Post-Colonial Psychology* (Albany: State University of New York Press, 1995). See also the work that Black feminist writer bell hooks has been doing on love. In the last chapter of her book, *Outlaw Culture,* for instance, she discusses the way that trauma has played out in the African American community. In 1998, the Durans teamed up with Maria Yellow Horse Braveheart to contribute an article titled, "Native American and the Trauma of History" to a collection edited by Russell Thornton called, *Studying Native America: Problems and Perspectives.* Syndicated newspaper columnist Roberto Rodríguez (who had attended my paper presentation at NACCS) has also explored this topic. The victim of police brutality, Rodríguez has done a lot of thinking about the links between rage and the need to heal psychologically from trauma that can be linked both to history and contemporary racism. Most recently, as I was in the final stages of

preparing this manuscript for publication (and to make late use of them), I ran across two articles by historian Yolanda Chávez Leyva in the September and October issues of the Esperanza Peace and Justice Center's newsletter. She is working on a larger project, which I assume will become a book at some point.

4. Renato Rosaldo, personal conversation, Mexico City, NACCS Conference, 1998.
5. Ana Castillo, *Massacre of the Dreamers: Essays on Xicanisma* (Albuquerque: University of New Mexico, 1995), 148.
6. Gloria Anzaldúa, *Borderlands/La Frontera: The New Mestiza* (San Francisco: Spinsters/Aunt Lute, 1987), 3.
7. Elena Avila, "La Llorona Has Found Her Children," *Chicano Studies: Critical Connection between Research and Community*, ed. Teresa Córdova (National Association for Chicano Studies, 1992), 68.
8. Root includes emotional abuse, racism, anti-Semitism, poverty, heterosexism, dislocation, ageism, and so forth among the stress factors that lead to "insidious trauma." She says the effects are cumulative and compounded by experience over the course of a lifetime. Maria P. P. Root, "Reconstructing the Impact of Trauma on Personality," in *Personality and Psychotherapy*, ed. L. S. Brown and M. Ballou (New York: Guilford, 1992).
9. Root "Reconstructing the Impact"; Olivia M. Espín, in "Feminist Approaches," in *Women of Color: Integrating Ethnic and Gender Identities in Psychotherapy*, ed. Lillian Comas-Díaz and Beverly Greene (New York: Guilford, 1994), 268–269.
10. Examples of events that might cause post-traumatic stress: witnessing the killing of a spiritual leader or someone thought to be a caretaker or protector; having family members disappear who are later found brutally murdered; witnessing the severing of body parts, beheadings, hangings, and rapes (especially of a parent or child); seeing the murder or beating of a parent or child; experiencing the loss of more than one family member at a time, or of a significant portion of your community; witnessing or experiencing torture and persecution, solitary exile or confinement, or gang rape; imprisonment without cause and police brutality. Though mainstream people tend to think of such things in association with other countries, many of these events have been part of our history, and continue to be the reality for many people living in the United States. Juan García-Castañón and Gordon G. Cappelletty, "A Preliminary Report on Continuous-Traumatic Stress in a Northern California Central American Refugee Community," in *Community Empowerment and Chicano Scholarship*, ed. Mary Romero and Cordelia Candelaria (Berkeley, CA: National Association for Chicano Studies, 1992), 91–92.
11. Avila, "La Llorona," 68.
12. Lorna Dee Cervantes, "Poem for the Young White Man Who Asked Me How I, an Intelligent, Well Read Person, Could Believe in the War between the Races," in *Making Face, Making Soul/Haciendo Caras: Creative and Critical Perspectives by Women of Color*, ed. Gloria Anzaldúa (San Francisco: Aunt Lute, 1990), 4–5.
13. Castillo, *Massacre of the Dreamers*, 156.
14. Alentícia Tijerina, "Notes on Oppression and Violence," in *Making Face, Making Soul/Haciendo Caras: Creative and Critical Perspectives by Women of Color*, ed. Gloria Anzaldúa (San Francisco: Aunt Lute, 1990), 171–172.
15. For examples, see Gloria Anzaldúa's "Coatlicue State," in *Borderlands/La Frontera* (San Francisco: Spinster/Aunt Lute, 1987); Lucha Corpi, *Delia's Song* (Houston: Arte Público, 1989); the short story, "Caribou Cafe" in Helena Viramontes, *The Moths and Other Stories* (Houston: Arte Público, 1985); and "One Holy Night," in *Woman Hollering Creek*, ed. Sandra Cisneros (New York: Random House, 1991).
16. Pat Mora, *Nepantla: Essays from the Land in the Middle* (Albuquerque: University of New Mexico, 1993), 107.
17. Gloria Anzaldúa, "El día de la chicana," *Infinite Divisions: An Anthology of Chicana Literature* (Tucson: University of Arizona Press, 1993), 82.
18. See George Lipsitz, *The Possessive Investment in Whiteness* (Philadelphia: Temple University Press, 1998).
19. Jeanette Rodriguez, *Our Lady of Guadalupe: Faith and Empowerment among Mexican-American Women* (Austin: University of Texas, 1994), 69.
20. Emma Pérez, "Gulf Dreams," *Chicana Lesbians: The Girls Our Mothers Warned Us About*, ed. Carla Trujillo (Berkeley, CA: Third Woman Press, 1991), 105.

21. Cherríe Moraga, *The Last Generation: Prose and Poetry* (Boston: South End Press, 1993), 187.

22. See Castillo, *Massacre of the Dreamers*.

23. Irene I. Blea, *La Chicana and the Intersection of Race, Class, and Gender* (New York: Praeger, 1992), 36.

24. Elizabeth Salas, *Soldaderas in the Mexican Military: Myth and History* (Austin: University of Texas, 1990), 25–35; Antonia I. Castañeda, "The Political Economy of Nineteenth Century Stereotypes of Californianas," *Between Borders: Essays on Mexicana/Chicana History*, ed. Adelaida R. Del Castillo (Encino, CA: Floricanto Press, 1990), 213–228. Elizabeth Salas tells us that this shift in gendered deities was an "uneven process." As one might guess, it did not take place overnight. Aztec elite, who were not without opposition, first had to ruin the reputation of the Earth Mothers, turning them into monsters. Salas, *Soldaderas*, 5–6.

25. For an expanded discussion of these processes, see James Diego Vigil, *From Indians to Chicanos: The Dynamics of Mexican American Culture* (Prospect Heights, IL: Waveland Press, 1980).

26. Vigil, *From Indians to Chicanos*, 9, 16–34; Nancy Boyd-Franklin and Nydia García-Preto, "Family Therapy: A Closer Look at African American and Hispanic Women," in *Women of Color: Integrating Ethnic and Gender Identities in Psychotherapy*, ed. Lillian Comas-Díaz and Beverly Greene (New York: Guilford, 1994), 239–262; Joan W. Moore, *Going Down to the Barrio: Homeboys and Homegirls in Change* (Philadelphia: Temple University Press, 1991), 11–68.

27. Mary Clearing Sky, "Historic Trauma and Unresolved Grieving in Native American Populations," Paper presented at the CIC Conference University of Illinois, Champaign-Urbana 31 October, 1992; Maria Felix-Ortiz and Michael D. Newcomb, "Risk and Protective Factors for Drug Use Among Latino and White Adolescents," *Hispanic Journal of Behavioral Sciences* 14, no. 3 (August 1992): 292–293.

28. Caméla Jaramillo "Postscript," *Making Face, Making Soul/Haciendo Caras: Creative and Critical Perspectives by Women of Color*, ed. Gloria Anzaldúa (San Francisco: Aunt Lute, 1990), 78.

29. Rodriguez, *Our Lady of Guadalupe*, 1, Vigil, *From Indians to Chicanos*, 6–7.

30. Lourdes Torres, "The Construction of the Self in U.S. Latina Autobiographies," in *Third World Women and the Politics of Feminism*, ed. Chandra Talpade Mohanty, Ann Russo, and Lourdes Torres (Bloomington: Indiana University Press, 1991), 275.

31. See Tucsona writer Silviana Wood's story "Dreams by Appointment Only," in *Woman of Her Word: Hispanic Women Write* (2nd ed.), ed. Evangelina Vigil (Houston: Arte Público, 1987) for a poignant look at the psychological hoops through which Latinas on welfare must jump—even with well-intentioned social workers.

32. Clearing Sky, "Historic Trauma,"; Avila, "La Llorona," 69; Beverly Engel MFCC, *The Right to Innocence: Healing the Trauma of Childhood Sexual Abuse* (Los Angeles: Jeremy Tarcher, 1989), 184–188.

33. Espín, "Feminist Approaches," 269.

34. Clearing Sky, "Historic Trauma,"; Espín, "Feminist Approaches," 268–269; Beverly Greene, "Lesbian Women of Color: Triple Jeopardy," in *Women of Color: Integrating Ethnic and Gender Identities in Psychotherapy*, ed. Lillian Comas-Díaz and Beverly Greene (New York: Guilford, 1994).

35. Carey McWilliams dealt with this denial of the true history in Chapter 2, "The Fantasy Heritage" in *North From Mexico: The Spanish-Speaking People of the United States* (New York: Greenwood, 1968). Carl Gutiérrez-Jones approaches the problem through literature and art—analyzing representations that hide the true nature of Anglo American conquest history. In his book, *Rethinking the Borderlands* (Berkeley: University of California Press, 1995), Gutiérrez-Jones calls the chapter "Mission Denial: The Development of Historical Amnesia." See also, Helen Delpar, *The Enormous Vogue of Things Mexican: Cultural Relations between the United States and Mexico, 1920–1935* (Tuscaloosa: University of Alabama, 1992).

36. Corpi, *Delia's Song*, 157–158.

37. Though many Native American and Chicana scholars have found his analysis problematic, see Ramón Gutiérrez's, *When Jesus Came, the Corn Mothers Went Away: Marriage, Sexuality, and Power in New Mexico, 1500–1846* (Palo Alto, CA: Stanford University Press, 1991). Although he fails to fully explore the violence with which the Spanish incorporated or dispensed with Indian people, he does present a picture of the Catholic concepts that

attempted to teach shame and guilt. In Antonia I. Castañeda's contribution "Sexual Violence in the Politics and Policies of Conquest: Amerindian Women and the Spanish Conquest of Alta California," in *Building with Our Hands: New Directions in Chicana Studies*, ed. Adela de la Torre and Beatríz M. Pesquera (Berkeley: University of California, 1993), we learn of some of the despicable acts committed against Indian women by the Spanish. She quotes a passage in a letter written by Fray Junipero Serra from the northern frontier in 1773 to the Viceroy in Mexico City, in which he describes the morning ritual of soldiers who would ride out to the rancherías. As the people fled at the sight of them, the soldiers would lasso Indian women, who were then raped in front of men, who were shot if they attempted to rescue the women. Serra's letters, Castañeda tells us, are typical of many others, of journal entries, and histories written by Spanish chroniclers Bernal Díaz del Castillo and Bartolemé de las Casas "Sexual Violence in the Politics and Policies of Conquest" (15). Attacks on women, she tells us in another article, were "the first recorded acts of Spanish domination and aggression." Antonia I. Casteñada, "Presidarias y Pobladoras: The Journey North and Life in Frontier California," in *Chicana Critical Issues*, ed. Norma Alarcón, et al., Mujeres Activas en Letras y Cambio Social (Berkeley, CA: Third Woman Press, 1993), 78.

38. See also Tey Diana Rebolledo, "Mujeres Andariegas: Good Girls and Bad," 9 in *Women Singing in the Snow: A Cultural Analysis of Chicana Literature* (Tucson: University of Arizona, 1995), for the legacy of Spanish/Catholic thought on women, women's bodies as the site of sin, and the construction of "good" and "bad" images for women. See Patricia Preciado Martin, *Songs My Mother Sang to Me: An Oral History of Mexican-American Women* (Tucson: University of Arizona, 1992) for a look at how women's lives were conducted within this social order, during the latter part of the nineteenth and early twentieth centuries.

39. Douglas Monroy, *Thrown among Strangers: The Making of Mexican Culture in Frontier California* (Berkeley: University of California Press, 1990), 435–440; Castañeda, "Presidarias y Pobladoras," 73–94; Rodríguez, *Our Lady of Guadalupe* 1–14.

40. Sandra Cisneros, "Guadalupe the Sex Goddess: Unearthing the Racy Past of Mexico's Most Famous Virgin," *Ms* (July/September 1996), 44.

41. Castillo, *Massacre of the Dreamers*, 70.

42. Castillo, *Massacre of the Dreamers*, 71.

43. Not all Chicana Lesbians experience a horrified reaction from their families when coming out. Many factors can intervene to mitigate the effect of traditional Spanish/Catholic teachings. Families may be more enlightened through their own insights and previous experiences, the existence of homosexuality already in (and out in) the family, through acculturation or education, and through empathy and the recognition of oppression. In a poem titled "Mother," Odilia Mendez tells of her mother's subjugation and abuse by her father. At the end she says, "I put my arms around you and love you, Mother, / hoping that I can love as well as you . . . when you need me the most. / To women, from separate worlds / made from the same clay. / I reveal my lovers to you, Mother, and you don't object. / You tell me you know that I am different." Odilia Mendez, "Mother," in *Compañeras: Latina Lesbians—An Anthology* (New York: Latina Lesbian History Project, 1987), 168. Juanita M. Sánchez tells a similar story in her poem "Paso a paso." In it she describes all the things various members of her family wanted her to do, and how she simply took her own path. She ends the poem hinting at their disappointment, but finding acceptance, nonetheless. "nothing turned out like / they wanted but / my mother did say, / 'if you want to be with a woman, / que le hace, as long as you/re happy.'" Juanita Sánchez, "Paso a paso," in *Chicana Lesbians: The Girls Our Mothers Warned Us About*, ed. Carla Trujillo (Berkeley, CA: Third Woman Press, 1991), 15. Aletícia Tijerina, "I am the Lost Daughter of My Mama's House," in *Compañeras: Latina Lesbians—An Anthology* (New York: Latina Lesbian History Project, 1987), 38.

44. Engel, *Right to Innocence*, 10.

45. See also E. D. Hernández, "Discussion, Discourse and Direction: The Dilemmas of a Chicana Lesbian," Emma Pérez, "Sexuality and Discourse: Notes from a Chicana Survivor," Carla Trujillo's "Chicana Lesbians: Fear and Loathing in the Chicano Community," *Chicana Lesbians: The Girls Our Mothers Warned Us About*, ed. Carla Trujillo (Berkeley, CA: Third Woman Press, 1991).

46. Anzaldúa, *Borderlands/La Frontera*, 21.

47. Anzaldúa, *Borderlands/La Frontera*, 20.

48. Clearing Sky, "Historic Trauma," Engel; *Right to Innocence*, 9–16.
49. Marina Rivera, "Mestiza," in *Infinite Divisions: An Anthology of Chicana Literature*, ed. Tey Diana Rebolledo and Eliana S. Rivero (Tucson: University of Arizona, 1993), 99.
50. Clearing Sky, "Historic Trauma,"; Engel, 41–84.
51. Clearing Sky, "Historic Truama."
52. This is currently being debated in psychotherapy literature. One school sees shame and guilt as distinctly separate categories of cognitive, affective response. Another sees guilt as simply another manifestation of shame, which is categorized as one of nine innate affects. For the first view, see Stuart Schneiderman, *Saving Face: America and the Politics of Shame* (New York: Knopf, 1995). For the second view, see Gershen Kaufman, *Shame: The Power of Caring* (Rochester, VT: Schenkman, 1992).
53. Vicki Underland-Rosow, *Shame: Spiritual Suicide* (Shorewood, MN: Waterford Publications, 1996). Also available at www.ic.mankato.mn.us/web/shame/shame.html.
54. Kaufman, *Shame*, 73.
55. Cervantes, "Poem for the Young," 4–5.
56. Gloria Anzaldúa, "La Prieta," *This Bridge Called My Back: Writings by Radical Women of Color*, ed. Cherríe Moraga and Gloria Anzaldúa (New York: Kitchen Table Press, 1983), 201.
57. Carmen Morones, "Grace," in *Making Face, Making Soul/Haciendo Caras: Creative and Critical Perspectives of Women of Color*, ed. Gloria Anzaldúa (San Francisco: Aunt Lute Foundation, 1990), 243.
58. See the chapter "It Is Painful" in Tomás Rivera's, *And the Earth Did Not Devour Him* (Houston: Arte Público Press, 1995), for an example. Here, the son is fearful and ashamed because he has been suspended from school after hitting a white boy who has been taunting him with racial slurs. He feels shame because his going to school has been so important to his family, and he feels he is letting them all down—and also that he may be living up to the criticism of Mexicans in general by not going to school. Rudolfo A. Anaya, in *Bless Me Ultima* (Berkeley: TQS Publications, 1972), tells of a similar incident in the life of his protagonist Antonio.
59. See Schneiderman's *Saving Face* in which he traces the philosophies of Alexander Hamilton (who believed in capital and free trade markets, as well as industry, but placed the nation over individual states rights) and Thomas Jefferson (who favored individual liberty and democracy). Schneiderman uses the work of Alexis de Tocqueville to show how shame in the United States has been used to promote hard labor and the cohesiveness of the family unit in service to Hamilton's and Jefferson's views.
60. See Thomas L. Dumm, *Democracy and Punishment: Disciplinary Origins of the United States* (Madison: University of Wisconsin Press, 1987), 6.
61. See Alfredo Mirandé, *Gringo Justice* (Notre Dame, IN: University of Notre Dame Press, 1987.)
62. Kaufman, *Shame*, xiii.
63. Kaufman, *Shame*, 37.
64. Clearing Sky, "Historic Trauma"; Lillian Comas-Díaz, "Feminist Therapy with Hispanic/Latina Women: Myth or Reality?" in *The Psychopathology of Everyday Racism and Sexism*, ed. Lenora Fulani (New York: Harrington Press, 1988), 39–59.
65. Clearing Sky, "Historic Trauma."
66. "Repeated attacks on our native tongue diminish our sense of self. The attacks continue throughout our lives . . . if you want to really hurt me, talk badly about my language. Ethnic identity is twin skin to linguistic identity—I am my language. Until I can take pride in my language, I cannot take pride in myself . . . I cannot accept the legitimacy of myself." Anzaldúa, *Borderlands/La Frontera*, 58–59. Melba J. T. Vasquez, "Latinas," in *Women of Color: Integrating Ethnic and Gender Identities in Psychotherapy*, ed. Lillian Comas-Díaz and Beverly Greene (New York: Guilford, 1994), 121–122.
67. Anzaldúa, *Borderlands/La Frontera*, 58.
68. Comas-Díaz, "Feminist Therapy," 43–42.
69. Similar tensions can also occur between Mexican immigrants and Mexican Americans. Mexicans may also be from elite families and fail to empathize with Chicanas/os. Or if they have been extremely economically deprived, they may see life in the United States as so much better than they might have had at home that they whole-heartedly embrace the culture (to which they have yet to assimilate). There are, of course, many poor Mexicans who

come here knowing both possibilities—that they are economically better off here in the United States, but who also recognize the flaws in U.S. society around race, class, gender, and sexual identity. These people are likely to know the social and economic history of the United States from a Mexican perspective and thus quickly adopt much of Chicana/o political ideology.

70. A study done on a Central American community in California showed that about one-third of the subjects had definite PTSD symptoms. Another third met some of the criteria. And the final third had "no manifestation of the disorder at all." I have no formal statistics or evidence of a similar study among Mexican Americans, so I cannot say that this three-way split applies. I would guess that the percentage of those actually suffering from PTSD is less than 33 percent because Mexican Americans are not currently refugees of the kind of violence that has taken place in Central America in the past twenty years. But, I do think at various times in our history it has been in greater evidence—though we were not testing for such things in 1848, 1910, or 1930. My concern is for the way in which the legacy of traumatic events and the associated psychological damage has continued to mark us as a people, as well as the way in which our social conditions maintain, (re)create, and reinforce that suffering. Even for those of us who exhibit only remnants of the original anxiety, we should be aware of how it might make us vulnerable to contemporary stress in equally harmful ways. García-Castañón and Cappelletty tell us that individuals who meet only some of the criteria are still at risk for developing the disorder in the future given the right circumstances. Juan García-Castañón and Gordon G. Cappelletty, "A Preliminary Report on Continuous-Traumatic Stress in a Northern California Central American Refugee Community," in *Community Empowerment and Chicano Scholarship*, ed. Mary Romero and Cordelia Candelaria (Berkeley, CA: National Association for Chicano Studies, 1992), 93. Clearing Sky, "Historic Trauma,"; Engel, *Right to Innocence*, 3–16; García-Castañón and Cappelletty, "A Preliminary Report," 93; American Psychiatric Association, *DSM-III: Diagnostic and Statistical Manual of Mental Disorders*, (3rd ed., rev.) (Washington, DC: APA, 1988), 247.

71. Clearing Sky, "Historic Trauma,"; Engel, *Right to Innocence*, 94–96.

72. Without soul you are without hope. You cannot take heart or be encouraged by anything. Gloria Anzaldúa, "Bridge, Drawbridge, Sandbar or Island: Lesbians-of-Color Hacienda Alianzas," in *Bridges of Power: Women's Multicultural Alliances*, ed. Lisa Albrecht and Rose M. Brewer (Philadelphia: New Society, 1990), 229.

73. Clearing Sky, "Historic Trauma,"; Engel, *Right to Innocence*, 9–16.

74. Jaramillo, "Postscript" 78.

75. Kaufman, *Shame*, 73–75.

76. Avila, "La Llorona," 68.

77. Clearing Sky, "Historic Trauma,"; APA, *DSM-III*.

78. Clearing Sky, "Historic Trauma."

79. As scholars, Chicanos trained in traditional methods, who either felt a natural affinity with these conventions or had no choice but to conform in order to succeed in the academy, may also respond dismissively out of the perception that they are being attacked, blamed, or betrayed by Chicanas. Women writers and theorists who expose the emotional force in the culture and the ways in which gender is (often painfully) inscribed in ethnicity can be dismissed for our lack of objectivity, trivialized for dealing with the psychological effects of pain rather than purely political or economic issues (as if the "human factor" were unimportant to such things). We may be ignored for not producing concrete data or purely descriptive history. While this can be a simple disagreement about scholarly methods, it may also be a way of avoiding the pain and the reality of the damage that has been inflicted. But there is another dimension to their criticism. This can be an example of internalized shame that is capable of autonomously activating through an inner or self-perceived cue, rather than an external one. In his book *Rethinking the Borderlands*, Carl Gutiérrez-Jones presents the problem of editors and teachers ignoring Chicana representations of male violence against women, either because it upsets proud nationalistic illusions of a united voice or because it betrays the romantic image of the nurturing community. But, he says, how are women to write about oppression without addressing one of its "most blatant expressions: rape?" Gutiérrez-Jones, *Rethinking the Borderlands*, 110.

80. Engel, *Right to Innocence*, 7.

81. Of course we also see these painful things in the prose, poetry, and autobiographies of male writers. But male theorists, critics, historians, and so forth do not generally see this subjective experience or expression as an appropriate topic for "objective" scholarship. Though this too is changing as men begin to see, understand, and deal with their own wounds, as well as their ambivalence around the social constructions of masculinity.

82. See Gloria Anzaldúa's confrontation with what she calls the "shadow beast," in *Borderlands/La Frontera.*

83. Avila, "La Llorona," 68.

84. Avila, "La Llorona," 69.

85. Edna Escamill, "Corazon de una anciana," in *Making Face, Making Soul/Haciendo Caras: Creative and Critical Perspectives by Women of Color*, ed. Gloria Anzaldúa, (San Francisco: Aunt Lute, 1990), 133.

86. Anzaldúa, *Borderlands*, 87, 88.

87. Engel, *Right to Innocence*, 48; Anzaldúa, *Borderlands.*

88. Engel, *Right to Innocence*, 87.

89. Avila, "La Llorona," 68.

90. Engel, *Right to Innocence*, 88; Espín, "Feminist Approaches," 273–274; Lillian Comas-Díaz and Beverly Greene, "Connections and Disconnections" and "Gender and Ethnicity in the Healing Process," in *Women of Color: Integrating Ethnic and Gender Identities in Psychotherapy*, ed. Lillian Comas-Díaz and Beverly Greene (New York: Guilford, 1994), 364–366; Vasquez, "Latinas," 134.

91. If as children we express anger and are berated for doing so in a way that makes us feel we are bad (rather than teaching us that our action was an inappropriate expression of anger), we may begin to interpret things that make us angry as cues to respond with shame. This confusion can carry over into adulthood if we express anger and our feelings are ignored or trivialized. In order to respond in healthy ways, we must tune our affective system to recognize and value genuine anger, rather than to automatically respond with shame. Kaufman, *Shame*, 44–45.

92. Kaufman, *Shame*, 44–45; Comas-Díaz and Greene, *Women of Color*, 378; Engel, *Right to Innnocence*, 91.

93. Engel, *Right to Innocence*, 92.

94. Engel, *Right to Innocence*, 91; Espín, "Feminist Approaches," 273–274; Comas-Díaz and Greene, *Women of Color*, 364–366; Vasquez, "Latinas," 134.

95. This type of response to the world may also be primarily or secondarily the result of chemical imbalance in the brain, linked with or separate from traumatic events or memories.

96. See Bruno Bettleheim and M. Janowitz, *The Dynamics of Prejudice* (New York: Harper & Row, 1950), 108.

97. Avila, "La Llorona," 69.

98. Luis J. Rodriguez, *Always Running—La Vida Loca: Gang Days in L.A.* (Willimantic, CT: Curbstone Press, 1993).

99. Engel, *Right to Innocence*, 1982.

100. In the past several years, many Chicanas/os have been invited by Native Americans to take part in sweats and other healing or visionary rituals. Some choose to participate out of a deep sense of returning to some lost part of their indigenous culture; others, like whites, are desperately searching for spirituality outside organized Western or Eastern religions. Some of us choose not to embark on this journey, feeling that it is not something that belongs to us. It is a road with many pitfalls and must be traveled carefully and with respect. In discussing this with several Native Americans, most of them Lakota, Dakota, or Ojibway, some are welcoming, others puzzled, and some wary of Mexican American motivations. But a Navajo friend dismissed it immediately and finally, saying, "They can't sweat out their Spanish blood." *Donde hay amor, hay dolor.* (Where there is love, there is pain.) While I understand this sentiment, it is still very painful to contemplate.

101. Anita Valerio, "It's in My Blood, My Face—My Mother's Voice, the Way I Sweat," *This Bridge Called My Back: Writings by Radical Women of Color* (2nd ed.) ed. Cherríe Moraga and Gloria Anzaldúa (New York: Kitchen Table Press, 1983), 43.

102. Clearing Sky, "Historic Trauma,"; Engel, *Right to Innocence.*

103. Garcia-Castañón and Cappelletty, "A Preliminary Report," 95.

104. Garcia-Castañón and Cappelletty, "A Preliminary Report," 97–98.

105. Clearly this is not possible for all people. Some are only in a position to focus on physical and/or psychological survival. But those of us who have the energy and resources to be self-reflexive should not have to apologize for doing so. This is worthwhile and we can be more help to others if we are healthy. Self-protection sometimes means saying "no" to all those requests on our time and creative energy. Elena Avila writes that, "The high drive pace that the dominant society tempts us with is making us ill. Let us call upon the courage that it takes to remember all of who we are and beckon our souls back home" ("La Llorona," 69).

106. Espín, "Feminist Approaches," 269; Clearing Sky, "Historic Trauma,"; Engel, *Right to Innocence*, 142–156.

107. Anzaldúa, "El dia de la chicana," 82.

108. Tijerina, "I am the Lost Daughter," 173.

109. Clearing Sky, "Historic Trauma,"; Engel, *Right to Innocence*, 48–50, 129–170.

110. Chéla Sandoval, "Feminism and Racism: A Report on the 1981 National Women's Studies Association Conference," in *Making Face, Making Soul/Haciendo Caras: Creative and Critical Perspectives of Women of Color*, ed. Gloria Anzaldúa (San Francisco: Aunt Lute Foundation, 1990), 63.

Chapter 2

1. Lorna Dee Cervantes, "Poem for the Young White Man Who Asked How I, An Intelligent, Well-Read Person Could Believe in a War between the Races," in *Infinate Divisions: An Anthology of Chicana Literature*, ed. Tey Diana Rebolledo and Eliana S. Rivero (Tucson: University of Arizona Press, 1993), 286–287.

2. Masao Miyoshi, "Sites of Resistance in the Global Economy," in *Cultural Readings of Imperialism: Edward Said and the Gravity of History*, ed. Keith Ansell Pearson, Benita Parry, and Judith Squires (New York: St. Martin's, 1997), 49.

3. Nasrin Jewell, "Women and Work: Irani Women in the Global Economy," Public lecture for the Center for Advanced Feminist Studies Colloquium Series. University of Minnesota, Minneapolis, 8 November 1999.

4. The All-American Disney Corporation for instance, operates its cruise line out of U.S. ports and profits primarily from U.S. travelers. But its ships are registered in another country in order to avoid paying U.S. corporate taxes.

5. Miyoshi, "Sites of Resistance," 49.

6. Miyoshi, "Sites of Resistance," 49.

7. Miyoshi, "Sites of Resistance," 50.

8. Joreen's theory is that structurelessness does not exist, that without deliberate and formal organization, any group will structure itself. The strong or most aggressive will establish unquestioned authority over others and the structurelessness itself will mask this power that has no obligation to anyone else. Joreen, *The Tyranny of Structurelessness* (Pittsburgh, PA: Know, Inc., 1986).

9. Miyoshi, "Sites of Resistance," 50.

10. Ziauddin Sardar and Borin Van Loon, *Introducing Cultural Studies* (New York: Totem Books, 1998), 164.

11. In their book *Introducing Cultural Studies* Sardar and Van Loon tell us that Malaysian born intellectual Anwar Ibrahim posits the theory that the strength of Asian cultures could create a kind of symbiosis between the East and West. This would result in a mutually enriching global culture that would replace the current exploitive form of globalization.

12. José Burciaga, *Drink Cultura* (Santa Barbara: Capra Press, 1993), 57.

13. Sarder and Van Loon, *Introducing Cultural Studies*, 165.

14. "Anzaldúa to Serros" represents for me a historical, generational, and theoretical continuum, which includes Ana Castillo, Cherríe Moraga, Denise Chávez, Pat Mora, Sandra Cisneros, and Diana García among others.

15. Sardar and Van Loon, *Introducing Cultural Studies*, 166–167.

16. Miyoshi, "Sites of Resistance," 55.

17. Sardar and Van Loon, *Introducing Cultural Studies*, 162–163.

18. Sardar and Van Loon, *Introducing Cultural Studies*, 162–163.

19. Sardar and Van Loon, *Introducing Cultural Studies*, 162.

20. Sardar and Van Loon, *Introducing Cultural Studies,* 162–163.
21. Sardar and Van Loon, *Introducing Cultural Studies,* 162.
22. Sardar and Van Loon, *Introducing Cultural Studies,* 163.
23. Ben Agger, *Cultural Studies as Critical Theory* (London: Falmer Press, 1992), 173.
24. Miyoshi, "Sites of Resistance," 53.
25. Miyoshi, "Sites of Resistance," 53.
26. Miyoshi, "Sites of Resistance," 53.
27. Miyoshi, "Sites of Resistance," 54.
28. Sardar and Van Loon, *Introducing Cultural Studies,* 9.
29. I am thinking of people like Adam Smith, Descartes, Kant, Hegel, Marx, Freud, Lacan, Saussure, Gramsci, Lévi-Strauss, Habermas, Jameson, Adorno, Marcuse, Derrida, Foucault, Fanon, Bahba, Spivak, Said, Showalter, Hartmann, Cixous, Irigaray, Anzaldúa, hooks, Gilroy, Rosaura Sánchez, Sandoval, and so forth.
30. Stuart Sim and Borin Van Loon, *Introducing Critical Theory* (New York: Totem Books, 2001), 20 Sardar and Van Loon, *Introducing Cultural Studies,* 9.
31. Sim and Van Loon, *Introducing Critical Theory,* 164.
32. Agger, *Cultural Studies,* 153, 170.
33. Debra Castillo, "Response Cutting/edge," in *Latin American Women's Writing: Feminist Readings in Theory and Crisis* (New York: Clarndon Press/Oxford, 1996), 216.
34. Castillo, "Response," 216; Deborah McDowell, "Interview with Susan Fraiman," *Critical Texts: A Review of Theory and Criticism* 6, no. 3: 13–29.
35. Edén Torres, "Ella que tiene jefes y no los ve, se queda en cuerros," in *Is Academic Feminism Dead? Theory and Practice,* ed. Social Justice Group at the Center for Advanced Feminist Studies, University of Minnesota (New York: NYU Press, 2000).
36. Miyoshi, "Sites of Resistance," 55.
37. Miyoshi, "Sites of Resistance," 55.
38. Miyoshi, "Sites of Resistance," 62.
39. Miyoshi, "Sites of Resistance," 62.
40. Castillo, "Response," 218–219.
41. Miyoshi, "Sites of Resistance," 62.
42. Miyoshi, "Sites of Resistance," 59.
43. The student goes by one name, Thane. I believe she said this in a feminist pedagogy grad seminar.
44. Castillo, "Response," 218–219.
45. Chéla Sandoval. "Theorizing White Consciousness for a Post-Empire World: Barthes, Fanon, and the Rhetoric of Love," in *Displacing Whiteness: Essays in Social and Cultural Criticism,* ed. Ruth Frankenberg (Durham, NC: Duke University Press, 1999), 92.
46. Sandoval, "Theorizing," 92.
47. Miyoshi, "Sites of Resistance," 56.
48. Miyoshi, "Sites of Resistance," 59.
49. Miyoshi, "Sites of Resistance," 59.
50. Agger, *Cultural Studies,* 154.
51. Miyoshi, "Sites of Resistance," 59.
52. Agger, *Cultural Studies,* 154.
53. Agger, *Cultural Studies,* 154.
54. Agger, *Cultural Studies,* 154.
55. Rey Chow, *Writing Diaspora* (Bloomington: Indiana University Press, 1993); Suzanne Pharr, *Homophobia–A Weapon of Sexism* (Little Rock, AR: Chardon Press, 1988), 53–64.
56. Pharr, *Homophobia,* 57.
57. Castillo, "Response," 219–220; Gayatri Spivak, "Theory in the Margin: Coetzee's *Foe* reading Defoe's *Crusoe/Roxana,*" in *Consequences of Theory,* ed. Jonathan Arac and Barbara Johnson (Baltimore: Johns Hopkins University Press, 1991), 166.
58. Agger, *Cultural Studies,* 169.
59. Miyoshi, "Sites of Resistance," 62.
60. Miyoshi, "Sites of Resistance," 62.
61. Miyoshi, "Sites of Resistance," 62–63.
62. Agger, *Cultural Studies,* 5.
63. Sandoval, "Theorizing," 102.

Chapter 3

1. bell hooks, *Outlaw Culture: Resisting Representations* (New York: Routledge, 1994) 209.
2. Tom Heany, "Issues in Freirean Pedagogy," *Thresholds in Education* (1995), available at thea@chicagol.nl.edu p. 1.
3. Gwen McCrea, "Response to Freire," Unpublished paper (2000), 1.
4. Roxana Ng, "Teaching against the Grain: Contradictions and Possibilities," in *Anti-Racism, Feminism, and Critical Approaches to Education*, ed. Roxana Ng, Pat Staton, and Joyce Scane (Westport, CT: Bergin and Garvey, 1995), 130–131.
5. Ng, "Teaching," 130–131.
6. This may be true of other universities as well. At Minnesota, it is still true to some extent. There are very few women of color teaching here, and fewer still from working-class backgrounds. I am one of three Chicanas—all of us in different colleges—and all hired in the past five years.
7. Henry A. Giroux, *Postmodernism, Feminism, and Cultural Politics: Redrawing Education Boundaries* (Albany: State University of New York Press, 1991), 47.
8. Rick Hesch, "Aboriginal Teachers as Organic Intellectuals," *Anti-Racism, Feminism, and Critical Approaches to Education*, ed. Roxana Ng, Pat Staton, and Joyce Scane (Westport, CT: Bergin and Garvey, 1995), 107. I expect my students to teach, interpret and analyze as well as critique from this perspective also. Thus I do not expect mainstream students to become people of color, for men to become women, nor for heterosexuals to choose another sexual identity. But I do expect them to find some way of empathizing with others, and this must come from their own lives if it is to have meaning beyond the course.
9. Ng, "Teaching," 133.
10. Ng, "Teaching," 129–150.
11. Ng, "Teaching," 129–150.
12. Ng, "Teaching," 129–150.
13. hooks, *Outlaw Culture*, 226.
14. Baldwin in hooks, *Outlaw Culture, 230.*
15. hooks, *Outlaw Culture, 224.*
16. hooks, *Outlaw Culture, 230.*
17. Hesch, "Aboriginal Teachers," 108.
18. Hesch, "Aboriginal Teachers," 106–108.
19. Debra Castillo, "Response Cutting/edge," *Latin American Women's Writing: Feminist Readings in Theory and Crisis* (New York: Clarndon Press/Oxford, 1996), 221–223.
20. McCrea, "Respone to Freire," 3.
21. Hesch, "Aboriginal Teachers," 107.
22. Leslie G. Roman, "White Is a Color!," in *Race, Identity and Representation in Education* (New York: Routledge, 1993), 79.
23. Heany, "Freirean Pedagogy," 2.
24. Heany, "Freirean Pedagogy," 3.
25. Heany, "Freirean Pedagogy," 5–6.

Chapter 4

1. Olga Angelina García Echeverría, "Blood Ain't Salsa," *Raza Spoken Here: Poesía Chicana,* Vol. I. Compact disc, Calaca Press, 1999.
2. Gloria Anzaldúa, *Borderlands/La Frontera: The New Mestiza* (San Francisco: Spinsters/Aunt Lute, 1987), 3.
3. Armond White, "Stepping Forward/Looking Back," *Film Comment* (March/April 2000): 34.
4. White, "Stepping Forward," 37.
5. Amy Kaminsky, "Identity at the Border: Narrative Strategies in María Novaro's *El jardín del Edén* and John Sayles's *Lone Star," Studies in 20th Century Literature: The Literature and Popular Culture of the U.S.–Mexican Border* (Winter 2001): 105.
6. Kaminsky, "Identity at the Border," 106.
7. Kaminsky, "Identity at the Border," 106.
8. White, "Stepping Forward," 32–39.

9. José E. Limón, *American Encounters: Greater Mexico, the United States, and the Erotics of Culture* (Boston: Beacon, 1998) 211–212.

10. Limón, *American Encounters*, 211–212.

11. Rosa Linda Fregoso, "Recycling Colonialist Fantasies on the Texas Borderlands," *Home, Exile, Homeland: Film, Media, and the Politics of Place*, ed. Hamid Naficy (New York: Routledge, 1999), 186.

12. Fregoso, "Recycling Colonialist," 186.

13. White, "Stepping Forward," 33.

14. Patrisia Gonzalez and Roberto Rodríguez, "It's Not All White." *XColumn@aol.com*, Universal Press Syndicate 13 September, 2002.

15. Gonzalez and Rodríguez, "It's Not All White."

16. Fregoso, "Recycling Colonialist," 185.

17. Fregoso, "Recycling Colonialist," 180.

18. Fregoso, "Recycling Colonialist," 184.

19. Fregoso, "Recycling Colonialist," 185.

20. Fregoso, "Recycling Colonialist," 175.

21. White, "Stepping Forward," 33.

22. Limón, *American Encounters*, 154; Emma Pérez, *The Decolonial Imaginary: Writing Chicanas Into History* (Bloomington: Indiana University Press, 1999), 126.

23. Limón, *American Encounters*, 152; Pérez, *Decolonial Imaginary*, 126.

24. Fregoso, "Recycling Colonialist," 176.

25. White, "Stepping Foward," 38.

26. Paulo Freire, *Pedagogy of the Oppressed*, trans. Myra Bergman Ramos (New York: Continuum, 1990), 161.

27. Alan Stone, "Prophet of Hope," Online film review, 28 May 2002, available at bostonreview. mit.edu/GR21.5/stone.html.

28. Lorna Dee Cervantes, "Oaxaca, 1974," *Infinite Divisions: An Anthology of Chicana Literature*, ed. Tey Diana Rebolledo and Eliana S. Rivero (Tucson: University of Arizona Press, 1993), 90.

29. Fregoso, "Recycling Colonialist," 169.

30. Chéla Sandoval, "Theorizing White Consciousness for a Post-Empire World: Barthes, Fanon, and the Rhetoric of Love," in *Displacing Whiteness: Essays in Social and Cultural Criticism*, ed. Ruth Frankenberg (Durham, NC: Duke University Press, 1999), 92–93.

31. Kaminsky, "Identity at the Border," 109.

32. Freire, *Pedagogy of the Oppressed*, 141.

33. Freire, *Pedagogy of the Oppressed*, 134.

34. Fregoso, "Recycling Colonialist," 188–189.

35. Freire, *Pedagogy of the Oppressed*, 141.

36. Sandoval, "Theorizing White Consciousness," 104.

37. See Roland Barthes, *Mythologies* (New York: Hill and Wang, 1972) and his discussion of poses, as well as Franz Fanon, *Black Skin, White Masks* (New York: Grove Press, 1967) for two views of internalized dominance.

38. Ben Agger, *Cultural Studies as Critical Theory* (London: Falmer Press, 1992), 160–161.

Chapter 5

1. Angie Chabram-Dernersesian, "On the Social Construction of Whiteness within Selected Chicana/o Discourses," in *Displacing Whiteness: Essays in Social and Cultural Criticism*, ed. Ruth Frankenberg (Durham, NC: Duke University Press, 1999), 108.

2. Rick Hesch, "Aboriginal Teachers as Organic Intellectuals," in *Anti-Racism, Feminism, and Critical Approaches to Education*, ed. Roxana Ng, Pat Staton, and Joyce Scane (Westport, CT: Bergin and Garvey, 1995), 108.

3. Gina Valdés, "The Border," in *Infinite Divisions: An Anthology of Chicana Literature*, ed. Tey Diana Rebolledo and Eliana S. Rivero (Tucson: University of Arizona Press, 1993), 186.

4. Franz Fanon, *Black Skin, White Masks* (New York: Grove, 1967), 32; Chéla Sandoval, "Theorizing White Consciousness for a Post-Empire World: Barthes, Fanon, and the Rhetoric of Love," in *Displacing Whiteness: Essays in Social and Cultural Criticism*, ed. Ruth Frankenberg (Durham, NC: Duke University Press, 1999), 98.

5. Ivan Illich, "To Hell with Good Intentions," Conference on Inter-American Student Projects, Cuernavaca, Mexico, 20 April 1968. Available at http://homepage.mac.com/tinapple/illich/1968_cuernavaca.html.
6. Illich, "To Hell with Good Intentions," 316.
7. Illich, "To Hell with Good Intentions," 316.
8. Sandoval, "Theorizing White Consciousness," 86.

Chapter 6

1. See Benedict Anderson's *Imagined Communities, Reflections on the Origin and Spread of Nationalism* for interesting ideas about the creation and maintenance of community and the way in which Marxist philosophy is transformed into nationalism.
2. Joshua Fishman, *Language Loyalty in the United States* (The Hague: Mouton, 1966) 32; Philip Gleason, "World War II and the Development of American Studies," *American Quarterly* 36 (1984): 344–352.
3. Linda Kerber, "Diversity and the Transformation of American Studies," *American Quarterly* 41, no. 3 (1989): 419.
4. Edward W. Said, *Culture and Imperialism* (New York: Knopf, 1993), 289.
5. Susan E. Keefe and Amado M. Padilla, *Chicano Ethnicity* (Albuquerque: University of New Mexico, 1987), 194.
6. Keefe and Padilla, *Chicano Ethnicity*, 7.
7. James A. Banks, *Multiethnic Education: Theory and Practice* (Boston: Allyn and Bacon, 1988). Adding modifiers to the word makes some of this complexity apparent. "Ethnic identification," for instance, is the already named or delineated category into which an individual places her- or himself. "Ethnic heritage" refers to the learned, studied, or consciously remembered history and culture of the group into which we are born. "Ethnic culture" is associated with shared values, behavioral and personality norms, symbolic representations, myths, and attitudes, and so forth of a particular group, that must also be learned, usually at the implicit level. The "ethnic core" has to do with behavioral and personality instinct, unconscious memory, and spiritual impulses that cannot fully be explained by environmental learning, which may also be the most indistinct factor in terms of cognition and language or the most difficult to conceptualize and articulate.
8. This element may also be invisible or impossible to grasp for members of the Mexican American community. For some of us, it becomes a blind spot. In many cases this is a legacy of the shaming process to which Mexican Americans are subject. What seems "essentially" Mexican about us is rejected. Richard Rodríguez has struggled with this throughout his career. He is a wonderful example of someone who inherited and learned his Mexicanness through a father who, he says, hated Mexico and a mother who loved it. (A paradox many of us have in common, though not necessarily in this specific form.) Despite his shame and denial, Rodríguez constantly exhibits behaviors instantly recognizable by Chicanas/os as "Mexican." Despite his insistence that Spanish is a private-colloquial language, and his glorification of English as a public, world-culture language, Rodríguez, both as a writer and as a speaker, even in English—creates and easily utters, traditional flower and song, the poetic foundation of Nahua communication and culture. This style is also reminiscent of Spanish ballads. Again, easily recognizable as "essentially" Mexican, by other Mestizas/os.
    After hearing him speak, an undergraduate student from East Los Angeles—a homegirl to be sure—said to me, "I don't understand him. I don't like what he says. But I like his words. The way he talks. It's flowery." She sensed the paradox—the love/hate relationship he has with his Mexicanness.
    Rodríguez's work exhibits what some critics call postmodern (and I call Mexican) discourse, in that he constantly slips out of concreteness and into contradiction and paradox. Circling ideas rather than pinpointing them, slipping in and out of definitions rather than creating solid, logical arguments. Some critics have described this trait as an acceptance of the "feminine," as opposed to the "masculine" style of drawing strict boundaries. But, I would say that it is a demonstration of an "Ometéotl" style—the blending of the feminine and masculine, of circular and linear, and so forth. Rodríguez does not follow strict lines. (For example: He vehemently opposes bilingual education, yet supports the immigration,

by whatever means, of Mexicans into the United States.) Though expository prose is his chosen form, Rodríguez is more poet than he is essayist in the academic or conventional sense. Clearly, his father and mother, like many "ethnic" parents, taught him a great deal about being Mexican, despite his efforts to deny this gift.

9. This is generally more true of written history and literature, but can certainly also be the case with oral forms. Though many storytellers are female, and much culture comes to us through women, traditional folklore and mythology are often patriarchal. (Though again, this is less true than recorded Western history and literature.) But a greater difference lies in the power of the oral practioner to shape and fashion the elements of the story. Female power, ways of knowing, and survival strategies have been much easier to transmit through oral tradition than discursive practice, precisely because it is relatively uncontrolled and has at least the potential to be quite revolutionary, though some cultures demand more strict adherence to precise repetition.

10. Michael M. J. Fischer, "Ethnicity and the Post-Modern Arts of Memory," in *Writing Cultures*, ed. James Clifford and George Marcus (Los Angeles: University of California, 1986), 210.

11. Natasha López, "Trying to be Dyke and Chicana," in *Chicana Lesbians: The Girls Our Mothers Warned Us About*, ed. Carla Trujillo (Berkeley, CA: Third Woman Press, 1991), 84.

12. Asunción Horno-Delgado, Eliana Ortega, Nina M. Scott, and Nancy Saporta Sternbach, *Breaking Boundaries: Latina Writing and Critical Readings* (Amherst: University of Massachusetts Press, 1989), 3.

13. Dorinda Moreno, quoted in Tey Diana Rebolledo and Eliana S. Rivero, eds., *Infinite Divisions: An Anthology of Chicana Literature* (Tucson: University of Arizona, 1993), 75.

14. I would add to this list of white scholars, several social commentators of color who also see race as incidental to ethnicity or culture or class—Thomas Sowell, Linda Chavez, Richard Rodríguez, Peter Bell, and Shelby Steele.

15. Alan Wald, "Theorizing Cultural Difference: A Critique of the 'Ethnicity School,'" *Melus* 14, no. 2 (Summer 1987): 21–33.

16. Wald, "Theorizing," 21–23.

17. Suzanne Oboler, *Ethnic Labels, Latino Lives: Identity and the Politics of (Re)Presentation in the United States* (Minneapolis: University of Minnesota Press, 1995), 90–91.

18. Wald, "Theorizing," 21–33; Werner Sollors, *Beyond Ethnicity: Consent and Descent in American Culture* (New York: Oxford University Press, 1986).

19. Oboler, *Ethnic Labels*, 90–91.

20. Oboler, *Ethnic Labels*, 90–91.

21. Mrinalini Sinha, "Gender in the Critiques of Colonialism and Nationalism: Locating the 'Indian Woman,'" in *Oxford Readings in Feminism: Feminism and History*, ed. Joan Wallach Scott (New York: Oxford University Press, 1996), 480.

22. Keefe and Padilla, *Chicano Ethnicity*, 192.

23. Chéla Sandoval, "Theorizing White Consciousness for a Post-Empire World: Barthes, Fanon, and the Rhetoric of Love," in *Displacing Whiteness: Essays in Social and Cultural Criticism*, ed. Ruth Frankenberg (Durham, NC: Duke University Press, 1999).

24. Oboler, *Ethnic Labels*, 90–91.

25. Lucha Corpi, *Delia's Song* (Houston: Arte Público, 1989), 128.

26. Oboler, *Ethnic Labels*, 90–91.

27. Bernice Zamora, *Releasing Serpents* (Houston: Bilingual Press, 1994), 82.

28. Tey Diana Rebolledo, *Women Singing in the Snow: A Cultural Analysis of Chicana Literature* (Tucson: University of Arizona, 1995), 189–196.

29. Rebolledo, *Women Singing*, 189–196. How scandalous! This has not gone unchallenged by Chicana writers, of course.

30. See Miriam Bornstein's poem "Toma de nombre," in Rebolledo and Rivero's *Infinite Divisions*, 79–80. Her married name she says carries with it an existing legend "de virginidad y mitos" (of virginity and myths), tied to her "con el lazo de buena mujercita mexicana" (with the rosary of the good little Mexican woman)." The female body, as Amy Kaminsky points out, "is one of the most heavily burdened bearers of meaning in culture." Amy Kaminsky, *Reading the Body Politic: Feminist Criticism and Latin American Women Writers* (Minneapolis: University of Minnesota Press, 1993), 98. Also quoted in Rebolledo, *Women Singing*, 190.

31. Zamora, *Releasing Serpents*, 21.

32. Oboler, *Ethnic Labels*, 21. It should be noted that this upper-class ideology was not universally accepted among Mexicans—neither abided by nor taken up unconditionally. The working poor often had no choice but to accept women as equal partners in the business of survival. Such women often had more socioeconomic freedom and latitude than the women of the Spanish elite. People still attached to indigenous ways, did not practice Catholicism—nor wholeheartedly accept its views of sin and women—in the same way that the upper classes did. Throughout greater Mexico's history, struggles initiated by the peasants, from the Indian/mestizo rebellions of the late 1600s to the current Zapatistas in Chiapas, have always included in their ideology the rights of women.

33. Sandra Cisneros, *The House on Mango Street* (Houston: Arte Público Press, 1989), 12–13.

34. Banks, *Multiethnic Education*, 20–29.

35. Suzanne Pharr, *Homophobia: A Weapon of Sexism* (Little Rock, AR: Chardon Press, 1988), 53–64.

36. Banks, *Multiethnic Education*, 20–29; Pharr, *Homophobia*, 53–64.

37. Oboler, *Ethnic Labels*, 28; Pharr, *Homophobia*, 53–64.

38. Banks, *Multiethnic Education*, 20–29; Irene I. Blea, *Toward a Chicano Social Science* (New York: Praeger, 1988), 140.

39. Banks, *Multiethnic Education*, 20–29; Blea, *Chicano Social Science*, 140.

40. Keefe and Padilla, *Chicano Ethnicity*, 8.

41. Keefe and Padilla, *Chicano Ethnicity*, 8. Extended families and kinship networks remain one of the "key cultural traits reinforcing ethnic social boundaries" that separates "Chicano/us" from "Anglo/Other."

42. Rubén Martínez, José Antonio Burciaga, and Cherríe Moraga have all talked about the transmission of cultural history in the barrio, through music, performance, graffiti, as well as traveling across the border and community conversation: Rubén Martínez, *The Other Side: Fault Lines, Guerrilla Saints and the True Heart of Rock 'n' Roll* (New York: Verso, 1992); José Antonio Burciaga, *Drink Cultura* (Santa Barbara, CA: Capra Press, 1993); Cherríe Moraga, *The Last Generation: Prose and Poetry* (Boston: South End Press, 1993).

43. While much of this has taken place in the public sector, racial discrimination against Mexicans is established in historical court documents and recorded political discourse. See Rodolfo Acuña, *Occupied America: A History of Chicanos* (3rd ed.) (Cambridge: Harper and Row, 1988); Oboler, *Ethnic Labels*; David J. Weber, *Foreigners in the Native Land: Historical Roots of the Mexican Americans* (Albuquerque: University of New Mexico, 1973); Arnoldo De Leon, *They Called Them Greasers: Anglo Attitudes Toward Mexicans in Texas, 1821–1900* (Austin: University of Texas Press, 1983).

44. Alfredo Mirandé and Evangelina Enríquez, *La Chicana: The Mexican American Female* (Chicago: University of Chicago Press, 1979), 228–232; Yolanda Chávez-Leyva, "Faithful Hard-Working Hands: Mexicana Workers During the Great Depression," in *Perspectives in Mexican American Studies*, vol. 5—*Mexican American Women: Changing Images,* ed. Juan R. García (Tucson: University of Tucson, 1995), 63–77.

45. Richard Santillán, "Midwestern Mexican American Women and the Struggle for Gender Equality: A Historical Overview, 1920's–1960's," *Perspectives in Mexican American Studies,* vol. 5—*Mexican American Women: Changing Images*, ed. Juan R. García (Tucson: University of Arizona, Mexican American Studies & Research Center, 1995), 79–119.

46. See Charles M. Wollenberg, *All Deliberate Speed: Segregation and Exclusion in California Schools, 1855–1975* (Berkeley: University of California Press, 1978); Guadalupe San Miguel, Jr., *Let All of Them Take Heed, Mexican Americans and the Campaign for Educational Equality in Texas, 1910–1981* (Austin: University of Texas, 1987). See also F. Chris García, ed., *La Causa Politica: A Chicano Politics Reader* (Notre Dame: University of Notre Dame, IN, 1974); Robert Lee Maril, *Poorest of Americans: The Mexican Americans of the Lower Río Grande Valley of Texas* (Notre Dame, IN: University of Notre Dame, 1989).

47. Juan Gómez-Quiñones, *Chicano Politics: Reality and Promise, 1940–1990* (Albuquerque: University of New Mexico, 1990), 31–58; Carlos Muñoz, Jr., *Youth, Identity and Power: The Chicano Movement* (London and New York: Verso, 1989), 42–44; Manuel A. Machado, Jr., *Listen Chicano! An Informal History of the Mexican American* (Chicago: Nelson Hall, 1978), 85–92. See Martha P. Cotera, *Diosa y Hembra: The History and Heritage of Chicanas in the U.S.* (Austin: Information Systems Development, 1976); Teresa L. Amott and Julie A. Matthaei, "The Soul of Tierra Madre: Chicana Women," in *Race, Gender and Work: A Multi-*

cultural Economic History of Women in the United States (Boston: South End Press, 1991). Amott and Matthaei, "The Soul of Tierra Madre"; Cynthia Orozco, "Beyond Machismo, La Familia and Ladies Auxiliaries: A Historiography of Women's Participation in Voluntary Associations and Politics in the United States, 1870–1990," in *Perspectives in Mexican American Studies*, vol. 5—Mexican American Women: Changing Images, ed. Juan R. García (Tucson: University of Arizona, Mexican American Studies and Research Center, 1995.) Santillán's "Midwestern Mexican American Women"; and the 1950s film script, *Salt of the Earth*: Michael Wilson and Deborah Silverton Rosenfelt, *Salt of the Earth* (New York: Feminist Press, 1978).

48. Banks, *Multiethnic Education*, 20–29.

49. Banks, *Multiethnic Education*, 20–29; Douglas E. Foley, *From Peones to Politicos: Class and Ethnicity in a South Texas Town, 1900–1987* (Austin: Center for Mexican American Studies, University of Texas, 1988), 93–138; Rudolfo A. Anaya and Francisco Lomelí, *Aztlán: Essays on the Chicano Homeland* (Albuquerque: El Norte Publications, 1989), 6–29; Mirandé and Enríquez, *La Chicana*, 228–234. Various groups did receive opposition—everything from conservative rhetoric to physical violence—in certain locales where the challenge to dominant culture sovereignty was greatest. See Foley's *From Peones to Politicos*, for example.

50. See work by Robert Blauner, Juan Gómez-Quiñonez, Carlos Muñoz, Mario Barrera, Charles Ornelas, and Tomás Almaguer for development of "internal colonial" model specific to the United States. See Gilbert Gonzáles and Rosaura Sánchez for critiques.

51. Rodolfo Acuña, *Occupied America: A History of Chicanos* (3rd ed.) (Cambridge: Harper and Row, 1988), 307–356; Foley, *From Peones to Politics*, 132, 139–141; Gilbert García, "Beyond the Adelita Image: Women Scholars in the National Association for Chicano Studies, 1972–1992," in *Perspectives in Mexican American Studies*, vol. 5—Mexican American Women: Changing Images, ed. Juan R. García (Tucson: University of Arizona, Mexican American Studies and Research Center, 1995), 35–53. The black eagle of the farm workers union is an example.

52. Marcela Christine Lucero-Trujillo, "The Dilemma of the Modern Chicana Artist and Critic," in *The Third Woman: Minority Women Writers of the United States*, ed. Dexter Fisher (Boston: Houghton Mifflin, 1980), 324.

53. Quetzal birds were part of the Aztec natural world. Its blue green feathers are associated with Quetzalcoatl, an important male deity. The Aztecs believed four worlds existed before this one. The Fifth Sun refers to the age we live in now, though we are in the transition period between the Fifth and Sixth Suns.

54. Marina Rivera, "Mestiza," in *Infinite Divisions: An Anthology of Chicana Literature*, ed. Tey Diana Rebolledo and Eliana S. Rivero. (Tucson: University of Arizona, 1993), 97.

55. Acuña, *Occupied America*, 307–356; Foley, *From Peones to Politics*, 132, 139–141.

56. Judith Baca, *Cultures in Contention* (Seattle, WA: Real Comet Press, 1985) 64.

57. Baca, *Cultures in Contention* 64; Gómez-Quiñones, *Chicano Politics*, 53–124; Mirandé and Enríquez, *La Chicana*, 234–243; Muñoz, *Youth*, 47–88.

58. Banks, *Multiethnic Education*, 20–29.

59. James Diego Vigil, *From Indians to Chicanos: The Dynamics of Mexican American Culture* (Prospect Heights, IL: Waveland Press, 1980), 184–213; Ramón Gutiérrez, *When Jesus Came the Corn Mothers Went Away* (Palto Alto, CA: Stanford U Press, 1991), 183–205.

60. Foley, *From Peones to Politics*, 139–222; Gómez-Quiñones, *Chicano Politics*, 124–187.

61. Foley, *From Peones to Politics*, 139–222; Gómez-Quiñones, *Chicano Politics*, 124–187.

62. Orozco, "Beyond Machismo," 11–18; Christine Marie Sierra, "The University Setting Reinforces Inequality," in *Chicana Voices: Intersections of Race, Class, and Gender*, ed. Teresa Córdova (Austin: Center for Mexican American Studies, University of Texas, 1986), 5–7; Irene Blea, *La Chicana and the Intersection of Race, Class, and Gender* (New York: Praeger, 1992), 1–20; Muñoz, *Youth*, 88–166.

63. García, "Beyond Adelita Image," 83.

64. Ocampo, Bernal, and Knight, writing about the link between acquiring a gender and an ethnic identity, tells us that children begin to develop long after they become aware of difference. The development of a strong identity is directly related to one's perceptions of constancy and meaning of a given element, and the concept of stability (i.e., it is not until race, ethnicity, or gender become in the child's mind a stable and unchangeable reality that the child begins to strongly identify as female or male, as Mexican, or as a brown person). In a

racist, ethnocentric environment, it is very possible that a Chicanita might begin to see ethnicity or race as a stable part of the Self before recognizing the importance and unchangeability of gender. We may also encounter or become aware of hostility toward us on the basis of race or ethnicty before we understand sexism, and thus need a meaningful group identity as protection against outsiders. But Chicanas can also grow up in families or environments where gender acts as a stable organizer of family or kinship attitudes, environments where there is less contact with non-Mexican American people, greater contact with conventional Catholicism, elite Hispanos with an increased sense of honor and sharply defined gender roles, among other possibilities. These children then have a vested interest in learning gender-appropriate behavior early. If this happens before race or ethnicity is perceived as a constant, gender identity is likely to precede ethnic or racial identity and may remain stronger throughout a lifetime. This helps to explain why some Chicanas place more or less emphasis on gender or race, though most of us understand the inseparability of the two. Catheryn A. Ocampo, Martha E. Bernal, and George Knight, "Gender, Race, and Ethnicity: The Sequencing of Social Constancies," in *Ethnic Identity: Formation and Transmission among Hispanics and Other Minorities*, ed. Martha E. Bernal and George P. Knight (Albany: State University of New York Press, 1993), 11–46; Sinha, "Gender in Critiques," 477–478.

65.   Carla Trujillo, "Chicana Lesbians: Fear and Loathing in the Chicano Community," in *Chicana Lesbians: The Girls Our Mothers Warned Us About*, ed. Carla Trujillo (Berkeley, CA: Third Woman Press, 1991), 186–193.

66.   Tiny, the woman the narrative voice loves throughout her life, dies of breast cancer. Moraga ties this death directly to the lesbian experience, remarking on the medical reality that women who have not been pregnant are at higher risk for breast cancer. But she sees this as just another way that life is not fair to lesbians.

67.   Cherríe Moraga, "La Ofrenda," *Chicana Lesbians: The Girls Our Mothers Warned Us About*, ed. Carla Trujillo (Berkeley, CA: Third Woman Press, 1991), 4–5.

68.   This gives rise to the many "we" categories in which I feel free and/or obligated to situate myself. Sinha, "Gender in Critiques," 477–478.

69.   While "radical feminism," even in the early stages of the modern women's movement gave some thought to lesbian issues, mainstream feminism either failed to address sexual identity issues or purposefully stayed away from them in response to the rampant homophobia inside the organizations and embedded in society's vilifying of the women's movement. Even now, in general feminist, histories or theoretical anthologies, it is not uncommon to find lesbian issues either nonexistent or limited to one article. It is ironic that the critique of feminism sees lesbianism as central, when in reality it is marginalized in mainstream feminist thought. In many publications, in fact, women of color have more visibility than do lesbians specifically.

Among Chicana feminist writers, however, lesbians are usually highly visible and prolific, producing much of the literature, history, and theory about Mexican American women. Though it is still true that they are ignored by most of the patriarchs of the Chicano movement, some scholars—more enlightened and less homophobic, straight and gay—are incorporating this knowledge in anthologies and into their own work. Or, at the very least, are consciously positioning themselves to speak of masculinity and related subjects, rather than pretending to represent a universal voice. See several essays in Héctor Calderón and José David Saldívar, eds., *Criticism in the Borderlands* (Durham, NC: Duke University Press, 1991); Genaro M. Padilla, *My History, Not Yours: The Formation of Mexican American Autobiography* (Madison: University of Wisconsin Press, 1993); José Limón, *Mexican Ballads, Chicano Poems* (Berkeley: University of California Press, 1992), and José Limón, *Dancing with the Devil* (Madison: University of Wisconsin Press, 1990) (Limón has also contributed work to anthologies specifically focused on women's issues); Ramón Saldívar, *Chicano Narrative* (Madison: University of Wisconsin Press, 1990); and Gutiérrez-Jones *Rethinking the Borderlands*, for examples.

70.   Elsa Barkley Brown, "Womanist Consciousness: Maggie Lena Walker and the Independent Order of Saint Luke," in *Oxford Readings in Feminism: Feminism and History*, ed. Joan Wallach Scott (New York: Oxford University Press, 1996) 453–469; Sinha, "Gender in Critiques," 477–482.

71.   Brown, "Womenist Consciousness," 453–469; Sinha, "Gender in Critiques," 477–482; Beatriz M. Pesquera and Denise M. Segura, "There Is No Going Back: Chicanas and Femi-

nism," in *Chicana Critical Issues: Mujeres Activas en Letras y Cambio Social,,* ed. Norma Alarcón, et. al. (Berkeley, CA: Third Woman Press, 1993), 95–115; Mirandé and Enríquez, *La Chicana,* 234–243; Alma M. García, "The Development of Chicana Feminist Discourse, 1970–1980," in *Unequal Sisters: A Multicultural Reader in U.S. Women's History,* ed. Ellen Carol DuBois and Vicki L. Ruiz (New York: Routledge, 1990), 418–431.

72. García, "Beyond Adelita Image," 418–431.
73. Sinha, "Gender in Critiques," 477–482; Brown, "Womenist Consciousness," 453–469; Carla Trujillo, "Chicana Lesbians: Fear and Loathing in the Chicano Community," in *Chicana Critical Issues: Mujeres Activas en Letras y Cambio Social.,* "Beyond Adelita Image," ed. Norma Alarcón, et al. (Berkeley, CA: Third Woman Press, 1993), 117–125; García, "Beyond Adelita Image," 418–431. Just as white women cannot be seen as being outside the sexualization and racialization of women of color, while less powerful than white men, they were nevertheless tangential to the construction of otherness for women of color.
74. Sinha, "Gender in Critiques," 477.
75. Trujillo, *Chicana Lesbians,* 117–125; García, "Beyond Adelita Image," 418–431; Orozco, "Beyond Machismo," 19–20.
76. Foremothers like: Sor Juana Inez de la Cruz—Mexican nun of seventeenth century Mexico who challenged the patriarchal Church and supported the struggles of mestizo and Indian peasants, sometimes called the Mexican mother of Chicana feminism. Doña Josefa Ortíz de Dominguez—instrumental in the struggle for Mexican independence. Carmen Serdan and Juana Belen Gutierrez de Mendoza—organizer of revolutionary forces and liberal journalist of the 1910 Revolution respectively. Petra Ruiz and Doña Juana Torres—two of many women soldiers during the Revolution. Doña Patricia de León—one of the founders of Victoria, Texas, forced to flee Anglo soldiers in the fight to create the Texas republic. Dolores Hernández—farm labor organizer shot by growers in 1933. Emma Tenayuca—famed 1930s labor leader of the Texas Pecan Shellers strike. Isabel Malagran Gonzales—writer, labor leader, teacher, and welfare rights activist in the late 1920s through the late 1940s. María L. Hernández—author, activist, and one of the founders of Orden Caballeros de America, a civil rights organizaiton formed in 1929. Jovita González—academic and writer recognized as the first Mexican American woman to write in English on Mexican American culture, being courageous and open about hostility between Mexicans and Anglos. Though they began their careers in 1920s, Señoras Hernández and González both remained active in civil rights struggles into the 1970s. See Cotera's, *Diosa y Hembra:* The History and Heritage of Chicanas in the U.S. (Austin: Information System Development, 1976), 44, for information on feminist organizations and conferences in Mexico.
77. Sinha, "Gender in Critiques," 480.
78. Banks, *Multiethnic Education,* 20–29.
79. Banks, *Multiethnic Education,* 20–29.
80. Foley, *From Peones to Politics,* 224–288; Gómez-Quiñonez, *Chicano Politics,* 189–205; Donna M. Gollnick and Philip C. Chinn, *Multicultural Education in a Pluralistic Society* (St. Louis, MO: Mosby, 1983), 27–31; Banks, *Multiethnic Education* 3–19.
81. The level of this "inspiration" has been argued. While some feel the Chicano movement is a direct result of African American social justice movements, others disagree. "There is a common belief—to a great extent misleading—that Chicanos have been following in the footsteps of the black movement. . . . [Yet] a prevailing [Mexican American] attitude toward Anglo society and its cultural domination has been indifference. For several centuries there have been blacks who were inspired to plead their case before the forum of public opinion, somehow maintaining a kernel of optimism and residual belief in the fundamental good will of at least a minority of whites. . . . It appears that Mexicans in the United States have rarely held such illusions about our vaunted democratic system. (Immigrants interviewed by Manuel Gamio during the 1920s were striking in their loyalty to Mexico and in their critical attitude toward U.S. cultural values and treatment of Mexicans. An aversion to the idea of U.S. citizenship was almost universal.) Of course, many individual Mexican Americans have struggled to make it economically, even disappearing socially and culturally into the Anglo middle-class. . . . Yet Chicano intellectuals and working people had been living their version of cultural nationalism long before Black militants brought the term to public attention. . . . Therefore we must be skeptical about the idea that the brown political dynamic is re-creating the Black's—the similarity of Brown Beret dress and rhetoric to

Black Panthers' notwithstanding. The historical and sociocultural context of Mexican-American life has been unique—it cannot be fitted into the pattern of black-white relations, nor to the model of European ethnic group immigration." Robert Blauner, *Racial Oppression in America* (New York: Harper and Row, 1972), 162–163.

82.   Brown, "Womenist Consciousness," 453–469; Sinha, "Gender in Critiques," 477–482; Pesquera and Segura, "There Is No Going Back," 95–115; Mirandé and Enríquez, *La Chicana* 234–243; García, "Beyond Adelita Image," 418–431.

83.   Chavez, for instance, does not call herself a Chicana. Neither does she want to be known as Mexican American. She is, she insists, simply "American." Yet, Chavez's conservative voice was being exploited by the right precisely because she is of Mexican descent. Her fame and prominence in political circles was directly linked to her rejection and denial of ethnic identity and history, or the way in which that rejection signaled submission to the "common" culture. Yet, let her walk into a store in any small town in western Minnesota or in Anglo Texas and she may be shocked to see how much outside that "common" culture she really is. Irene I. Blea, *Toward a Chicano Social Science* (New York: Praeger, 1988), 143.

84.   María Herrera-Sobek, "My All-American Son," in *Three Times a Woman*, ed. Alicia Gasper de Alba. (Tempe AZ: Bilingual Press, 1989) 80–81.

85.   Oboler suggests that the debate around the use of the word "Hispanic," mirrors a tension being discussed by Latin American intellectuals since the nineteenth century. Though Spanish colonialism lasted over three hundred years, many do not feel this justifies their continued identification with Spain. Most recognize that beneath the Spanish gloss they all share deep differences between their indigenous and postcolonial histories and cultures that hold more importance than their commonalities. Oboler, *Ethnic Labels*, 19–20.

86.   Gómez-Quiñonez, *Chicano Politics*, 124–187; Foley, *From Peones to Politics*, 224–266; Acuña, *Occupied America*, 377–451; Oboler, *Ethnic Labels*, 159. While there may be some benefits to developing a "pan-Hispanic," situational identity, in terms of creating a larger political culture or community resource, distinct historical experience, psycho-social development, and access to power often prevent such unity.

87.   Gutiérrez, *When Jesus Came the Corn Mothers Went Away*, 183–205.

88.   See the beginning of Ana Castillo's essay, "La Macha: Toward an Erotic Whole Self," in her book, *Massacre of the Dreamers,* for a poignant example of this behavior—in this case, a Chicano poet at a conference who objectifies Castillo, rather than taking her seriously as a writer or theorist. She describes the painful realization that her work will never be respected by the men with whom she felt aligned against racial and ethnic oppression. Ana Castillo, *Massacre of the Dreamers: Essays on Xicanisma* (New York: Plume, 1994), 121.

89.   Bernice Zamora, "So Not to Be Mottled," *Infinite Divisions: An Anthology of Chicana Literature*, ed. Tey Diana Rebolledo and Eliana S. Rivero (Tucson: University of Arizona, 1993), 132.

90.   Lucero-Trujillo, "The Dilemma," 402.

91.   Hijas de Cuahtémoc (feminist organization following the example of its parent group in Mexico), Encuentro Femenil (primarily concerned with education and liberation politics), the Comisión Femenil Mexicana Nacional (concerned with identifying and training female community leaders), the Chicana Service Action Center (which grew out of the Mexican Feminist Commission), the Chicana Rights Project (which was begun by MALDEF), and Mujeres Activas en Letras y Cambio Social (MALCS) which was organized by women who had met through the National Association of Chicano Studies. These organizations were accompanied by new journals and conferences specifically addressing and articulating the concerns of women.

92.   See and note the tone of nationalism in Moraga's piece "Codex Xerí: El Momento Histórico," though she moves beyond Mexican or Chicano identity and includes other oppressed peoples in a kind of global nationalism—or a "movements" nationalism. Moraga, *The Last Generation*, 184.

93.   Gómez-Quiñonez, *Chicano Politics*, 124–187; Gutiérrez, *When Jesus Came*, 183–205; Pesquera and Segura, "There Is No Going Back," 95–115.

94.   In the academy, however, the conventions of Chicana/o writings were still differentiated from canonized Euro or Anglo American literature, not directly on the basis of its differing perspective, but as "emerging literature." Ironically, narratives marked by similar ethnic forms such as bilingualism—novels by Jewish authors using Yiddish words and phrases, for example—had already been accepted into academic and/or popular culture, but were not

characterized by the mainstream as "emerging." Similarly, narratives that contained foreign, but less "ethnic" languages like French and German, or "high" culture phrases in Latin, not only escaped this characterization, but had been part of the canon for some time. Banks, *Multiethnic Education*, 20–29.

95. Banks, *Multiethnic Education*, 20–29.

96. This is a clear indication of cyclic process. The "melting-pot" theory, coined in the early part of the century during intense immigration, was supposed to signify the pluralistic ideals of the United States and the ongoing creation of a uniquely "American" culture that would result from the mixing of many ethnic groups. But, it was always a euphemism for assimilation to white, Anglo American culture. It was never intended that immigrant groups would retain any of their distinctive features.

    The exclusion of Native Americans, African Americans, Asians, and Mexicans from this imagined "melting-pot" nation was already well established long before the term was coined. It meant to include the European immigrants of the early 1900s, not the Mexican ones simultaneously arriving in the Southwest, or allow admittance to any other people of color. This is the reason it was rejected by civil rights activists, who knew it was a false promise. Oboler, *Ethnic Labels*, 28; Milton Gordon, *Assimilation in American Life* (New York: Oxford University Press, 1964), 115.

97. Banks, *Multiethnic Education*, 20–29; Susan Jeffords, *The Remasculinization of America: Gender and the Viet Nam War* (Bloomington: Indiana University Press, 1989), 116–143; Edward W. Said, *Culture and Imperialism* (New York: Knopf, 1993), 282–303.

98. Congressional Fact Sheets, March 1999, 15–18.

99. Linda K. Kerber, "Diversity and the Transformation of American Studies," *American Quarterly* 41, no. 3 (1989): 420.

100. Gloria Anzaldúa, "Bridge, Drawbridge, Sandbar or Island: Lesbians-of-Color Hacienda Alianzas," in *Bridges of Power: Women's Multicultural Alliances*, ed. Lisa Albrecht and Rose M. Brewer (Philadelphia: New Society, 1990), 142–148; Jonathan Kozol, *Savage Inequalities: Children in America's Schools* (N.Y. Crown, 1991), 206–233, Gutiérrez, *When Jesus Came*, 207–216.

101. Banks, *Multiethnic Education*, 19–26; bell hooks, *Outlaw Culture: Resisting Representations* (New York: Routledge, 1994), 83–90, 101–108; Oboler, *Ethnic Labels*, 80–100.

102. The mistaken impression that racism is only comprised of blatant acts of aggression, language, ignorant behaviors, and attitudes serves a similar function. It places the responsibility in the hands of a single person, ignoring the institutionalized, systematic, and pervasive racism that circumscribes our lives. Unconscious, unaware, and covert forms of racism are the spirit killers with which we do battle everyday.

103. Banks, *Multiethnic Education*, 20–29; Saldívar, *Chicano Narrative*, 171–199; Renato Rosaldo, *Culture and Truth: The Remaking of Social Analysis* (Boston: Beacon, 1989), 151–217; hooks, *Outlaw Culture*, 83–90, 101–108.

104. Banks, *Multiethnic Education*, 19–26; Patricia Nelson Limerick, *The Legacy of Conquest: The Unbroken Past of the American West* (New York: Norton, 1987) 322–349.

105. Gómez-Quiñonez, *Chicano Politics*, 207–214. Moraga, in part, has been inspired by the upheaval in Los Angeles after the Rodney King verdict. This replicates historical responses throughout much of the existence of the United States, as civil unrest and defiance have often been sparked by police brutality or trials and investigations in which policemen have been absolved of their crimes against people of color. See Americo Parades, *With a Pistol in His Hand*, (Houston: University of Texas Press, 1958); Alfredo Mirandé, *The Chicano Experience: An Alternative Perspective* (South Bend, IN: University of Notre Dame, 1985); Arnoldo De León, *They Called Them Greasers* (Houston: University of Texas Press, 1983); Lettie Austin, L. Fenderson, and S. Nelson, *The Black Man and the Promise of America* (New York: Scott Foresman, 1996); Sterling Tucker, *For Blacks Only* (New York: William B. Eerdmans Publishing Company, 1971); Robert Blauner, *Racial Oppression in America* (New York: Harper & Row, 1972); Manning Marable, *How Capitalism Underdeveloped Black America* (Boston: South End Press, 2000); August Meier and Elliot Rudwick, *From Plantation to Ghetto* (New York: Hill and Wang Publishing, 1976); and Gerald Leinwand, *Problems of American Society: Racism* (New York: Washington Square Press, 1969). Moraga says "I cling to the word 'nation' because without the specific naming of the nation, the nation will be lost (as when feminism is reduced to humanism, the woman is subsumed). Let us retain our radical naming but expand it to meet a broader and wiser revolution." That is, let us keep

a specific focus, but be more inclusive. Morago, "Queer Aztlán: the Re-formation of Chicano Tribe," in The Last Generation: Prose and Poetry (Boston: South End Press, 1993), 150, which is a kind of cycle that merges gay and lesbian identity with the revitalization of ethnicity.

106. See Oscar Zeta Acosta's recently reissued autobiographical novels, *The Revolt of the Cockroach People* (New York: Vintage Books, 1989); and *The Autobiography of a Brown Buffalo* (New York: Vintage Books, 1989). See also Carlos M. Jiménez, *The Mexican American Heritage* (Berkeley, CA: TQS Publications, 1993).

107. I do not say this to question anyone's firm concept of themselves as either heterosexual or homosexual/gynosexual. But, for me, Anzaldúa's concept of living in the borderland space rather than on one side or the other includes an awareness that love does not have genitals. While I certainly believe that many people are more heavily inclined to be one or the other, I do not think it is as steadfast and distinct as most cultures dictate. Gender identity is as socially constructed as any other category, even as it is true that our instincts and impulses may lead us to the conclusion that we are straight or gay or bisexual. While the latter two labels increase the possibilities, it still limits us to just three. Can we really be so simple? How then do we explain all the behaviors that go on between, around, despite, and outside those choices?

108. Corpi, *Delia's Song*, 105.

109. Carolyn McTighe Musil, "Foreword," *Bridges of Power: Women's Multicultural Alliances*, ed. Lisa Albrecht and Rose M. Brewer (Philadelphia: New Society, 1990), vii.

110. Anzaldúa, "Bridge, Drawbridge, Sandbar or Island," 225.

111. Anzaldúa, "Bridge, Drawbridge, Sandbar or Island," 217.

112. Roxanna Carillo, "Feminist Alliances: A View from Peru," *Bridges of Power: Women's Multicultural Alliances*, ed. Lisa Albrecht and Rose M. Brewer (Philadelphia: New Society, 1990), 205.

113. Internalized oppression has its corollary in internalized dominance. The two things present in coalition work make for some of the most incredibly frustrating, disheartening, and painful experiences of our activist lives. Some features of internalized dominance are: the existence or acceptance of prejudice, feelings of inborn or environmentally acquired superiority, self-righteousness, a sense that you are normal and others not like you are abnormal or deviant, guilt, fear of losing dominance, projection of your deepest fears onto others, denial or failure to see the reality of oppression, alienation from your physical being because the debasement of others narrows the range of human behaviors and emotions, alienation from natural surroundings because the "Other" is associated with nature. Prejudice, feeling and acting superior, and denial of reality that restricts one's ability to empathize, to love, or trust, or fully open to a defined "Other." This requires rigidity and self-repression. All of these things perpetuate exclusion and justify oppression. Gail Pheterson, "Alliances Between Women: Overcoming Internalized Oppression and Internalized Domination," *Bridges of Power: Women's Multicultural Alliances*, ed. Lisa Albrecht and Rose M. Brewer (Philadelphia: New Society, 1990), 35–36.

114. Anzaldúa, "Bridge, Drawbridge, Sandbar or Island," 225. This means that if white women and women of color are working together, women of color must set the "terms of engagement." If lesbians and straight women form an alliance, lesbians must take responsibility for articulating the larger group's concerns, with lesbians of color taking leadership before straight women of color. Ditto other possible combinations: men and women, gay men and straight men, men of color and white men, and so forth. Many situations will not always be so clear or easy to decide, because our relationships to power seem equally distant, and both sides must be considered. Consensus will be necessary and could depend on context. This is done not because some people are more or less oppressed than others, nor to give one group power or privilege over the other, but because it is often (not always) easier for those with numerous, overlapping forms of oppression to see not only their own burden clearly, but that of others as well. Whereas the opposite is seldom true. No matter how enlightened we are, we seldom understand the extent or power of our privilege. "Consensus," for instance, is a loaded word when we do not take into account power differentials. The reason groups tend to operate on dominant models is because of our failure to acknowledge such things as ideals rather than realities. True consensus can only happen if voices of opinion are equal or equalized, otherwise it is still majority or loudest opinion that wins. Janice L. Ristock, "Canadian Feminist Social Service Collectives: Caring and Contradictions,"

Bridges of Power: Women's Multicultural Alliances, ed. Lisa Albrecht and Rose M. Brewer (Philadelphia: New Society, 1990), 178.

115. Carillo, "Feminist Alliances," 205; Sinha, "Gender in Critiques," 480.

116. Though the history of Latin America and its relationship with the United States since the 1800s has been one of economic dominance and exploitation, it has grown past being a problem of national proportions. As Lisa Albrecht and Rose Brewer point out in *Bridges of Power: Women's Multicultural Alliances* (Philadelphia: New Society, 1990) 15, "the internationalization of the economy . . . generated profound consequences for women of color and white women globally." Which, the authors say, is one of the reasons why alliances and a less provincial worldview are particularly necessary.

117. Corpi, *Delia's Song*, 76.

118. Anzaldúa, "Bridge, Drawbridge, Sandbar or Island," 217.

119. See Gloria Anzaldúa's piece, "Bridge, Drawbridge, Sandbar or Island: Lesbians-of-Color Hacienda Alianzas." In it, Anzaldúa describes some of the difficulties of forming and maintaining alliances, things that keep us apart, various modes of behaving in the world, cautions to be kept in mind when choosing a strategy, and some of the terms to which we must agree to make coalitions work.

120. Carillo, "Feminist Alliances," 199; Ristock, "Canadian Feminist," 175.

Bibliography

Acuña, Rodolfo. *Occupied America: A History of Chicanos, 3rd Edition.* Cambridge: Harper & Row, 1988.

Agger, Ben. *Cultural Studies as Critical Theory.* London: Falmer Press, 1992.

American Psychiatric Association. *DSM-III—Diagnostic and Statistical Manual of Mental Disorders, Third Edition, Revised.* Washington, DC: APA, 1988.

Amott, Teresa L., and Julie A. Matthaei. *Race, Gender and Work: A Multicultural Economic History of Women in the United States.* Boston: South End Press, 1991.

Anaya, Rudolfo A. *Bless Me Ultima.* Berkeley, CA: TQS Publications, 1972.

Anaya, Rudolfo A. and Francisco Lomeli. *Aztlán: Essays on the Chicano Homeland.* Albuquerque, NM: El Norte Publications, 1989.

Anzaldúa, Gloria. *Borderlands/La Frontera: The New Mestiza.* San Francisco: Spinsters/Aunt Lute Books, 1987.

———. "Bridge, Drawbridge, Sandbar or Island: Lesbians-of-Color Hacienda Alianzas." In *Bridges of Power: Women's Multicultural Alliances,* edited by Lisa Albrecht and Rose M. Brewer. Philadelphia: New Society, 1990.

———. "El Dia de la Chicana." In *Infinite Divisions: An Anthology of Chicana Literature,* edited by Tey Diana Rebodello and Eliana S. Rivero. Tucson: University of Arizona Press, 1993.

———. "La Prieta." In *This Bridge Called My Back: Writings by Radical Women of Color,* edited by Cherríe Moraga and Gloria Anzaldúa. New York: Kitchen Table Press, 1983.

Avila, Elena. "La Llorona Has Found Her Children." In *Chicano Studies: Critical Connection Between Research and Community,* edited by Teresa Córdova. San José, CA: National Association for Chicano Studies, 1992.

Baca, Judith. *Cultures in Contention.* Seattle: Real Comet Press, 1985.

Banks, James A. *Multiethnic Education: Theory and Practice.* Boston: Allyn and Bacon, 1988.

Barthes, Roland. *Mythologies.* New York: Hill and Wang, 1972.

Bettleheim, Bruno, and M. Janowitz. *The Dynamics of Prejudice.* New York: Harper & Row, 1950.

Blauner, Robert. *Racial Oppression in America.* New York: Harper & Row, 1972.

Blea, Irene I. *La Chicana and the Intersection of Race, Class, and Gender.* New York: Praeger, 1992.

———. *Toward a Chicano Social Science.* New York: Praeger, 1988.

Bornstein, Miriam. "Toma de Nombre." In *Infinite Divisions: An Anthology of Chicana Literature,* edited by Tey Diana Rebolledo and Eliana S. Rivero. Tucson: University of Arizona Press, 1993.

Boyd-Franklin, Nancy, and Nydia García-Preto. "Family Therapy: A Closer Look at African American and Hispanic Women." In *Women of Color: Integrating Ethnic and Gender Identities in Psychotherapy,* edited by Lillian Comas-Díaz and Beverly Greene. New York: Guilford, 1994.

209

Brown, Elsa Barkley. "Womanist Consciousness: Maggie Lena Walker and the Independent Order of Saint Luke." In *Oxford Readings in Feminism: Feminism and History*, edited by Joan Wallach Scott. New York: Oxford University Press, 1996.

Burciaga, José Antonio. *Drink Cultura*. Santa Barbara, CA: Capra Press, 1993.

Calderón, Héctor, and José David Saldívar, eds. *Criticism in the Borderlands: Studies in Chicano Literature, Culture, and Ideology*. Durham, NC: Duke University Press, 1991.

Carillo, Roxanna. "Feminist Alliances: A View from Peru." In *Bridges of Power: Women's Multicultural Alliances*, edited by Lisa Albrecht and Rose M. Brewer. Philadelphia: New Society, 1990.

Casteñada, Antonia I. "The Political Economy of Nineteenth Century Stereotypes of Californians." In *Between Borders: Essays on Mexicana/Chicana History*, edited by Adelaida R. Del Castillo. Encino, CA: Floricanto Press, 1990.

———. "Presidarias y Pobladoras: The Journey North and Life in Frontier California." In *Chicana Critical Issues*, edited by Norma Alarcón. Berkeley, CA: Third Woman Press, 1993a.

———. "Sexual Violence in the Politics and Policies of Conquest: Amerindian Women and the Spanish Conquest of Alta California." In *Building With Our Hands: New Directions in Chicana Studies*, edited by Adela de la Torre and Beatríz M. Pesquera. Berkeley, CA: University of California Press, 1993b.

Castillo, Ana. *Massacre of the Dreamers: Essays on Xicanisma*. Albuquerque: University of New Mexico Press, 1995.

Castillo, Debra. "Response Cutting/Edge." In *Latin American Women's Writing: Feminist Readings in Theory and Crisis*, edited by Anny Brooksbank Jones. New York: Clarendon Press/Oxford University Press, 1996.

Catacalos, Rosemary. "(There Has To Be) Something More Than Everything." In *Daughters of the Fifth Sun: A Collection of Latina Fiction and Poetry*, edited by Bryce Milligan, Mary Guerrero Milligan, and Angela de Hoyos. New York: Riverhead Books, 1995.

Cervantes, Lorna Dee. "Oaxaca, 1974." In *Infinite Divisions: An Anthology of Chicana Literature*. edited by Tey Diana Rebolledo and Eliana S. Rivero. Tucson: University of Arizona Press, 1993.

———. "Poem for the Young White Man Who Asked How I, An Intelligent, Well-Read Person Could Believe in a War between the Races." In *Infinite Divisions: An Anthology of Chicana Literature*, edited by Tey Diana Rebolledo and Eliana S. Rivero. Tucson: University of Arizona Press, 1993. Also in: *Making Face, Making Soul/Haciendo Caras: Creative and Critical Perspectives by Women of Color*, edited by Gloria Anzaldúa. San Francisco: Aunt Lute Books, 1990.

Chabram-Dernersesian, Angie. "On the Social Construction of Whiteness within Selected Chicana/o Discourses." In *Displacing Whiteness: Essays in Social and Cultural Criticism*, edited by Ruth Frankenberg. Durham, NC: Duke University Press, 1999.

Chávez, Denise. *Last of the Menu Girls*. Houston, TX: Arte Público, 1986.

Chávez-Leyva. "Faithful Hard-Working Hands: Mexicana Workers During the Great Depression." In *Perspectives in Mexican American Studies*, Vol. 5—*Mexican American Women: Changing Images*, edited by Juan R. García. Tucson: University of Arizona Press, 1995.

Chow, Rey. *Writing Diaspora: Tactics of Intervention in Contemporary Cultural Studies*. Bloomington: Indiana University Press, 1993.

Cisneros, Sandra. "Guadalupe the Sex Goddess: Unearthing the Racy Past of Mexico's Most Famous Virgin." *Ms* (July/September 1996), 43–46.

———. *The House on Mango Street*. Houston: Arte Público Press, 1989.

———. *Woman Hollering Creek and Other Stories*. New York: Random House, 1991.

Clearing-Sky, Mary. "Historic Trauma and Unresolved Grieving in Native American Populations." Paper presented at the CIC Conference. 31 October 1992. Champaign-Urbana: University of Illinois.

Comas-Díaz, Lillian. "Feminist Therapy with Hispanic/Latina Women: Myth or Reality?" In *The Psychopathology of Everyday Racism and Sexism*, edited by Lenora Fulani. New York: Harrington Press, 1988.

———. "An Integrative Approach." In *Women of Color: Integrating Ethnic and Gender Identities in Psychotherapy*, edited by Lillian Comas-Díaz and Beverly Greene. New York: Guilford, 1994.

Comas-Díaz, Lillian, and Beverly Greene. "Connections and Disconnections." In *Women of Color: Integrating Ethnic and Gender Identities in Psychotherapy*, edited by Lillian Comas-Díaz and Beverly Greene. New York: Guilford, 1994.

———. "Gender and Ethnicity in the Healing Process." In *Women of Color: Integrating Ethnic and Gender Identities in Psychotherapy*, edited by Lillian Comas-Díaz and Beverly Greene. New York: Guilford, 1994.

———. *Women of Color: Integrating Ethnic and Gender Identities in Psychotherapy*. New York: Guilford, 1994.

Corpi, Lucha. *Delia's Song*. Houston, TX: Arte Público, 1989.

Cotera, Martha P. *Diosa y Hembra: The History and Heritage of Chicanas in the U.S.* Austin: Information Systems Development, 1976.

De Leon, Arnoldo. *They Called Them Greasers: Anglo Attitudes Toward Mexicans in Texas, 1821–1900*. Austin: University of Texas Press, 1983.

De León, Susana. Statement to rehearsal group of Cuatemoc Danzantes. November 1996. CreArte Gallery, Minneapolis.

Delpar, Helen. *The Enormous Vogue of Things Mexican: Cultural Relations between the United States and Mexico, 1920–1935*. Tuscaloosa: University of Alabama Press, 1992.

Dumm, Thomas L. *Democracy and Punishment: Disciplinary Origins of the United States*. Madison: University of Wisconsin Press, 1987.

Duran, Eduardo, and Bonnie Duran. *Native American Post-Colonial Psychology*. Albany: State University of New York Press, 1995.

Echeverría, Olga Angelina García. "Blood Ain't Salsa." C.D. *Raza Spoken Here: Poesía Chicana*, Vol. I. San Diego, CA: Calaca Press, 1999.

Engel, Beverly M.F.C.C. *The Right to Innocence: Healing the Trauma of Childhood Sexual Abuse*. Los Angeles: Jeremy Tarcher, 1989.

Escamill, Edna. "Corazon de Una Anciana." In *Making Face, Making Soul/Haciendo caras: Creative and Critical Perspectives by Women of Color*, edited by Gloria Anzaldúa. San Francisco: Aunt Lute Books, 1990.

Espín, Olivia M. "Cultural and Historical Influences on Sexuality in Hispanic/Latina Women: Implications for Psychotherapy." In *Pleasure and Danger: Exploring Female Sexuality*, edited by C. Vance. London: Routledge and Kegan Paul, 1984.

———. "Feminist Approaches." In *Women of Color: Integrating Ethnic and Gender Identities in Psychotherapy*, edited by Lillian Comas-Díaz and Beverly Greene. New York: Guilford, 1994.

Fanon, Franz. *Black Skin, White Masks*. New York: Grove Press, 1967.

Felix-Ortiz, Maria, and Michael D. Newcomb. "Risk and Protective Factors for Drug Use Among Latino and White Adolescents." *Hispanic Journal of Behavioral Sciences* 14:3 (August 1992): 291–306.

Fischer, Michael M. J. "Ethnicity and the Post-Modern Arts of Memory." In *Writing Cultures*, edited by James Clifford and George Marcus. Los Angeles: University of California, 1986.

Fishman, Joshua. *Language Loyalty in the United States*. The Hague: Mouton, 1966.

Foley, Douglas E. *From Peones to Politicos: Class and Ethnicity in a South Texas Town, 1900–1987*. Austin: Center for Mexican American Studies, University of Texas, 1988.

Fregoso, Rosa Linda. "Recycling Colonialist Fantasies on the Texas Borderlands." In *Home, Exile, Homeland: Film, Media, and the Politics of Place*, edited by Hamid Naficy. New York: Routledge, 1999.

Freire, Paulo. *Pedagogy of the Oppressed*. New York: Continuum, 2000.

García, Alma M. "The Development of Chicana Feminist Discourse, 1970–1980." In *Unequal Sisters: A Multicultural Reader in U.S. Women's History*, edited by Ellen Carol DuBois and Vicki L. Ruiz. New York: Routledge, 1990.

García, F. Chris. *La Causa Politica: A Chicano Politics Reader*. South Bend, IN: University of Notre Dame Press, 1974.

García, Gilbert. "Beyond the Adelita Image: Women Scholars in the National Association for Chicano Studies, 1972–1992." In *Perspectives in Mexican American Studies*, Vol. 5—Mexican American Women: Changing Images, edited by Juan R. García. Tucson: Mexican American Studies and Research Center, University of Arizona Press, 1995.

García-Castañón, Juan, and Gordon G. Cappelletty. "A Preliminary Report on Continuous-Traumatic Stress in a Northern California Central American Refugee Community." In *Community Empowerment and Chicano Scholarship*, edited by Mary Romero and Cordelia Candelaria. Berkeley, CA: National Association for Chicano Studies, 1992.

Giroux, Henry A. *Postmodernism, Feminism, and Cultural Politics: Redrawing Education Boundaries*. Albany: State University of New York Press, 1991

Gleason, Philip. "World War II and the Development of American Studies." *American Quarterly*, 36 (1984): 344–352.

Gollnick, Donna M., and Philip C. Chinn. *Multicultural Education in a Pluralistic Society*. St. Louis, MO: Mosby, 1983.

Gómez-Quiñones, Juan. *Chicano Politics: Reality and Promise, 1940–1990.* Albuquerque: University of New Mexico Press, 1990.

Gonzalez, Patrisia, and Roberto Rodríguez. "It's Not All White." Universal Press Syndicate. Available at http://www.latinola.com/story.php?story=470,] accessed September 13, 2002.

Greene, Beverly. "Lesbian Women of Color: Triple Jeopardy." In *Women of Color: Integrating Ethnic and Gender Identities in Psychotherapy,* edited by Lillian Comas-Díaz and Beverly Greene. New York: Guilford, 1994.

Gutiérrez, Ramón. *When Jesus Came, the Corn Mothers Went Away: Marriage, Sexuality, and Power in New Mexico, 1500–1846.* Palo Alto, CA: Stanford University Press, 1991.

Gutiérrez-Jones, Carl. *Rethinking the Borderlands.* Berkeley, CA: University of California Press, 1995.

Heany, Tom. "Issues in Freirean Pedagogy." *Thresholds in Education.* Available at http://www.nl.edu/ace/resources/documents/FreireIssues.html, accessed June 20, 1995.

Hernández, E. D. "Discussion, Discourse and Direction: The Dilemmas of a Chicana Lesbian." In *Chicana Lesbians: The Girls Our Mothers Warned Us About,* edited by Carla Trujillo. Berkeley, CA: Third Woman Press, 1991.

Herrera-Sobek, Maria. "My All-American Son." In *Three Times a Woman: Chicana Poetry,* ed. Alicia Gaspar de Alba. Tempe: Bilingual Press, 1989.

Hesch, Rick. "Aboriginal Teachers as Organic Intellectuals." In *Anti-Racism, Feminism, and Critical Approaches to Education,* edited by Roxana Ng, Pat Stanton, and Joyce Scane. Westport, CT: Bergin & Garvey, 1995.

hooks, bell. *Outlaw Culture: Resisting Representations.* New York: Routledge, 1994.

Horno-Delgado, Asunción, Eliana Ortega, Nina M. Scott, and Nancy Saporta Sternbach. *Breaking Boundaries: Latina Writing and Critical Readings.* Amherst: University of Massachusetts Press, 1989.

Illich, Ivan. "To Hell With Good Intentions." Speech. Conference on Inter-American Student Projects, 20 April 1968. Cuernavaca, Mexico. http://homepage.mac.com/tinapple/illich/1968_cuernavaca.html.

Jaramillo, Canéla. "Postscript." In *Making Face, Making Soul/Haciendo caras: Creative and Critical Perspectives by Women of Color,* edited by Gloria Anzaldúa. San Francisco: Aunt Lute Books, 1990.

Jeffords, Susan. *The Remasculinization of America: Gender and the Viet Nam War.* Bloomington: Indiana University Press, 1989.

Jewell, Nasrin. "Women and Work: Irani Women in the Global Economy." Public lecture for the Center for Advanced Feminist Studies Colloquium Series, November 8, 1999. University of Minnesota, Minneapolis.

Joreen. "The Tyranny of Structurelessness." *Know, Inc.* Pittsburgh: Know, Inc., 1986.

Kaminsky, Amy . "Identity at the Border: Narrative Strategies in María Novaro's *El jardín del Edén* and John Sayles's *Lone Star.*" *Studies in 20th Century Literature: The Literature and Popular Culture of the U.S.–Mexican Border* 25:1 (Winter 2001): 91–118.

———. *Reading the Body Politic: Feminist Criticism and Latin American Women Writes.* Minneapolis: University of Minnesota Press, 1993.

Kaufman, Gershen. *Shame: The Power of Caring.* Rochester, VT: Schenkman, 1992.

Keefe, Susan E., and Amado M. Padilla. *Chicano Ethnicity.* Albuquerque: University of New Mexico Press, 1987.

Kerber, Linda K. "Diversity and the Transformation of American Studies." *American Quarterly* 41.3 (1989): 415–431.

Kozol, Jonathan. *Savage Inequalities: Children in America's Schools.* New York: Crown, 1991.

Limerick, Patricia Nelson. *The Legacy of Conquest: The Unbroken Past of the American West.* New York: Norton, 1987.

Limón, José E. *American Encounters: Greater Mexico, the United States, and the Erotics of Culture.* Boston: Beacon Press, 1998.

———. *Mexican, Chicano Poems: History and Influence in Mexican-American Social Poetry.* Berkeley, CA: University of California Press, 1992.

———. *Dancing with the Devil.* Madison: University of Wisconsin Press, 1990.

Lipsitz, George. *The Possessive Investment in Whiteness.* Philadelphia: Temple University Press, 1998.

López, Natasha. "Trying to be Dyke and Chicana." In *Chicana Lesbians: The Girls Our Mothers Warned Us About,* edited by Carla Trujillo. Berkeley, CA: Third Woman Press, 1991.

Lucero-Trujillo, Marcela Christine. "The Dilemma of the Modern Chicana Artist and Critic." In *The Third Woman: Minority Women Writers of the United States,* edited by Dexter Fisher. Boston: Houghton Mifflin, 1980.

Machado, Manuel A. Jr. *Listen Chicano! An Informal History of the Mexican American*. Chicago: Nelson Hall, 1978.

Maril, Robert Lee. *Poorest of Americans: The Mexican Americans of the Lower Río Grande Valley of Texas*. South Bend, IN: University of Notre Dame Press, 1989.

Martin, Patricia Preciado. *Songs My Mother Sang to Me: An Oral History of Mexican-American Women*. Tucson: University of Arizona Press, 1992.

Martínez, Demetria. "The Conquest." In *Chicana (W)rites on Word and Film*, edited by María Herrera-Sobek and Helena María Viramontes. Berkeley, CA: Third Woman Press, 1995.

Martínez, Rubén. *The Other Side: Fault Lines, Guerrilla Saints and the True Heart of Rock 'n' Roll*. New York: Verso, 1992.

McCrea, Gwen. "Response to Freire." Unpublished paper, University of Minnesota, 2000.

Mc Dowell, Deborah. "Interview with Susan Fraiman." *Critical Texts: A Review of Theory and Criticism* 6, no. 3 (1989): 13–29.

McWilliams, Carey. *North from Mexico: The Spanish-Speaking People of the United States*. New York: Greenwood, 1968.

Mendez, Odilia. "Mother." In *Compañeras: Latina Lesbians—An Anthology*, edited by Juanita Ramos. New York: Latina Lesbian History Project, 1987.

Mirandé, Alfredo. *Gringo Justice*. South Bend, IN: University of Notre Dame Press, 1987.

Mirandé, Alfredo, and Evangelina Enríquez. *La Chicana: The Mexican American Female*. Chicago: University of Chicago Press, 1979.

Miyoshi, Masao. "Sites of Resistance in the Global Economy." In *Cultural Readings of Imperialism: Edward Said and the Gravity of History*, edited by Keith Ansell-Pearson, Benita Parry, and Judith Squires. New York: St. Martin's Press, 1997.

Mora, Pat. *Nepantla: Essays from the Land in the Middle*. Albuquerque: University of New Mexico Press, 1993.

Moraga, Cherríe. "La Ofrenda." In *Chicana Lesbians: The Girls Our Mothers Warned Us About*, edited by Carla Trujillo. Berkeley, CA: Third Woman Press, 1991.

———. *The Last Generation: Prose and Poetry*. Boston: South End Press, 1993.

Morones, Carmen. "Grace." In *Making Face, Making Soul/Haciendo Caras: Creative and Critical Perspectives of Women of Color*, edited by Gloria Anzaldúa. San Francisco: Aunt Lute Books, 1990.

Muñoz, Carlos Jr. *Youth, Identity and Power: The Chicano Movement*. London & New York: Verso, 1989.

Ng, Roxana. "Teaching against the grain: Contradictions and possibilities." In *Anti-Racism, Feminism, and Critical Approaches to Education*, edited by Roxana Ng, Pat Staton, and Joyce Scane. Westport, CT: Bergin and Garvey, 1995.

Oboler, Suzanne. *Ethnic Labels, Latino Lives: Identity and the Politics of (Re)Presentation in the United States*. Minneapolis: University of Minnesota Press, 1995.

Ocampo, Catheryn A., Martha E. Bernal, and George Knight. "Gender, Race, and Ethnicity: The Sequencing of Social Constancies." In *Ethnic Identity: Formation and Transmission Among Hispanics and Other Minorities*, edited by Martha E. Bernal and George P. Knight. Albany: State University of New York Press, 1993.

Orozco, Cynthia. "Beyond Machismo, La Familia, and Ladies Auxiliaries: A Historiography of Mexican-Origin Women's Participation in Voluntary Associations and Politics in the United States, 1870–1990." In *Perspectives in Mexican American Studies*, Vol. 5—*Mexican American Women: Changing Images*, edited by Juan R. García. Tucson: Mexican American Studies and Research Center, University of Arizona Press, 1995.

Padilla, Genaro M. *My History, Not Yours: The Formation of Mexican American Autobiography*. Madison: University of Wisconsin Press, 1993.

Pérez, Emma. *The Decolonial Imaginary: Writing Chicanas Into History*. Bloomington: Indiana University Press, 1999.

———. "Gulf Dreams." In *Chicana Lesbians: The Girls Our Mothers Warned Us About*, edited by Carla Trujillo. Berkeley, CA: Third Woman Press, 1991.

———. "Sexuality and Discourse: Notes from a Chicana Survivor." In *Chicana Critical Issues: Mujeres Activas en Letras y Cambio Social*, edited by Norma Alarcón. Berkeley, CA: Third Woman Press, 1993. Also in: *Chicana Lesbians: The Girls Our Mothers Warned Us About*, edited by Carla Trujillo. Berkeley, CA: Third Woman Press, 1991.

Pesquera, Beatriz M., and Denise M. Segura. "There Is No Going Back: Chicanas and Feminism." In *Chicana Critical Issues: Mujeres Activas en Letras y Cambio Social*, edited by Norma Alarcón. Berkeley, CA: Third Woman Press, 1993.

Pharr, Suzanne. *Homophobia: A Weapon of Sexism.* Little Rock, AR: Chardon Press, 1988.

Pheterson, Gail. "Alliances Between Women: Overcoming Internalized Oppression and Internalized Domination." In *Bridges of Power: Women's Multicultural Alliances,* edited by Lisa Albrecht and Rose M. Brewer. Philadelphia: New Society, 1990.

Ramirez, Manuel. *Multicultural/Multiracial Psychology: Mestizo Perspectives on Personality and Mental Health.* New York: Pergamon Press, 1983.

Rebolledo, Tey Diana. *Women Singing in the Snow: A Cultural Analysis of Chicana Literature.* Tucson: University of Arizona Press, 1995.

Rebolledo, Tey Diana, and Eliana S. Rivero, eds. *Infinite Divisions: An Anthology of Chicana Literature.* Tucson: University of Arizona Press, 1993.

Rivera, Marina. "Mestiza." In *Infinite Divisions: An Anthology of Chicana Literature,* edited by Tey Diana Rebodello and Eliana S. Rivero. Tucson: University of Arizona Press, 1993.

Rivera, Tomás. *And the Earth Did Not Devour Him.* Houston, TX: Arte Público Press, 1995.

Rodriguez, Jeanette. *Our Lady of Guadalupe: Faith and Empowerment among Mexican-American Women.* Austin: University of Texas Press, 1994.

Rodriguez, Luis J. *Always Running—La Vida Loca: Gang Days in L.A.* Willimantic, CT: Curbstone Press, 1993.

Rodríguez, Richard. "All Immigrants Are Outlaws." *Minneapolis Star-Tribune* (7 November, 1994): A10.

———. *Days of Obligation: An Argument with My Mexican Father.* New York: Viking, 1992.

———. *Hunger of Memory: The Education of Richard Rodríguez.* New York: Bantam Books, 1982.

Roman, Leslie G. "White Is a Color!" In *Race, Identity and Representation in Education,* edited by Cameron McCarthy and Warren Crichlow. New York: Routledge, 1993.

Root, Maria P.P. "Reconstructing the Impact of Trauma on Personality." In *Personality and Psychotherapy,* edited by L. S. Brown and M. Ballou. New York: Guilford, 1992.

Rosaldo, Renato. Personal conversation with author. 1998 National Association of Chicano and Chicana Studies. Mexico City, Mexico.

Said, Edward W. *Culture and Imperialism.* New York: Knopf, 1993.

Salas, Elizabeth. *Soladaderas in the Mexican Military: Myth and History.* Austin: University of Texas Press, 1990.

Saldívar, Ramón. *Chicano Narrative: The Dialectics of Difference.* Madison: University of Wisconsin Press, 1990.

Sánchez, Juanita. "Paso a Paso." In *Chicana Lesbians: The Girls Our Mothers Warned Us About,* edited by Carla Trujillo. Berkeley, CA: Third Woman Press, 1991.

Sandoval, Chéla. "Feminism and Racism: A Report on the 1981 National Women's Studies Association Conference." In *Making Face, Making Soul/Haciendo Caras: Creative and Critical Perspectives of Women of Color,* edited by Gloria Anzaldúa. San Francisco: Aunt Lute Books, 1990.

———. "Theorizing White Consciousness for a Post-Empire World: Barthes, Fanon, and the Rhetoric of Love." In *Displacing Whiteness: Essays in Social and Cultural Criticism,* edited by Ruth Frankenberg. Durham, NC: Duke University Press, 1999.

San Miguel, Guadalupe Jr. *"Let All of Them Take Heed": Mexican Americans and the Campaign for Educational Equality in Texas, 1910–1981.* Austin: University of Texas Press, 1987.

Santillán, Richard. "Midwestern Mexican American Women and the Struggle for Gender Equality: A Historical Overview, 1920's–1960's." In *Perspectives in Mexican American Studies,* Vol. 5— *Mexican American Women: Changing Images,* edited by Juan R. García. Tucson: Mexican American Studies and Research Center, University of Arizona Press, 1995.

Sardar, Ziauddin, and Borin Van Loon. *Introducing Cultural Studies.* New York: Totem Books, 1998.

Schneiderman, Stuart. *Saving Face: America and the Politics of Shame.* New York: Knopf, 1995.

Sierra, Christine Marie. "The University Setting Reinforces Inequality." In *Chicana Voices: Intersections of Race, Class, and Gender,* edited by Teresa Córdova. Austin: Center for Mexican American Studies, University of Texas Press, 1986.

Sim, Stuart, and Borin Van Loon. *Introducing Critical Theory.* New York: Totem Books, 2001.

Sinha, Mrinalini. "Gender in the Critiques of Colonialism and Nationalism: Locating the 'Indian Woman.'" In *Oxford Readings in Feminism: Feminism and History,* edited by Joan Wallach Scott. New York: Oxford University Press, 1996.

Sollors, Werner. *Beyond Ethnicity: Consent and Descent in American Culture.* New York: Oxford, 1986.

Spivak, Gayatri Chakravorty. *In Other Worlds: Essays in Cultural Politics.* New York: Methuen, 1987.

——. "Theory in the Margin: Coetzee's *Foe* Reading Defoe's *Crusoe/Roxana*." In *Consequences of Theory*, edited by Jonathan Arac and Barbara Johnson. Baltimore: Johns Hopkins University Press, 1991.

Stone, Alan. "Prophet of Hope." Available at http://bostonreview.mit.edu/GR21.5/stone.html, accessesd May 28, 2002.

Tijerina, Aletícia. "I Am the Lost Daughter of My Mama's House." In *Compañeras: Latina Lesbians— An Anthology*, edited by Juanita Ramos. New York: Latina Lesbian History Project, 1987.

——. "Notes on Oppression and Violence." In *Making Face, Making Soul/Haciendo caras: Creative and Critical Perspectives by Women of Color*, edited by Gloria Anzaldúa. San Francisco: Aunt Lute Books, 1990. Also in: *Compañeras: Latina Lesbians—An Anthology*, edited by Juanita Ramos. New York: Latina Lesbian History Project, 1987.

Torres, Edén. "Ella que tiene jefes y no los ve, se queda en cueros." In *Is Academic Feminism Dead? Theory and Practice*, edited by The Social Justice Group at the Center for Advanced Feminist Studies, University of Minnesota. New York: New York University Press, 2000.

Torres, Lourdes. "The Construction of the Self in U.S. Latina Autobiographies." In *Third World Women and the Politics of Feminism*, edited by Chandra Talpade Mohanty, Ann Russo, and Lourdes Torres. Bloomington: Indiana University Press, 1991.

Trujillo, Carla, ed. *Chicana Lesbians: The Girls Our Mothers Warned Us About*. Berkeley, CA: Third Woman Press, 1991.

Underland-Rosow, Vicki. *Shame: Spiritual Suicide*. Shorewood, MN: Waterford Publications, 1996.

Valdés, Gina. "The Border." In *Infinite Divisions: An Anthology of Chicana Literature*, edited by Tey Diana Rebolledo and Eliana S. Rivero. Tucson: University of Arizona Press, 1993.

Valerio, Anita. "It's in My Blood, My Face—My Mother's Voice, the Way I Sweat." In *This Bridge Called My Back: Writings by Radical Women of Color* (2nd ed.), edited by Cherríe Moraga and Gloria Anzaldúa. New York: Kitchen Table Press, 1983.

Vasquez, Melba J. T. "Latinas." In *Women of Color: Integrating Ethnic and Gender Identities in Psychotherapy*, edited by Lillian Comas-Díaz and Beverly Greene. New York: Guilford, 1994.

Vigil, James Diego. *From Indians to Chicanos: The Dynamics of Mexican American Culture*. Prospect Heights, IL: Waveland Press, 1980.

Villanueva, Alma. "The Ceremony of Orgasm." In *Infinite Divisions: An Anthology of Chicana Literature*, edited by Tey Diana Rebolledo and Eliana S. Rivero. Tucson: University of Arizona Press, 1993.

Viramontes, Helena. *The Moths and Other Stories*. Houston, TX: Arte Público, 1985.

Wald, Alan. "Theorizing Cultural Difference: A Critique of the 'Ethnicity School.'" *Melus* 14.2 (Summer 1987): 21–33.

Weber, David J. *Foreigners in the Native Land: Historical Roots of the Mexican Americans*. Albuquerque: University of New Mexico Press, 1973.

White, Armond. "Stepping Forward/Looking Back." *Film Comment* (March/April 2000): 36.

Wilson, Michael, and Deborah Silverton Rosenfelt. *Salt of the Earth*. New York: Feminist Press, 1978.

Wollenberg, Charles M. *All Deliberate Speed: Segregation and Exclusion in California Schools, 1855–1975*. Berkeley, CA: University of California Press, 1978.

Wood, Silviana. "Dreams by Appointment Only." In *Woman of Her Word: Hispanic Women Write* (2nd ed.), edited by Evangelina Vigil. Houston, TX: Arte Público, 1987.

Yellow Horse Braveheart, Maria. "Native American and the Trauma of History." In *Studying Native America: Problems and Perspectives*, edited by Russell Thornton. Madison: University of Wisconsin Press, 1999.

Zamora, Bernice. *Restless Serpents*. Houston, TX: Bilingual Press, 1994.

Index